Four Shakespearean Period Pieces

Four Shakespearean
Period Pieces

MARGRETA DE GRAZIA

The University of Chicago Press ❋ *Chicago and London*

The University of Chicago Press, Chicago 60637
The University of Chicago Press, Ltd., London
© 2021 by The University of Chicago
Published 2021
Printed in the United States of America

30 29 28 27 26 25 24 23 22 21   1 2 3 4 5

ISBN-13: 978-0-226-78519-6 (cloth)
ISBN-13: 978-0-226-78522-6 (paper)
ISBN-13: 978-0-226-78536-3 (e-book)
DOI: https://doi.org/10.7208/chicago/9780226785363.001.0001

Library of Congress Cataloging-in-Publication Data

Names: De Grazia, Margreta, author.
Title: Four Shakespearean period pieces / Margreta de Grazia.
Description: Chicago ; London : The University of Chicago
    Press, 2021. | Includes bibliographical references and index.
Identifiers: LCCN 2020051720 | ISBN 9780226785196 (cloth) |
    ISBN 9780226785226 (paperback) | ISBN 9780226785363 (ebook)
Subjects: LCSH: Shakespeare, William, 1564–1616—Criticism
    and interpretation.
Classification: LCC PR2976 .D36 2021 | DDC 822.3/3—dc23
LC record available at https://lccn.loc.gov/2020051720

To Colin Thubron

Contents

Figures

Introduction

In a certain way it is always too late to ask the question of time.
J. DERRIDA, *Margins of Philosophy*

A curious transvaluation is taking place in our study of the past. As key terms are being reappraised, negatives are becoming positives and vice versa. *Anachronisms*, previously condemned as errors in the order of time, are being hailed as correctives or alternatives to that order, features not to be extirpated but entertained, perhaps even cultivated. At the same time, the schema violated by anachronism, *chronology*, is on the defensive, as are the historical units of time we call *periods*. Once the mainstay of historical studies, chronology and periods are now suspected of limiting and distorting the past they were formerly entrusted to represent. Also on the decline is the master *narrative of secularization* they have been sustaining in which an epochal break from a devout past precipitates an ever-advancing trajectory toward secularity. The explanatory force long enjoyed by that narrative is now being challenged if not rejected.

Four Shakespearean Period Pieces begins by sketching out the alterations the four terms italicized above appear to be undergoing. But this is only to prepare the way for the book's focus: the work these terms have done in the study of Shakespeare. Each of them entered commentary on Shakespeare centuries after Shakespeare. And each of them is currently under reappraisal. The book begins with a chapter on *anachronism*, once an embarrassment in Shakespeare studies but now a plausible heuristic, and it proceeds with chapters on *chronology*, *periods*, and the *secularization narrative*, respectively, all formations once crucial to the reproduction and understanding of Shakespeare that are now under stress. Before turning to Shakespeare, however, we need first to rough out the larger epistemic overturn that is this book's working postulate, beginning with the term that is no longer a simple marker of opprobrium: *anachronism*.

We think we know what an anachronism is: an error in the order of time. To be more specific, it is an error in the order of "chronology" imagined as advancing uniformly in one direction, like an arrow. It is also an error in the order of historical "periods": self-contained totalities, enframed like pictures. Chronology and periods conjoin to form a diachronic time line sectioned into synchronic time frames; the former gives direction, the latter coherence. Anachronism foils both.

It is no wonder, then, that red flags go up when anachronisms are detected.[1] They disrupt the mainstays of history: chronological seriality and period integrity. We speak of them as if they were crimes, to be *detected* and *exposed*: those who *commit* them are said to be *guilty*. The offense is slight when the anachronism pertains to concrete things in the past, like events, persons, and objects; they are petty infractions, easily set right. The offense is more serious when the anachronism pertains to abstractions reflecting the thoughts, beliefs, and feelings of the past. Bound up with our own categories for apprehending the world, such anachronisms can be hard to identify and harder to reform. They are the bane of historical work because they violate the cardinal principle of historicism: the recognition of historical difference between periods of the past and, above all, between the present and the past. This is a methodological failure, to be sure: a collapse of the distance that objectivity requires between the *now* of the historian and the *then* of the historical object. But it is also an ethical failure. With periods as with persons, we have an obligation to respect difference. In history as in anthropology, the reduction of the other to the same constitutes an effacement of the other, and for Levinas, of the self as well.[2]

Indeed, our way of talking about historical periods encourages us to think of them as persons. We anthropomorphize them, attributing to each a distinctive character with distinguishing features—a spirit or a style, for example, or a temperament, even a pathology. Above all, periods, like persons, are said to have a particular way of viewing and experiencing the world, a Kantian Weltanschauung that translates variously as worldview, world picture, mindset, or episteme. And this is where problems arise. For the historian also belongs to a period and therefore holds its regulatory way of looking at the world.[3] Anachronism occurs when a contemporary worldview is assumed to correspond with that of the period in question.

It is not surprising, therefore, that the strongest critique of anachronism comes from the historian of worldviews or mentalités. Lucien Febvre has urged that the study of any given past should restrict itself to the terms that period would itself have used and understood, especially in regard to mental processes. Without such a restraint, historians risk projecting their own conceptual categories onto the past, thereby committing "psychological anachronism . . . the most insidious and harmful of all."[4] Febvre singled out one particular anachronism for the strongest possible censure: the attribution of atheism or skepticism to an earlier age of faith. How was disbelief possible in what was, to his mind, an age of belief? The offense was serious enough to provoke a hefty monograph condemning it.[5] To assume secularity in a period steeped in Christianity was Febvre's sole example of "the worst of all sins, the sin that cannot be forgiven—anachronism."[6] With religion itself in the balance, the doctrinal severity of the charge is unmistakable: the unforgivable sin is the denial of the Holy Ghost, damnable and unpardonable, in this world and the next.

And yet a change of critical opinion is in the air. No longer vilified, anachronisms are now being seen as productive, creative, and useful. A spate of recent titles reflects this turnabout: "The Return of Anachronism," "The Rhetoric of Anachronism," "The Sovereignty of Anachronism," "Towards a New Model of Renaissance Anachronism," "The Concept of Anachronism and the Historian's Truth."[7] Each of these studies puts anachronism to positive use as a literary hermeneutic, as an adjudicator between the claims of formalist and historicist criticism, as a figure of the psychoanalytic symptom, as a new temporal dimension for past artifacts, and as a heuristic by which to enlarge historical possibility. A reversal appears to be occurring: the feature once thought to vitiate the study of the past is now beginning to show signs of promise.

Anachronisms, it seems, are no longer the errors they used to be.

>>><<<

While the critical prestige of anachronism is on the rise, that of chronology and periods is in decline. *Chronology* was once valued for its neutrality: devoid of bias, it appeared capable of synchronizing all calendrical systems into a single advancing time line onto which anything might be situated. Now, however, in various areas of critical thought, it is mistrusted as coercive and exclusionary. Most of the critiques bear the imprint of Walter Benjamin's critique in "Theses on the Philosophy of History," exposing the bias of the empty and homogeneous temporal continuum that, while appearing neutral, instantiates in the name of progress an oppressive capitalist world order.[8] Postcolonialism has argued that the advancing chronological continuum has precluded parity between the West and the non-West; the non-West, having gotten at best a late start, can only lag behind the perpetually front-running West.[9] In psychoanalysis, the unconscious is seen to resist uniform rectilinear time, erupting in symptomatic dreams, memories, slips, traumas, and latencies. Queer theorists have countered the exclusions of "straight time" with "queer temporalities" that refuse the linearity subtending a range of discourses from historicist practice to biological reproduction.[10] Poststructuralists have also challenged rectilinear time. For Roland Barthes, the chronological sequencing of narrative is illusory; if the time of a narrative's utterance were marked (and thereby severed from the time of the narrative itself), that rupture would "dechronologize the thread of history" and thereby restore a time that is "complex, parametric and not in the least linear."[11] For Derrida, it is only a residual logocentrism that allows us to imagine the punctuality of any given moment or the coherence of any attendant logic of seriality.[12] These critiques have shaken the authority of the continuum that has long given us our epistemological and institutional bearings.

Periods, too, once indispensable to the study of the past, have been subjected to critique. Formerly they provided frames within which the past could be organized into coherent units, each with a distinctive character discernible through its various social, economic, and cultural emanations. Even if these multiple aspects advanced and developed unevenly and at different paces, they were still seen to cohere as an "expressive totality."[13] Historical contrast has been basic to how the past has been taught and researched, at least since the early twentieth century.[14] But recently any number of manifestos are decrying the constraints of period divisions and urging their dismantling.[15] Even Fredric Jameson, the staunch defender of periods, while insisting on their indispensability, has never denied their inadequacy.[16] Questions have been asked about their construction: Why do they start and end where they do? What determines the cultural dominant around which other features are expected to rally and cohere? And what about those elements that fall outside its parameters? Periods are now recognized as arbitrary demarcations introduced and observed to suit the argument of any given study. Liberties are being taken even with the numerically fixed units of the century and the decade: according to the project at hand, they are clipped or stretched at either end to make short or long spans. At the same time, there is an awareness of how ideologically charged the cutoffs can be, perhaps none more than that between the medieval and the modern, for that epochal divide upholds other binaries: between the religious and the secular, between feudal-ism and capitalism, between superstition and science.[17]

Chronology and periods have proven particularly supportive of narratives that, like traditional novels, progress through time in stages, including the most consequential of them: the grand narrative, master narrative, or metanarrative of secular moder-nity. As has been noted of Hegel's *Philosophy of History*, world history can be seen to follow a bildungsroman structure: like a novel of formation, with consciousness as the protagonist, it advances sequentially and dialectically through time toward the perfection that is absolute freedom.[18] The groundbreaking modern thinkers—among them Marx, Durkheim, Weber, and Freud—all shared the belief that as religion gradually receded, the forces of modernization would advance. It was only a mat-ter of time before the lagging rest of the world, extricated from its own backward past, would follow the same trajectory into a modern and secular future. (Voltaire, it was alleged, gave the process fifty years.[19]) As recently as 2007, Charles Taylor, in his monumental *A Secular Age*, holds to this narrative (on the prin-ciple that it is better to improve a master narrative than repudiate it) in covering the period between 1500 (when it was virtually impossible *not to believe* in God) to 2000 (when it was almost impossible—or at least very hard—*to believe* in God). His story is basically one of progressive disenchantment in which the Reformation retains its divisive epochal function, effecting "the transfer out of embodied 'enfleshed' forms of religious life, to those which are more 'in the head.'"[20]

The sway of the secularization narrative can hardly be over-stated. It is repeated in miniature in any number of accounts de-signed to mark the onset of modernity: an epochal figure breaks from the spellbound medieval past to inaugurate an ever-advancing modernity. In Protestant history, Luther hammers his ninety-five theses to the church door at Wittenberg. In philosophy, Descartes, alone in his study, predicates existence on his own cogitation. In science, Galileo, peering through his telescope, confirms a helio-centric cosmos. And each start-up effects the same secular break from old-faith bondage: for Luther, from the papacy; for Descartes, from the tradition of monastic scholasticism; for Galileo, from church dogma.

And yet the break is rarely an absolute voiding of Christianity. Sacral elements persist but are redirected toward the worldly ends that in turn make up the defining features of modernity. Examples of this conversion are legion: sociologist Max Weber's account of the modern work ethic as a secularization of saintly or monastic asceticism; philosopher Ludwig Feuerbach's thesis that the notion of the purely human (or anthropocentric) is a secularization of the divine logos; historian Karl Löwith's thesis that progressive history secularizes Judeo-Christian eschatology; jurist Carl Schmitt's contention that the key concepts of modern political theory are secularized theological concepts; political historian Ernst Kantorowicz's study of the dual nature of the king's two bodies (politic and mortal) in the image of the Word made flesh; European cultural historian Norman Cohn's identification of modern anarchic and revolutionary impulses with the millenarian and messianic force of medieval uprisings; early modern historian Keith Thomas's account of the transformation of superstitious magic to rational science; Michel Foucault's technologies of psychoanalysis as secularized priestly confessional practices; Theodor Adorno's aesthetic theory maintaining that "the theological heritage of art is the secularization of revelation."[21] The list could go on. Secularization itself has been given a theological heritage in the doctrinally charged mystery of kenosis, whereby Christ is said to have "self-emptied" himself of divinity in order for the Word to be made flesh (Phil. 2:6–7).[22] So proliferative is the list that Hans Blumenberg describes it as "secularization 'run wild'": virtually any modern phenomenon can be recast as a secularized version of a Christian antecedent by the simple formula *"B is the secularized A."*[23]

As the number of modern secularizations proliferated, the status of the modern itself was thrown into question. If the modern era consisted of so many replays or redactions of medieval Christian theology, what claim could it make to being a discrete period, a period in its own right, rather than a derivation or attenuation of what had come before? This was a problem for the period that prided itself on having broken definitively with its Christian background. Blumenberg attempts to identify a purely secular feature that belongs singularly to the modern age, one with no compromising theological precedents. He proposes "self-assertion," a program of epistemological self-grounding that presupposes no divine dispensation or intervention.[24]

But the demise of the secularization thesis is not, of course, only a discursive or academic matter. World events indicate no decline of religious belief, so it can no longer be said, at least not axiomatically, that religion is tapering off or that modernity requires secularity or that forward movement or progress is the course of either modernity or secularity.[25] If the present is to continue calling itself "a secular age," it is only by redefining *secular* to include belief as well as unbelief—as indeed Taylor does in his tome by that title: religion of whatever stripe is as much "an option" or "human possibility" as irreligion: both are "alternative ways of living our moral/spiritual life."[26]

With the narrative of secular modernity in disrepute, with the integrity of period concepts contested, and with the neutrality of chronology debated, where is one to turn?

Anachronism looks like a promising antidote to these expiring disciplinary determinants. And yet some caution is needed here, for it is hardly independent of the schema it ostensibly disrupts. With every charge of anachronism, the rule of chronology and periods is reinstated. The violation of the prohibition secures the authority of the standard. Anachronism belongs to the same schema as chronology and periods, as is illustrated by still another of modernity's etiologies. In this one, the quattrocento Italian humanist Lorenzo Valla ushers in modern historical consciousness by invalidating the Donation of Constantine, the decree by which the Emperor Constantine allegedly transferred imperial lands to the church.[27] By detecting the decree's many anachronisms, it is said, Valla exposed it as a forgery. His sensitivity to anachronism is believed to have demonstrated a grasp of historical change, of the difference between the particulars of Constantine's fourth century (its offices, customs, events, and idioms) and those of the forger's later century. Here, as in the other foundational narratives of modernity, Valla's epochal feat is applauded for its sacrilegious boldness in confronting the spurious authority of the church.

Again and again, modernity predicates to itself the origins by which it would be defined and casts the time before it as its foil or negation. Once modernity identifies itself with historical consciousness, the medieval is relegated to the time *before* historical consciousness, a period whose constitutive credulity is expressed by its belief in forged documents as well as in the relics, miracles, and real presence of the old faith. Once again, the decisive break between the medieval and the modern is marked: on the far side, darkness and superstition; on the near, rationality and secularity.[28]

>>><<<

If the shifts sketched out above are any indication, the key terms by which the past has been studied are undergoing transformation. *Four Shakespearean Period Pieces* has been written in the light (or is it the shadow?) of this reappraisal. The book takes those same four key interdependent regulates and traces the work they have done in the reproduction of the most valued author in the language: Shakespeare as text, Shakespeare in criticism, and Shakespeare on stage. Here, too, the same reversal seems to be underway, as the challenge raised at the conceptual level has influenced practices within Shakespeare studies. Within the bounds of that field, these temporalizing terms can be viewed more precisely both as they have traditionally worked and as they now appear to be weakening. Here, too, anachronisms, no longer errors to be castigated, appear to be enjoying new favor.

In Shakespeare, anachronisms were once seen as something of an embarrassment. His plays abound in them in references to persons, things, events, customs, laws, and beliefs belonging to a notably later date than that of a play's action. Items from the time of Shakespeare routinely crop up in ancient settings: clocks and codices in Republican Rome; lace and billiards in Cleopatra's Egypt; tithes and primogeniture in King Lear's ancient Albion. Even the three inventions widely acknowledged to distinguish the moderns from the ancients appear in his plays: the compass, gunpowder, and the printing press.[29] In Coriolanus's Rome, the will of the *populus* is said to fly off in all directions on the navigational compass, an instrument not available in England until the thirteenth century. Firearms are mentioned at least fifty times in *King John*, though gunpowder was not in use in the West until two centuries after that king's reign. The handgun was later still, yet in the *Henry IV* plays Shakespeare introduces a bellicose character named after one and gives him the military rank of ensign or ancient, producing the oxymoronic Ancient Pistol. In *2 Henry VI*, Jack Cade complains of printing and paper technologies decades before their arrival in England. In Caesar's Rome, Brutus turns down a page of a codex in order to mark his place; so, too, does Imogen in the Britain of Caesar's contemporary Cymbeline. Perhaps more disjunctive still is the presence of Christianity in BC settings: the seven deadly sins in *Troilus*, pulpits in Caesar's Rome, a millenarian prophecy in BC *King Lear*, and allusions to the Bible and oaths on Christ's body in plays like *Lear* set before the Incarnation.

Shakespeare may have been careless of chronology, but not Shakespeareans. Since the earliest efforts to establish a chronology of Shakespeare's works at the end of the eighteenth century, chronology has been a priority of Shakespeare studies. When the New Shakspere Society was founded in 1873, its mandate was "to make out the succession of his plays."[30] No feature of the canon has been tackled with more industry and ingenuity than the dating of the plays. In the classroom, in editions of his collected or complete works, even in criticism, Shakespeare's plays and poems are now generally encountered in the order in which Shakespeare is thought to have written them. Both literary biography and historical criticism build on chronology: only after the date of a play's composition has been set, say at 1599 or 1606,

can that play be related to Shakespeare's experience (his life) or
to current events (his times) of 1599 or 1606. Formalist criticism
also relies on chronology. It gives the corpus a canon ordered in
time, a continuum connecting Shakespeare's first and last works.
Between those termini, development can be charted—of style or
of thought, for example—with its own internal progression irre-
spective of the author's life and times.

Nor has the study of Shakespeare been imaginable without
situating him in a historical period. A period provides a context, a coherent network of beliefs and ideas characteristic of an
age. Sometimes Shakespeare is seen to represent his times, his
work informed by his historical milieu. Sometimes he is thought
to transcend them, his genius confirmed by his transtemporal
clairvoyance. Though the period in which he is situated is often named after the century (sixteenth and seventeenth) or the
sovereign (Elizabethan or Jacobean) or even after the playwright
himself (the Age of Shakespeare), two period designations have
dominated: Renaissance and early modern. While the two terms
draw him in opposite directions, the former connecting him
with the ancient past and the latter with the modern future, both
work toward the same end of removing him from the dogma and
mystification of the Middle Ages.

Yet in Shakespeare studies, as in critical work more generally,
the validity of chronology and periods is uncertain. The failure of
the 1623 folio compilers to date their catalogue of plays has long
been a source of lament. The dates when his works were written
are still only conjectural. For every play and for the Sonnets, we
know the latest date by which Shakespeare must have written
a work, but the earliest eludes us. The challenge is even greater
now that some plays are thought to exist in more than one text.
For the three texts of *Hamlet*, for example, we have three different dates. Collaboration also complicates dating. If Shakespeare worked on *Macbeth* in 1606 and Middleton reworked it
in 1610, when was the play written? And on whose chronological time line should it appear? Since the mid-twentieth century,
the standard order for reproducing Shakespeare's works has

been chronological, but in this century, exceptions are emerg-
ing. The Arden Shakespeare orders the works alphabetically, and
the Royal Shakespeare Company Shakespeare reverts back to the
1623 folio's generic groupings. In the New Oxford Shakespeare,
the plays exist in three forms, each in a different order: the modern edition in order of composition, the old-spelling edition in
order of first publication, and the digital edition in alphabetical
order.[31]

Shakespeare's period designation is also uncertain. Though
Shakespeare was once securely a Renaissance or an early modern
author, in a number of recent studies he has been pulled back into
the very period against which Renaissance and early modern were
defined to become "medieval Shakespeare."[32] The recent coinages
"premodern" and "transreformational" boldly dissolve the epochal
wall between the medieval and the early modern. But even when
the wall remains, it is permeable. Either the Roman faith survives
the repression of the Reformation, or the Reformation rather than
breaking off from the old faith, deepens and purifies by disembed-
ding it from the world.[33]

Thus reperiodized, Shakespeare cannot retain his role in the
world-historical narrative. In the twentieth century, E. K. Chambers's foundational history of the early English stage set down "the
pre-existing conditions which . . . made the great Shakespearean
stage possible."[34] One of its key chapters, "The Secularization
of the Plays," famously describes that process as a passing of the
drama from the naves and choirs of the clergy to the marketplaces
and guildhalls of the laity until it reaches the purpose-built com-
mercial theaters of Shakespeare's London.[35] More recently, eccle-
sial edifices and possessions have been seen to follow the same
secularizing course: after the dissolution of the monasteries, the
Dominican Blackfriars and the Carmelite Whitefriars convert to
private theaters, liturgical vestments to playhouse costumes, con-
secrated vessels to tiring-house props, and church rituals and sacraments to sensational stage effects.

As English stage history prepares the way for Shakespeare's
secular arrival, so, too, does English literary history. The founding
work of new historicism, Stephen Greenblatt's *Renaissance Self-*

Fashioning, follows a trajectory in which the Renaissance begins in a struggle against the authority of the church and of the monarch enthroned to defend it, first by Catholic Sir Thomas More and then by Protestant William Tyndale, followed by Wyatt's anguished relation to power, Spenser's subservience to it, and Marlowe's flouting of it until finally Shakespeare emerges unshackled to assume full creative autonomy.[36] In Greenblatt's subsequent criticism, too, the release from religious ties—"a drastic swerve from the sacred to the secular"—is the precondition of Shakespeare's artistic achievement.[37] And he finds the same process at work in the plays themselves as Shakespeare appropriates the abandoned forms and beliefs of the old faith and turns them to theatrical effect. (In *Hamlet*, even the Eucharist "assumed an apparently secular form."[38]) By staging exorcisms, miracles, and purgatorial ghosts, Shakespeare's theater demystified them, exposing them as mere show, devoid of transcendent power, divine or demonic. "Does this mean that Shakespeare was participating in a secularization process?" Greenblatt asks outright.[39] Almost, but not quite, for Shakespeare's art in Greenblatt retains something of the enchantment of the sacral forms it exploits, but with a difference: rather than concealing its own artifice, it admits, even celebrates it. This is, perhaps, an intimation of what Adorno intends in ascribing a "theological heritage" to art.

For another influential critic of Shakespeare, Stanley Cavell, the "theological heritage" of Shakespeare's stage takes the form not of art but of epistemology. Shakespeare's great tragedies dramatize what happens when a world no longer sustained by faith turns to knowledge for what knowledge cannot possibly deliver: the certainty once proffered by revelation. The unknowability of a post-Reformational providence spreads to doubt of the world and of others, resulting in the self-corroding and world-destroying skepticism that, for Cavell, runs through the philosophical tradition. He locates its onset not in the solitary confinement of Descartes's *Meditations* but a generation earlier, on Shakespeare's open stage.[40] In the four great tragedies, the protagonists strive desperately for certainty while recoiling from the only bulwark against it: presence, not that of Christ in

the sacraments but of the self attuned to "ordinary language."[41]
For Sarah Beckwith, following Cavell, the Reformation strikes
a fatal blow, particularly through the abolition of the sacrament
of penance, but in the late romances Shakespeare discovers that
"ordinary language" in the form of "the grammar of forgiveness"
has the efficacy of that abrogated sacrament and gives access to
the recognition and reconciliation debarred from the tragedies.[42]

There is no missing the secularizing direction of Shakespeare
criticism in the turn to political theology, notably in the work of
Julia Lupton. She has tracked the shift from divinely sanctioned
kingship to popularly mandated constitutionalism from the vantage of the ruled rather than the ruler. Shakespearean characters follow the same progressive program as the polity—from
exclusivity to universal acceptance, from covenants to contracts,
from vertical hierarchy to horizontal equality, from obligations
to rights—in what she terms "the passage of exegetical rhythms
and sacral figures into the modern zones of civil society, national
citizenship, and secular literature."[43] The secularizing mechanism Carl Schmitt had deployed to critique liberalism is redeployed by Lupton in its defense. Thus, Shakespeare criticism has
assigned a secularizing agency to Shakespeare's plays, tracing a
movement either from religious mystery to aesthetics, from faith
to epistemology, or from divine right to liberal democracy.

But now the secularizing tilt of Shakespeare's plays can
no longer be assumed. Within a mere generation, the field of
Shakespeare studies has shifted from one in which few critics
raised religious issues to one in which few do not. Even some
who believe that Shakespeare was not religious maintain that
his plays were. The Bible once was accorded the same status in
Shakespeare as pagan myth: a literary resource for which questions of faith were moot. Now confessional and doctrinal issues
loom large in discussions of the plays, of their early audience,
and of the institution of the theater as well as of Shakespeare's
own beliefs. The opposition between players and preachers at the
heart of the "antitheatrical prejudice" is now debated; pulpit and
stage are seen to share some of the same social and ethical com-

mitments. Conflicts reside instead within the various denominations of Christianity so that such ecumenical possibilities as the "postconfessional" or the "postsecular" are being entertained.[44] Today's religious climate has thrown even presentists back to the sixteenth century, [45] as if current sectarianism cannot be viewed without recourse to a sixteenth century that is now looking more and more like the "age of belief" defended so fiercely by Febvre.

In Shakespeare studies, as in critical discourse at large, the coordinates for organizing past time are no longer disciplinary givens. The chronology of Shakespeare's works, his period status, and his role as a secularizing agent, once widely assumed, are now requiring defense. Anachronisms, however, are attracting critical interest, though no longer to demonstrate Shakespeare's modern grasp of historical difference.[46] Indeed, his anachronisms are being nudged away from the jurisdiction of history. They are being seen as an antidote to "historical correctness" in the name of fantasy, the imaginary, and a specifically literary history.[47] Or as rhetorical troping, a figure of literary style.[48] Or as a typological hermeneutic that encourages analogies across rather than through time.[49] Several recent studies have found in anachronism a mechanism by which to exempt objects and subjects on stage from the requirements of temporal continuity and coherence, allowing props (like Desdemona's handkerchief) and actors (like *Lear*'s Fool) their errant and disruptive temporalities.[50] Dramatic form itself is seen to be shaped by anachrony: Shakespeare's plots move unevenly, by temporal compression and dilation;[51] a constitutive "law of contretemps" drives action unhappily off course.[52] Thus *anachronism* is proving quite serviceable in Shakespeare studies to mark the workings of fiction, rhetoric, hermeneutics, performance, and genre. It is becoming so familiar a critical term that it has lost its stigma as the exception that proves the rule of the order of time.

>>><<<

Four Shakespearean Period Pieces takes advantage of the current instability of these four concatenated terms—*anachronism, chronology, period,* and *secular modernity*—in four freestanding but interrelated essays. With the exception of *anachronism,* each of these terms was available to Shakespeare but in senses now obsolete or unfamiliar. Shakespeare never uses *chronology,* though if he had, it might well have carried the sense it is given in rhetorical and poetic treatises of his day: a story about time—diurnal, seasonal, historical—rather than a succession of dates.[53] Shakespeare's use of *period* adheres to its Greek roots that indicate the completion of a course (astronomical, political, syntactic, biological), a coming around full circle rather than a duration between two termini. His use of *modern* also sticks closer to its ancient roots, the Latin *modernus* functioning as what linguists now term a *deictic*: a variable indexing of the present as determined by the time of the utterance, a rolling marker of the present time, like "now" or "nowadays," indefinite in duration and character but always to be superseded. *Secular* is not in Shakespeare's glossary, but again, had it been, it would have denoted a status within the church hierarchy rather than one outside or apart from it.

The only chapter rubric Shakespeare could not have known in any sense is *anachronism.* The word was not used in England until a couple of decades after his death, and even then only in recondite technical treatises on universal chronology, in Greek letters in Latin texts, in contexts far removed from the literary or dramatic.[54] That it was not available to Shakespeare, that *anachronism* is itself an anachronism, does not mean that we should drop it from subsequent critical discussion, as Quentin Skinner, following Febvre, once urged. Historians, he argued, should restrict their discussion of subjects from the past to the language past subjects themselves would have intended and understood.[55] Were that restriction enforced, however, conversation might prove quite thin, for much of our analytic and critical vocabulary was not available until a couple of centuries after Shakespeare.[56] Not to attend to such anachronisms is to miss an opportunity, for they can reveal just those points when the past resists the apparatus by which we represent it. A case in point is *anachronism* itself, a word that when applied to a time that predates its coinage is perfectly self-referential: it exemplifies what it names.

>>><<<

Though widely credited with the epoch-making exposure of anachronism, Valla never uses the word; it is his modern commentators who do.[57] His recent translator singles out the example of *satrap*, the title of a high official, as one of the most "egregious" and "the most damning" of the "grotesque anachronisms" detected by Valla in the Donation of Constantine.[58] "Palea" (or "Chaff"), as Valla dubs the Donation's anonymous author (35), lists *satraps* among the Romans who, he claims, approved Constantine's imperial gift to the papacy (42).[59] Recent scholars, having proven that "the word *satrap* was not applied to high officials in Rome before the mid-eighth century," have concluded that fourth-century Constantine could not have written the document: it is a forgery.[60] But this conclusion is not Valla's. He never charges his straw man with having projected his own eighth-century usages on to the fourth-century emperor. He objects strenuously to the word *satrap*, but on rhetorical rather than historical grounds. The word offends decorum: "Do emperors talk that way? Are Roman decrees normally drafted like that?" (42). Valla argues not only that Constantine never used the word but also that no one ever did, at least not in Rome or the Roman provinces. This is not because the word belonged to another period but because it belonged to the language of the non-Roman, the outsider or barbarian. Valla tags his opponent *barbara*—identifying him with the invading Nordic hordes that destroyed Rome and corrupted Latin culture—and accuses him of "linguistic barbarisms" (*barbariem sermonis*) and "foolishness of words" (*verborum stoliditatem*): "Uncultivated people (*barbari homines*) commonly talk and write this way" (44, 55, 58).[61] The difference between Valla and Palea is not that only the former understands the principle of historical difference but that only he knows how to argue with fluency, agility, and subtlety. His own virtuosity puts the imposter to shame most notably when Valla appropriates the rhetorical figure on which Palea's decree depends.

That figure is *prosopopeia*, or impersonation, "the personation of characters," the technique of inventing speeches and putting them "into the mouths of characters likely to utter them," praised by both Cicero and Quintilian.[62] The device enables the orator or writer to converse with the dead or absent. Palea impersonates the voice of Constantine to confer imperial territories on the Pope; Valla also impersonates Constantine to deny that conferral. In recovering that ancient voice, neither Renaissance Valla nor medieval Palea makes Constantine speak the Latin of his own late antiquity. Valla puts his own fifteenth-century Latin in the mouth of fourth-century Constantine and does the same for eighth-century Palea, whom he also impersonates.[63] He wants to address the deceased "as if they were present," and they respond to him in kind as if they were his contemporaries. Valla terms Palea a *hypocrite*, Greek (*hypokrites*) for stage actor—the professional impersonator—but Valla is also one, for he, too, pretends to be someone he is not, though with notably more skill and élan than his rival (65).[64] It is not for his historically precocious grasp of historical difference that Valla should be commended but for his mastery of rhetorical technique.

If Valla's epochal status depends on his grasp of anachronism in *On the Donation*, it needs to be rethought. The errors and infelicities he castigates in his rhetorical showpiece are not anachronisms but solecisms, barbarisms, and catachreses. Dates and periods are irrelevant to his excoriating critique.[65] Nor was Valla's attack in *On the Donation* received as a strike against the church—until, that is, a century later when polemicized by the Reformers.[66] In 1508, the Vatican commissioned Raphael to design a fresco of the Donation of Constantine. The fresco, most likely executed by Giulio Romano, situates the event not in Constantine's fourth century but in the recently renovated St. Peter's Basilica. The profile portrait of the enthroned pontiff receiving the gift is not of Constantine's contemporary, Sylvester I, but of Romano's, Clement VII.[67] If this is an anachronism, surely in the high Renaissance it cannot be the result of what one Renaissance scholar has termed "diachronic innocence."[68] The fresco represents not the alleged event of centuries past but rather the validity in the present of the transfer it effected. The fresco's modernity attests to the currency and perpetuity of papal sovereignty.

Shakespeare commentary, too, was once too quick to write off anachronisms as errors in the reckoning of time. This book's first chapter, "Shakespeare's First Anachronism," focuses on criticism's first application of the stigma to Shakespeare: the charge of anachronism in Hector's citation of Aristotle in *Troilus and Cressida*. It is often paired with another literary anachronism, Virgil's treatment of Dido and Aeneas as contemporaries when they were reckoned to have lived two centuries apart. Like the word *anachronism* itself, preoccupation with the date of the Trojan War derives from seventeenth-century chronologists: it is the cardinal date of ancient history, the starting point from which the diverse world calendars were synchronized. Eighteenth-century commentators look for the same kind of synchrony in Shakespeare. Scores of violations are flagged in editions, and various excuses are made for them, from the printers' illiteracy to Shakespeare's flaunting of poetic license. But this chapter turns the tables: it is not chronological transgressions that call for explanation but rather the expectation that all elements of a play be in sync with the time of the play's action. For the semantic scope of Shakespeare's plays is keyed not to the time of their setting in the remote past but to the moment of their enactment in the present. Aristotle is unknown to the play's Homeric Trojans and Greeks, but not to its audience. We might call this a discrepancy between what the characters know and what the audience knows, then, not anachronism but irony. Here, as for Valla, what is at issue is not the computation of time but the arts of language, or more specifically, a dramaturgy whose particular prerogative it is to speak in the present while its action pretends to be happening in the past.

It is not only Shakespeare's indifference to chronology that Shakespeareans have regretted but also that of the compilers of the 1623 folio volume that defined his canon: why did they not record the dates when the plays were written? Chapter 2, "Shakespeare in Chronological Order," ventures an answer: because they were not interested in Shakespeare's development. Genre was the first folio's organizing principle, as its title made clear: *Mr. William Shakespeares Comedies, Histories, & Tragedies.* Subsequent editions—the seventeenth-century folios and the eighteenth-century multivolume octavos and quartos—retained the generic schema, sometimes with adjustments and refinements. Not until the late eighteenth century was a chronology for the order in which Shakespeare wrote his works attempted, and not until the middle of the twentieth did that order become standard in editions of his collected works. Since then, chronology has remained the bedrock of Shakespeare studies, providing the basis for how we interrelate the plays and contextualize them. And yet this chronology is becoming increasingly untenable, and not only because the dates of the plays' composition, unlike those of their performance or of their publication, remain conjectural. It is because chronology, the schema that attributes each play to one hand at one point in time, cannot accommodate the complexities (coauthorship, revision, and adaptation) that are now seen to constitute the canon.

Chapter 3, "Period Drama in the Age of World Pictures," turns from the chronologizing of Shakespeare's plays in print to their periodizing on stage. In the only visualization we have of a Shakespearean play from his lifetime, periodization is moot. In the Longleat drawing of *Titus Andronicus*, only Titus's costume might belong to the fifth-century time frame of the play: the attire and weaponry of the others are modern. If *Titus* had been performed in 1800, however, all characters would have been uniformly in ancient attire as ascertained by historical and archaeological research. The turn of the nineteenth century marks the beginning of period drama: costumes, props, and settings are synchronized with the historical time of the play's action. With such a radical change, theater takes on a new mimetic function: instead of holding up a mirror to the audience, it presents a picture of a world from the past set off by the picture-frame stage. At the same time, historical painting (Benjamin West) and the historical novel (Walter Scott) commit to period coherence, and philosophy backs them with an epistemological correlate: the Weltanschauung, or world picture, by which each world-historical epoch is distinguished.[69]

With Chapter 4, "Secularity before Revelation," the book ends as it began, with an anachronism, this time from the heathen world of *King Lear*. Lear's BC Fool delivers a prophecy that, as he points out, will not be given until the time of Merlin, King Arthur's seer, in the next millennium: "This prophecy Merlin shall make, for I live before his time."[70] The Fool's anticipation of Merlin, like Hector's of Aristotle, has a long history of being flagged as an anachronism. But prophecy is an extraordinary kind of speaking ahead of time, and the Fool speaks a prophecy of a prophecy. It is an extreme kind of prolepsis, in keeping with the play's own operational tactic of gesturing toward a salvational program that in Albion had not yet been revealed in the eighth century before Christ. Those gestures are highly theatricalized in *Lear*: the apocalyptic storm, the fallen man's resurrection, the "Turlygod" (an anagram?) beggar from Bedlam in loincloth who compels charity by displaying his wounds, the image of the "promised end" that looks more like the Pietà than the Parousia. Anachronism, in this play, disrupts not only chronology but also eschatology. By the twentieth century, what was once the play's faltering intimation of a typology still under wraps is taken for something else: a godless world, the hallmark of its secular tragic greatness. If there is one temporal marker observed by Shakespeare's stagecraft, more often in the breach than in the keeping, it is the BC-AD axis.

>>><<<

Four Shakespearean Period Pieces could be said to take part in the ostensible transvaluation of the four critical regulates that are its subject. It focuses on aspects of Shakespeare studies where the long-term sway of chronology, periods, and secularity can no longer be taken for granted. Yet this book often resorts to those very categories. It uses the word *anachronism* while querying its proleptic application to Shakespeare. It cannot avoid chronology and the logic of one thing after another that it upholds. Its critique of periods is conspicuously period based, often hovering over the eighteenth century. (Indeed, the entire book's argument could itself be seen as a brazen act of periodization: a new epistemic order is overtaking the old—"a change is in the air.") The final chapter, in accounting for the godforsaken world of *Lear*, ends up adopting, albeit with a difference, the secularization mechanism whose overuse it also decries.

Reliance on disciplinary heuristics, it is hoped, need not preclude their critique. One can live in a glass house and still throw stones.

Shakespeare's First Anachronism

It is better to recognize the necessity of anachronism as something positive.
G. DIDI-HUBERMAN, "Before the Image, Before Time"

Hector's citation of Aristotle in *Troilus and Cressida* is Shakespeare's first anachronism. Or rather, it is the first instance of something in Shakespeare's plays being *called* an anachronism, an error in the order of chronological time. As commentators are still noting, the error is colossal: almost a millennium separates the Trojan hero from the Greek philosopher. But it is only an error by a standard alien to Shakespearean drama: that of world chronology, the highly technical study that introduced the term *anachronism* into English. By that standard, the play's dialogue should be keyed to the date of the play's action in the twelfth century BC. Instead, the dialogue of *Troilus and Cressida*, like that of all Shakespeare's plays, references the present of its composition and first performances. Hector did not know of Aristotle; Shakespeare and his audience did. The semantics of Shakespeare's plays is generally modern, that is, indexed to the time of their writing. If that is the norm, how can any instance of it be taken to be error? The error here is not Shakespeare's, and it is not chronological: it is the commentators', and it is categorical. "Aristotle" names not the Greek who lived from 384 to 322 BC but the philosopher who set down the guiding principles, rational and ethical, for action. This is the Aristotle who is absent from the world of *Troilus and Cressida*, and his absence makes all the difference.

>>><<<

In the seventeenth-century quarto and folio editions of *Troilus and Cressida*, Hector invokes Aristotle during the debate over whether the Trojans should return the abducted Helen or continue the fight to keep her. When his two younger brothers, Paris and Troilus, rashly argue for the latter, Hector chides them by invoking Aristotle.[1]

> Hect. *Paris* and *Troylus*, you have both said well:
> And on the cause and question now in hand,
> Have gloz'd, but superficially; not much
> Unlike young men, who *Aristotle* thought
> Unfit to heare Morall Philosophie.

Eighteenth-century editors were baffled by Hector's naming Aristotle. Could Shakespeare possibly have thought that the fourth-century BC Greek philosopher predated the twelfth-century BC Trojan hero?

When Nicholas Rowe, Shakespeare's first eighteenth-century editor, encountered Hector's citing of Aristotle, he did what he did whenever he noted what he assumed to be a textual error: he tacitly corrected it. He replaced "Aristotle" with a metrically equivalent and chronologically indeterminate "graver Sages." In his edition, Hector's two brothers

> Have gloss'd, but superficially; not much
> Unlike young Men, whom graver Sages think
> Unfit to hear moral Philosophy.[2]

Alexander Pope, Shakespeare's next editor, follows Rowe's precedent, footnoting the emendation and justifying it in his preface. He classifies "Hector's quoting Aristotle" among the folio's numerous "blunders and illiteracies," like the ungrammatical Latin of such stage directions as "*Actus tertia, Exit Omnes, Enter three Witches solus.*" Such errors betray a degree of ignorance beyond Shakespeare's alleged unfamiliarity with the ancients. Anyone who had "the least tincture of a School or the least conversation with such as had" would have known that Aristotle postdated Hector. Pope instead blames the folio's publishers, whose "ignorance shines almost in every page."[3]

It is the emendation of "*Aristotle*" to "graver Sages" that Lewis Theobald targets in his scathing 194-page critique of Pope's 1725 edition, *Shakespeare restored: or, a specimen of the many errors, as well committed, as unamended, by Mr Pope in his late edition of this poet.*[4] In the appendix, a two-page essay on "transgressions in Time" includes the marginal subheadings "Anachronism consider'd" and "Anachronisms familiar with Shakespeare."[5] This is the first application of *anachronism* to Shakespeare's text. The note begins by exposing the error the emendation had concealed: "'Tis certain, indeed, that *Aristotle* was at least 800 Years subsequent in Time to *Hector.*" It proceeds to expose a second anachronism, "every whit as absurd," in the very next line. "Philosophy" itself also postdated Hector: "*Pythagoras* was the first who invented the Word *Philosophy.* . . . And he was near 600 Years after the Date of *Hector.*"[6] It was not Shakespeare's publishers who committed these anachronisms, as Pope had alleged, but Shakespeare himself, as Theobald sets out to prove with a generous sampling of many more instances from his works. His first specimens of temporal offenses are from the plays set in antiquity: a few more from *Troilus* (Ajax's nerves are likened to those of Milo, "who was not in Being till 600 Years after that *Greek*") as well as from *Coriolanus* (Galen is named, "who was not born till the second Century of the Christian Æra").

That Shakespeare should have committed anachronisms in plays set in the ancient past was to be expected. Throughout the seventeenth century, commentators, both biographical and critical, invariably stressed Shakespeare's limited knowledge of the ancients, the result, it was said, of his low-level provincial education.[7] But why should such slips crop up in plays about the past of his own nation, a past he knew well, as was apparent, according to Theobald, in his use of "the *English* Annals" as sources for his history plays?

> Yet, in his King *Lear*, he has ventur'd to make *Edgar* talk of the *Curfew*, a Thing not known in *Britain* til the *Norman* Invasion: In his King *John* he above fifty times mentions *Cannons*, tho *Gunpowder* was not invented till above a Century and a half after the Death of that Monarch: and what is yet more singular, (as he could not be a Stranger to the Date of a remarkable Man, who liv'd so near his own Time) twice in the Story of *Henry* VI. he makes mention of *Machiavel.*[8]

These many examples of "Innovation upon Chronology" were not, Theobald insists, inadvertent. Like Hector's anachronism, they were "the Effect of Poetick Licence in [Shakespeare], rather than Ignorance." And Shakespeare was not above flaunting his use of this "Licence." In pagan *King Lear*, Theobald points out, the Fool, after delivering a "Dogrel Prophecy" chock-full of contemporary references, concludes by drawing attention to his own flagrant prolepsis: "*This Prophecy* Merlin *shall make; for I do live before his time.*" Theobald imagines Shakespeare deriding the very prerogative he exploits: "he may be presum'd to sneer at his own Licentiousness."[9]

But it is Theobald who is sneering, in his self-appointed responsibility to castigate excesses of poetic liberty. Theobald concludes his long note in *Shakespeare restored* by offering to provide "ten Times the Number" of anachronisms he has just discussed, and indeed he flags at least that many in the notes to his own 1733 edition of Shakespeare's plays: "I thought it my Duty, to discover some *Anachronisms* in our Author."[10] In both his 1726 critique of Pope's edition as well as in the preface and notes to his own edition, Theobald locates so many anachronisms in both modern and ancient drama that he might have concluded that they were typical of the genre rather than an aberration. He notes their frequency in English playwrights besides Shakespeare both before and after the Restoration. In Beaumont and Fletcher's tragicomedy *The Humorous Lieutenant,* one of the successors of Alexander the Great appears with pistol in hand "1500 Years before Fire-arms were ever thought of," and in Dryden and Lee's *Oedipus,* the "Theatre at Athens" is mentioned, though surely those two dramatists had enough "Dramatical Chronology" to know that no theaters existed in the time of Oedipus.[11] A translator of Greek drama, Theobald also cites numerous examples from ancient comedy and tragedy, postponing, he explains, the discovery of "the Anachronisms of Aeschylus" until the publication of his own translation of his tragedies.[12] Their frequency among the ancient playwrights authorizes their modern successors: "Poets of our own Nation may be justified in these Liberties by Examples of the Antients."[13]

All the same, critical intervention is needed. Ideally, for Theobald, a play's allusions would observe its historical setting as closely as possible so that "if there was not Chronological Truth, there was at least Chronological Likelihood." Thus, in the *Henry VI* plays, he has no objection to the two mentions of Machiavelli because the dates of the Italian politician "are very near the Time of the Action," the reign of Henry VI. The discrepancy is so slight, he maintains, that it might pass unnoticed by an English audience. But when Hector cites Aristotle or the Fool quotes Merlin, Shakespeare "goes out of his Jurisdiction," and it is the editor's duty to catch out these "voluntary Transgressions of Time" and subject them to "the Penalty of the Criticks Laws."[14]

After Theobald, Shakespeare's editors continue to flag anachronisms as if it were their prescribed duty. And Hector's anachronism remains the prime example. Samuel Johnson asks why commentators should be troubled by the Trojan's anachronism when it is only one among many: "We need not wonder to find *Hector* quoting *Aristotle,* when we see the loves of *Theseus* and *Hippolyta* combined with the Gothick mythology of fairies."[15] George Steevens attributes the anachronism to the frequent computational errors found in the romances on which most of the comedies and tragedies were based.[16] Edward Capell condemns "Aristotle" as a "violent anachronism" while regretting that the precise source of the error remains unknown.[17] For Edmond Malone, Shakespeare's anachronisms are his own, and they are chronic. As he observes in noting another anachronism in *Troilus and Cressida*—Ulysses's comparison of Ajax to "bull-bearing Milo," the sixth-century BC wrestler—"our author here, as usual, pays no regard to chronology."[18] His indifference extends to modern English history, as Malone points out, in his notes to *1 Henry IV*, for example: "*Turkies* were not brought into England till the time of Henry VIII," and Shakespeare has "fallen into an anachronism, in furnishing his tavern in Eastcheap with sack in the time of Henry IV," when sack was not sold in taverns (only in apothecary shops) "till the 33d year of King Henry VIII. 1543."[19] These lapses in the order of time were particularly galling to the editor who, as will be discussed in chapter 2, was obsessed from the start to the finish of his career with chronologizing Shakespeare's plays. As he repeats in all three of the chronological essays he published, "It is certain that there is nothing in which [Shakespeare] is less accurate, than the computation of time."[20]

Editors up through the present have continued the tradition of highlighting the Trojan anachronism. Consider the following glosses in recent editions of *Troilus and Cressida*:

An obvious (and trivial) anachronism.

Arden 2 (1982)

Shakespeare may not have realized that Aristotle lived after the date of the Trojan War.

Oxford Shakespeare (1982)

The mention of Aristotle in ancient Troy is, of course, an anachronism.

Riverside (1997)

Aristotle (384–22 BC) lived long after the Trojan War (c. early 12th century BC) and Homer (probably ninth BC), and the anachronism offended some early editors of Shakespeare like Rowe, but these dates were imperfectly understood in the Renaissance.

Arden 3 (1998)

An obvious anachronism, since Aristotle lived several centuries after the Trojan War.

New Cambridge Shakespeare (2003)

The reference to Aristotle is, of course, an anachronism.

New Penguin Shakespeare (2006)

Aristotle famous Greek philosopher; in fact, he lived several centuries after the Trojan war.

RSC Shakespeare (2007)

This is an anachronistic reference to Aristotle's *Nicomachean Ethics*.

Norton Shakespeare (2015)

Editors no longer systematically draw attention to Shakespeare's anachronisms, of course. But that they should continue to mark this one bears witness to a deep-seated expectation: a play's dialogue should be in sync with its historical setting.[21] The red flag still pops up, as if to warn the reader that the play has lost its chronological footing.

>>><<<

On Shakespeare's stage, would an anachronism even have registered?[22] Would there have been any visual indication of the vast distance that separated the time of the play's early spectators from that of the play's action just before the fall of Troy? No scenery specified a time; if props were used—a tent from which Achilles and Patroclus emerge and return, a wall from which Pandarus and Cressida observe the procession of Trojans—they would have been generic.[23] Before the closing of the theaters in 1642, ancient Trojan and Greek as well as Roman characters appear to have been mainly attired in apparel roughly contemporary with that of their modern English counterparts.[24] So, too, they would have read modern codices, written in modern table books, and marked time with modern clocks. Garments might indicate a character's gender, ethnicity, nationality, rank, age, occupation, and order of being (supernatural, allegorical), but not his or her historical period.[25]

FIGURE 1.1. Artist unknown, *The Somerset House Conference* (1604). PHOTO-GRAPH: © National Portrait Gallery, London

When dressed for battle, the ancient warriors of *Troilus and Cressida* would have donned the same modern swords, helmets, breastplates, and shoulder armor that the players would have worn when staging more recent historical battles at Dunsinane (1054), for example, or Agincourt (1415). When the Trojan and Greek peers met in council, they might have appeared in ruffed doublets and hose, perhaps not unlike those worn by the delegates in the 1604 group portrait of the Somerset House Conference (fig. 1.1), where the terms to end another war, between England and Spain, were being negotiated. Certainly the inventories of theatrical apparel we have for the Admiral's Men suggest a good selection of attire suitable for dignitaries. "Senators caps" and "senators gown" are inventoried in Philip Henslowe's account books as well as numerous ruff collars, black doublets, and robes in velvet and damask.[26]

That plays set in the ancient world were performed primarily in varieties of dress similar to those worn by their audiences is often thought to have had an economic rationale. The cost of making ancient apparel for a cast of scores may well have been exorbitant for acting companies accustomed to acquiring ready-made clothes, with minor exceptions, through purchase, loan, or gift.[27] But it is not only on stage that the past is not visually differentiated from the present. The same indifference to historical setting is apparent, for example, in the woodcut illustrations on the title pages of two other plays set during the ten-year duration of the Trojan War: Thomas Heywood's *The Iron Age* (fig. 1.2) and *The Second Part of the Iron Age* (fig. 1.3), both published in 1632 though performed in 1612.

These woodcuts are not visual records of plays performed twenty years before their publication, as their elaborate scenic backgrounds confirm. They are instead images keyed to the playbooks themselves.[28] The first, "The Combate betwixt *Hector* and *Aiax*," illustrates the stage direction at the end of *actus secundus*: "*Hector* takes up a great peece of a Rocke, and casts it at *Aiax*; who teares a young Tree up by the rootes and assailes *Hector*."[29] Hector's armor, cap-a-pie, is fully modern, from his brimmed and crested ("morion") helmet to his protective steel-plated footwear. At his feet lie an embossed spiked shield and a broken broadsword with a bird's head on its hilt. The second woodcut compresses three successive episodes: the meeting of the sinister Sinon and Thersites, the exit of the Greeks with javelins from the Trojan horse (with the avenger Pyrrhus in the lead), and the burning of Troy—"Troy, no Troy but fire."[30] The deceitful Sinon conceals himself in a generic cloak, but brook-backed Thersites is in modern, even smart attire: a feathered hat, boots with roweled spurs, doublet and pantaloons, and a sheathed longsword.[31] In both woodcuts, the city of Troy, before and after its destruction, is also modern: behind medieval crenellated fortifications, with an arched portal that remains intact in the first (with gridded portcullis) but is breached in the second, as if by the horse's

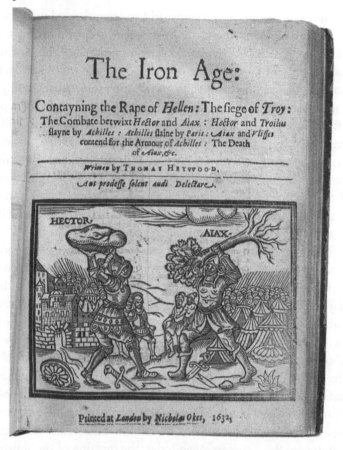

FIGURE 1.2. Hector and Ajax in combat. Thomas Heywood, title page to *The Iron Age* (London, 1632). Used by permission of the Folger Shakespeare Library (133214)

entry. In the latter, steeples are just discernible on the horizon of billowing flames.

As on Shakespeare's stage, the printed woodcuts show no interest in visually differentiating Troy's twelfth century BC from London's seventeenth AD. It is tempting to classify them with the medieval book illuminations the art historian Erwin Panofsky drew on to distinguish the Renaissance from the Middle

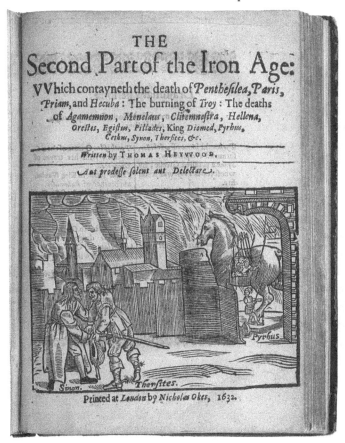

THE
Second Part of the Iron Age:

VVhich contayneth the death of *Penthefilea*, *Paris*,
Priam, and *Hecuba* : The burning of *Troy* : The deaths
of *Agamemnon*, *Menelaus*, *Clitemnestra*, *Hellena*,
Oreftes, *Egiftus*, *Pillades*, King *Diomed*, *Pyrhus*,
Cethus, *Synon*, *Therfites*, &c.

Written by T H O M A S H E Y W O O D.

Aut prodeffe folent aut Delectare.

Printed at London by Nicholas Okes, 1632.

FIGURE 1.3. Sinon and Thersites embracing outside the gates of Troy. Thomas Heywood, title page to *The Second Part of the Iron Age* (London, 1632). Used by permission of the Folger Shakespeare Library (115901)

Ages. In the earlier period, subjects were borrowed from the classical past but presented in terms of the present, so that, for example, in the illuminations to the Carolingian *Commentary on Martianus Capella*, Achilles, Patroclus, Dido, and Aeneas are depicted playing chess clad in medieval garb.[32] The 1612 woodcut shows no signs of the "historical consciousness" by which Panofsky and the many scholars influenced by him differentiated the Renaissance from earlier ages as well as their own present.[33]

When Hector's naming of Aristotle registers as an anachronism, the play is being imagined "in period," that is, in keeping with the style of the historical time in which it had been set by its sources. But if that remote date were not indicated on stage by synchronous costume, props, and scenery—if there were no illusion of a uniform antiquity to unsettle—would spoken anachronisms have flared up? As chapter 3 will discuss, it was not until around 1800 that attempts were made to dress actors unvaryingly "in period." Even after the Restoration, when the budget for theatrical costume increased under royal sponsorship, male characters in Greek and Roman plays were attired in classicized apparel, while women still wore contemporary, often fashionable, gowns. The engraved frontispiece to *Troilus and Cressida* in Rowe's 1709 edition (fig. 1.4) depicts the climactic scene in which Troilus (behind the curtain and restrained by Ulysses) witnesses Cressida handing his love token to Diomedes.[34] Diomedes (like Ulysses and Troilus) is clad in breastplate, plumed helmet, and tunic, while Cressida wears a modish contemporary gown with plumed headdress.

But what about the object—the sleeve—they hold between them, the pledge Troilus gave to Cressida that she here gives to Diomedes who will on the battlefield wear it in his helm to taunt Troilus? In the 1709 illustration, the engraver, no doubt asking himself the same question, fashions it to quite precisely replicate the dangling bell sleeve on Cressida's Rococo gown. But Troilus's sleeve is an identifiable article of Elizabethan clothing, detachable and to be tied or pinned to a doublet.[35] In ancient Troy, the prop is another of the play's copious anachronisms. But to dismiss it as that, as so often, misses the point. *Sleeve* in early modern English is used to reference the covering not only of a man's arm but of his sword. *Sleeve* and *sheath* are synonyms, and as anyone in Shakespeare's audience with schoolboy Latin would have known, the Latin translation of *sheath* goes some way to explaining why Troilus shatters at the sight of Cressida coyly

FIGURE 1.4. Diomedes and Cressida. Elisha Kirkall after François Boitard, frontispiece to *Troilus and Cressida*, *The Works of Mr. William Shakespear*, ed. Nicholas Rowe, 4:1810 (London, 1709). Photograph: Beinecke Rare Book and Manuscript Library, Yale University (Ig 17 09R)

surrendering his sleeve to Diomedes: "To Sheath, or put into a sheath. *1 Vagino, invagino recondere in vaginam.*"[36]

Only later in the century was a play's action visually cordoned off from the present of performance by the proscenium stage and a curtain that, when dropped, completed the enclosure of the stage; only then were characters given historically authentic clothing, weaponry, and props based on antiquarian and archaeological research. Shakespeare's plays set in historical time were thereby visually distanced from the "now" of the audience and set back to the "then" of the play's historical source.

Once plays located in the historical past are visually "historicized," the earlier tradition of performing Shakespeare in dress like that being worn by the audience appears absurdly anachronistic.

Two centuries after the performance of Shakespeare's plays, the antiquarian Francis Douce ridicules the contemporary costumes worn by the generation of Shakespearean actors before him:

> Many persons now recollect the state of the English stage in Garrick's time, when that excellent performer used to exhibit his Hamlet in a common French suit of black velvet and a cocked hat, and his Macbeth in a scarlet coat with broad gold lace like the uniform of a modern general. Quin is said to have played Othello in a flowing powdered periwig.[37]

Also "as an object of amusement," Douce compiles a partial list of "The Anachronisms and Some Other Incongruities of Shakspeare."[38] Here, as with Panofsky, the observation of historical difference is seen to mark the present off from a dimmer past.

As far as is known, throughout the three-hundred-year interval between the Stationers' register entry in 1603 and the play's revival at the turn of the twentieth century, Shakespeare's *Troilus and Cressida* was never performed on the English stage.[39] The play was not produced until 1898 in Berlin when, for the first time, the kind of archaeological evidence that had existed for the Greeks and Romans was unearthed for the Trojans.[40] Heinrich Schliemann's excavations from Troy and Mycenae were exhibited in Berlin in 1882, displaying the hoard of artifacts known as the "Treasure of Priam," including diadems, shields, goblets, and lances. When he discovered the most famous and evocative of the artifacts, a gold mask, Schliemann was said to have wired to the king of Greece from the excavation site: "I have gazed upon the face of Agamemnon."[41] The first English production in 1907 was also in classical dress, set before Doric columns with assorted Greek artifacts as props, offering a picture of Greek or Trojan life of the Homeric period. William Poel's 1912 setting of the play was also produced in researched historical dress, though not of the Trojan War but of Shakespeare's own time.[42] As the program notes explained, the Greeks were outfitted as Elizabethans and the Trojans in flamboyant masque costumes based on Inigo Jones's drawings. To further ground the play in Shakespeare's time, the notes connected the play to George Chapman's 1598 translation of the *Iliad* and proposed that Achilles was intended to represent the intransigent Earl of Essex, the dedicatee of the translation.[43] Hector's naming of Aristotle would have been perfectly in keeping with the courtly Tudor ambience.

It would have been in sync, too, when the play was staged around 1600. Indeed, fathers and schoolmasters in the play's first audiences might well have had occasion to quote to their headstrong sons and pupils the very passage that Hector cites. Aristotle's dictum from *Nicomachean Ethics* that young men were unfit for philosophy was itself commonplace, quoted by Erasmus, Richard Mulcaster, Nicholas Grimald, and Francis Bacon as well as circulating in popular handbooks and paraphrases.[44] And if the play was indeed written for or performed at the Inns of Court, as numerous scholars have argued,[45] the reference to Aristotle during what has been termed the "Aristotelian revival" might have been particularly timely.[46] "Aristotle," then, might have had the same topical reference as the Prologue's unconventional appearance in bellicose armor that many scholars have taken to signal the rivalry between theatrical companies known as the War of the Theatres.[47] Prologues and epilogues, delivered on the edges of the play's action and addressed directly and exclusively to the audience, tend toward topicality and colloquialism. In the epilogue, Pandarus anticipates that his final exit will be hissed (rather than applauded) by a "galled goose of Winchester," a prostitute from the same diocese of Winchester as the Globe Theatre itself, who is infected by the venereal disease from which he also suffers. He promises shortly to bequeath the same disease to the audience, the syphilis he earlier termed the "Neapolitan bone-ache" for its reputed origin in modern Naples.[48]

Only if a play were staged to conform with the period of its action could anachronism disrupt its representational surface. In a performance keyed to the time of performance, however, references to contemporary persons and events are the norm. Like all Shakespeare plays set in antiquity, *Troilus* abounds in such references. As the play set farthest back in antiquity, it may contain more than any other. It features anachronisms pertaining to weaponry (scimitars, beavers, gauges), food (mince pie, potatoes), dress (plackets, leather jerkins, chivalric sleeves, gauntlets), custom (playing at bowls, dancing "high lavolt," "taborins"), technology (wall hangings, compassed windows, table books with clasps, a codex book, a shoehorn, spectacles), law (primogeniture, chivalry, pressing to death, fee farm, tithes), disease (the "Neapolitan bone-ache," lazars), professions (tapster, drayman), and idioms (the rude Italian for female genitalia, *chipochia*).[49] Productions that set action before pedimented temples and Hellenized sculptures, for example, might well be disturbed by the dialogue's allusions to chapmen, Friday fast days and Sunday feast days, canonization, angels, cherubim, the conjuring of devils, the seven deadly sins, the world's end, the state of grace, and in expletives like "God-a-mercy," "the Lord be praised," and "'sfoot." While notably out of kilter with the time of the Trojan War, these terms would have all been at home in the time of the play's early stagings. They are not errors in the order of time but rather modernisms, updatings attuned to the present of the play's enactment.

>>><<<

Hector's naming of Aristotle was not the first literary anachronism to receive critical attention in the eighteenth century. Commentators on Virgil's *Aeneid*, from the late fourth-century grammarian Servius to the Italian humanists and the French neoclassicists, had noted that a gap of centuries separated Aeneas from Dido, the fall of Troy from the building of Carthage.[50] In England, John Dryden's dedicatory essay to his 1697 translation of the *Aeneid* defended "the Famous anachronism, in making *Æneas* and *Dido* Contemporaries. For 'tis certain that the Heroe liv'd almost two hundred years before the Building of *Carthage*."[51] Following the earlier commentators, Dryden appealed to poetic license, explaining that the liberties Virgil took with time enhanced the quality of his heroic poem by making it both more delightful and more instructive. The romance between the Trojan hero and the Carthaginian queen provided "the most pleasing entertainment of the *Æneis*," and its violent dissolution explained the inveterate hostility between Carthage and Rome: "This was the Original, says [Virgil], of the immortal hatred betwixt the two Rival Nations."[52]

While approving of Virgil's anachronism, Dryden is disinclined to extend the privilege to lesser poets. "Chronology at best is but a Cob-web Law," he maintains, meaning not that the law is easily broken, as he is often taken to mean, but rather that only poets of Virgil's stature, like the largest insects, can escape its hold: "he broke thro' it with his weight."[53] Indeed, one might wonder whether Dryden would extend the privilege to any poet but Virgil. He compares the poet's license to break the law of chronology to the sovereign's privilege to abrogate the laws of the land: "A Monarch may dispense with, or suspend his own Laws," not unconditionally but only "when he finds it necessary so to do, especially if those Laws are not altogether fundamental."[54]

Dryden raises the question of anachronism in a purely literary context in a defense of Virgil's preeminence that covers a full range of literary topics, including the relation of epic poetry to drama, the Aristotelean rules, the moral purpose of epic, and Latin versus English metrics. But the term originated in another discourse altogether. It is to Joseph Justus Scaliger, "the father of chronology," that the first uses of *anachronism* have been credited. Around the turn of the seventeenth century, Scaliger revolutionized traditional chronology through what Anthony Grafton has termed "technical" or "systematic" chronology.[55] In this system, the world's calendars and genealogies were synchronized according to a single fixed scale, which Scaliger called the "Julian Period." As Grafton demonstrates, technical chronology played a central role in scholarship up through the Enlightenment, engaging the most innovative and erudite scholars of the time.[56] Scaliger's computations were reproduced, debated, and emended by a wide range of scholars, including Johannes Kepler, Denis Pétau, Christopher Helvicus, and Isaac Newton.

The subject was also popularized through a number of chronological primers or digests, such as Thomas Hearne's *Ductor historicus, or, A short system of universal history* (1698), which offers
"A Chronology of the most Celebrated Persons and Actions
from the Creation to this Time" accompanied by "Definitions,
and Explications of Terms used in History and Chronology."[57]
Edmund Coote's popular *The English School-Master* (1596) prefaces his brief chronology with "Directions to the Ignorant,"
instructing the student to read the dated events "so often, un-
till thou canst runne them over as fast as any other English."[58]
James Ussher's universal chronology, which retained Scaliger's
Julian period while emending his chronology, was reproduced
in the marginal notes of editions of the Authorized King James
Bible from 1701 until well into the twentieth century.[59] By the
eighteenth century, chronology was a subject in its own right,
recommended to students of both history and theology by
such authorities as Samuel Johnson, John Locke, and Edward
Gibbon.[60]

The scholar named "the father of chronology" might also be
credited with having fathered anachronism. In the prolegomenon
to the expanded 1598 edition of Scaliger's *Opus de emendatione
temporum* (first published in 1583), the term appears three times
in Greek to flag erroneous dates that had skewed attempts to
devise a comprehensive world chronology.[61] Sir Walter Raleigh,
who draws on Scaligerian chronology throughout his *History of
the World* (1614), follows his usage, anglicizing the term. Fearing his own chronological table might include erroneous dates,
he invites their correction: "It may serve to free the Booke, and
likewise the Reader . . . from anie notorious *Anachronicisme*."[62] In
his notes to Michael Drayton's *Poly-olbion* (1622), John Selden,
known as the "English Scaliger," when discriminating between
fictive and historical accounts, protests that the Brutus legend is
full of "intollerable Antichronismes," errors in what he termed
synchronism, the concurrence of events or persons.[63] According
to the *OED*, the first use of *anachronism* in its familiar English

form is in the posthumously published tract of John Gregory, "De Aeris & Epochis," also based on Scaliger, which includes "the Several Accounts of Time among all Nations, from the Creation to the Present Age" (1649). Gregory follows Selden in defining *anachronism* as an "error" in "synchronism."[64] Dryden's attention to anachronism in Virgil also derives, at two removes, from Scaligerian chronology. He borrows heavily from Jean Regnault de Segrais's preface to his 1668 French translation of the *Aeneid*. Segrais in turn credits his long discussion "de l'Anacronisme" to Samuel Bochart, a renowned Huguenot scholar of antiquities who relied on Scaliger's chronologies to correlate his Hebrew, Greek, Roman, and Arabic sources. In his remarks on book four of the *Aeneid*, Segrais includes a letter from Bouchart on Virgil's anachronism in which he calculates the discrepancy by aligning the Hebrew biblical genealogies with Tyrrenhian chronicles.[65]

The noncontemporaneity of Dido and Aeneas can also be found in Scaliger. In *Opus de emendatione temporum*, he calculates an interval of 299 years between the destruction of Troy and the founding of Carthage: "Tot annis Aeneas Dioden antecessit."[66] His calculations are reproduced in subsequent chronologies, as in Helvicus's *Theatrum historicum*, first published in 1609 and reissued six times before being translated into English as *The Historical and Chronological Theatre of Christopher Helvicus* (1687).[67] Hearne, also familiar with Scaliger, accuses Virgil of being "guilty of an Anachronism" in having made "*Aeneas* and *Dido* Cotemporaries [*sic*], whereas they lived 300 Years distant one from another."[68] Virgil's poem continues to provide the prime illustration of chronological error into the next century, as in Ephraïm Chambers's entry on *anachronism* in his *Cyclopædia; or, An Universal Dictionary of Arts and Sciences* (1728): "in matters of chronology, an error in the computation of time. . . . Such is that of *Virgil* who placed *Dido* in *Africa* at the time of *Aeneas* tho, in reality, she did not come there until 3000 [*sic*] Years after the taking of *Troy*."[69] Both Samuel Johnson in his 1755 *Dictionary* and

Denis Diderot in his 1751 *Encyclopédie* illustrate the term with the anachronistic contemporaneity of Dido and Aeneas.[70]

That Virgil's anachronism should have become the locus classicus for the category is not surprising. The date it compromised was of cardinal importance to world chronologists. In the third century BC, Eratosthenes dated the fall of Troy to 1184/1183 BC on the Julian and Gregorian calendars, and that date became the fixed point from which other dates were determined and coordinated, including events in the Old Testament.[71] The date was key to Scaliger's dating of both ancient and biblical history. The year 1184 was the earliest nonbiblical date to be printed in the margins of the King James bibles to align with Jephthah's rule over the Israelites in Judges 11.[72] Any refixing of that date would offset world chronology, as indeed did Isaac Newton's radical revision in the culmination of a lifetime study of chronology, published posthumously in 1724 to great controversy. In attempting to reduce all ancient pagan chronologies to the temporal framework of Scripture, he set the traditional chronological cornerstone back some three hundred years.[73] His redating on the basis of logarithms, stellar coordinates, and solstitial and equinoctial colures had the unintended benefit of reducing the gap between the fall of Troy and the building of Carthage to a mere twenty years.[74] Edward Gibbon, in his *Essay on the Study of Literature* (1764), was among those who applauded Newton's chronology for having made Dido and Aeneas's encounter in Virgil less "irreconcileable to chronological truth." So, too, did Diderot: "I prefer Newton's chronology," he wrote in a short entry in his *Pensées détachées* (1775), "because, if he has calculated accurately, it makes Aeneas the contemporary of Dido."[75] For the same reason, Joseph Priestley, in devising his chronology for his *New Chart of History* (1769), preferred Newton's date to Scaliger's or Ussher's: "The classical reader, I hope, will not be displeased with seeing Dido and Aeneas placed side by side, after having been so long, and so far separated by tasteless chronologers."[76] James Martyn, in a section of his commentary on the *Aeneid* (1770) titled "A

Vindication of the Poet Virgil from the charge of an Anachronism," demonstrated how, as a result of Newton's updating of the Trojan War, the "mighty chronological error of Virgil is reduced from about three hundred years, to no more than nine." He notes "with pleasure" the mutual reinforcement of the chronologer and the poet: "as Sir Isaac Newton has, though undesignedly, justified Virgil, so the authority of that noble poet is a confirmation of the amendment of ancient chronology, which has been made by our great philosopher."[77] As Scaliger's chronology had exposed Virgil's anachronism, so Newton's revised chronology dispelled it.

There is one more famous literary anachronism from antiquity singled out in the early eighteenth century, one that, like Virgil's and Shakespeare's, inserts persons and events from later centuries into the time of the Trojan War and its aftermath. Its detector is, again, Lewis Theobald. In his discussion of Shakespeare's anachronisms, he enumerates many others from ancient drama. The first on the list is from a tragedy he had translated: "The Great Sophocles, in his *Electra*, supposes that *Orestes* was thrown from his Chariot, and kill'd, at the *Pythian Games*; which Games, as the Scholiast tells us, were not instituted till 600 Years afterwards."[78] The reference is to the false report of Orestes's death in a chariot race, delivered to his mother and sister by Orestes's old tutor. In the *Poetics*, Aristotle had cryptically referred to "the account of the Pythian games in *Electra*" as an example of the improbability that tragedy should avoid.[79] The medieval scholiasts or commentators on Aristotle thought the offending improbability must have been Clytemnestra's belief in the false news of her son's death: had it been true, word would have reached her by swifter messengers than the aged tutor.[80] For Theobald, in a long note to his 1714 translation of *Electra*, what constitutes improbability is simply a misdating: "the *Pythian Games* were not instituted till above five [hundred] Years after Orestes was Dead."[81] Sophocles's "Alteration in the *Epocha*" rendered the account "absurd," and to disastrous effect: "this

Falshood ruin'd all the probability of the Piece, of which it was the Foundation." In his own translation, Theobald retained the reference to the Pythian games but cut the long account by almost half, regarding it as "too tedious and *Graphical* a Description of the *Pythian Games* to be relish'd at this time of Day."[82]

Theobald makes the same mistake with Sophocles as with Shakespeare. As Bernard Knox has argued, Greek drama takes place in the present of the dramatist and his audience: "The contemporary reference in all Attic tragedy is so obvious and insistent that the term 'anachronism,' often applied to details of the tragic presentation of mythical material, is completely misleading."[83] As Theobald himself realizes, the Pythian games, while unknown to Orestes, would have been familiar to Sophocles's audience. For Theobald, however, anachronisms are glitches to be marked by the vigilant editor rather than a given of the genre. He must invoke a special dispensation to allow the dramatist to take liberties with "chronological truth."

But no special dispensation is needed to account for references that postdate a play's "chronological truth." Plays are keyed to the "now" of their composition and always open to updating at any subsequent staging. The dramatist's commitment is to his present audience rather than to any earlier historical context. The oddity is not that the dialogue of a play set in the past should extend its semantic reach to the present but rather that editors and critics should have ever expected it to be otherwise. As Schiller once observed and as modern theater historians have reiterated, "all dramatic form makes of the past a present."[84]

So it is with *Troilus and Cressida*. The action of the play, we are told, occurs "after seven years' siege" (1.3.12). But in the play's opening lines, the Prologue translates the Homeric epic's there and then to the drama's here and now with three emphatic temporal deictics: "*Now* on Dardan plains," "*Now* expectation . . . sets all on hazard," and "*Now* good or bad, 'tis but the chance of war" (Prol.13, 20–22, 31, italics added). The time, like the verb tense of these declaratives, is the present. The audience of "fair beholders" experiences the action as it happens before them rather than through the *post facto* lens of narration. The immediacy of its enactment authorizes the contemporaneity of its reference.

>>><<<

This is not to say that *Troilus and Cressida* ignores the remoteness of its historical setting. Signs of antiquity pervade its vernacular dialogue. Archaisms counter its modernisms.[85] Hellenisms and especially Latinisms acoustically situate the play in a long by-gone era. Greek derivatives (*mastic, caduceus, colic, paradox*) are scattered amid Greek proper names. Catalogs recur: of places (the recital of the six gates of Troy: "Dardan and Timbria, Helias, Chetas, Troien, / And Antenorides" [Prol. 16–17]), of warriors retiring from the battlefield ("That's Aeneas," "That's Antenor," "That's Hector" [1.2.180ff.]), and of their fighting there ("The fierce Polydamas / Hath beat down Menon" and so on [5.5.6–14ff.]). In contrast to terse vernacular monosyllables, polysyllabic Latinisms abound: *maculation, propugnation, modicum, deceptious, unplausive, assubjugate, orgulous, mirable, oppugnancy, protractive, uncomprehensive, persistive, recordation, protestation, neglection, flexure, unrespective, abruption.*

The Prologue locates the play in the faraway time when Troy still stood: "In Troy, there lies the scene." It dates the action quite precisely within the ten-year duration of the Trojan War: "after seven years' siege." As we have seen, 1184/1183 was a key date for Scaligerian chronologists in their erudite attempts to coordinate pagan and Christian calendars. But in the Roman historiographical tradition, the Trojan War was the earliest event from which time was counted. According to the classicist Denis Feeney, in Roman accounts like those of Livy and Lucretius, "Troy is the farthest back one can go in order to find examples of human beings doing verifiable things. . . . Beyond that point it is not possible to go."[86] Its destruction marked the beginning of the historical record; behind that epochal watershed were myths about the gods rather than records of the heroic deeds of men. For Horace there may have been heroes and deeds before Troy, but no poets existed to record them, as he famously laments:

> There lived before King Agamemnon many
> men of courage: but all unlamented and
> unknown are crushed in lasting
> darkness, they lack a poet.[87]

For the Romans, Feeney concludes, "Troy is the event horizon."[88]
    The Trojan War serves as the terminus a quo for early modern
historians of antiquity as well. In his *History of the World*, Raleigh
quotes and translates Horace's ode lamenting the lack of records
before Troy: "Ere Agamemnon," deeds were covered in darkness,
"unwept for, and unknowne."[89] Ben Jonson draws on the same
ode in one of his epistles:

> There were brave men before
> Ajax or Idomen, or all the store
> That Homer brought to Troy; yet none so live:
> Because they lacked the sacred pen could give
> Like life unto 'em.[90]

Like Raleigh, Helvicus is unwilling to go "further than the Destruction of Troy" in the account of the ancients in his world
history, since he has no "ancient writer for my President." In
The Historical and Chronological Theatre (1687), he notes that,
"The Destruction of TROY [is] the most ancient and most
noted Epocha among the Gentiles."[91] In *Ductor historicus*, Hearne
separates "civil history" from "ecclesiastical" history, and its inaugural event is "the taking of Troy."[92] England's own history
originated there as well, as in Geoffrey of Monmouth's *The History of the Kings of Britain*, which spans two thousand years, beginning with the founding of Britain by the eponymous Brute,
Aeneas's great grandson, three generations after the fall of Troy.
So, too, in Holinshed's *Chronicles*, England's historical narrative
begins when "Brute with his remnant of Troians arriue in this
Ile," and is dated first in relation to the creation of the world and
then to the fall of Troy: "the yeare of the world 2850, after the
destruction of Troy 66."[93] In sixteenth- and seventeenth-century

almanacs, and in Ussher's chronology, too, the fall of Troy is the earliest event in nonbiblical history, predating other events from which time is reckoned in the Greco-Roman world: the institution of the Olympian games, the reign of Alexander, the founding of Rome, the death of Caesar.[94]

Troilus and Cressida, then, is situated at the outermost rim of ancient history, as far back in classical antiquity as the record extends. It antedates by centuries the time of King Lear and Lear's biblical contemporaries, the Hebrew prophets Isaiah and Elijah.[95] In the Greco-Roman world, history is just beginning; before Troy there is only dateless myth. The Trojan War, as Feeney observes, "is a key marker of the transition from a period of myth to a period of history . . . the moment of passage from a more blessed time of heroes and gods to the continuous time of history."[96] *Troilus* never mentions the war's mythic *casus belli*: the rivalry among the three goddesses for the golden apple. Its reference to past events stops at the abduction of Helen or the time just before: Nestor recalls having fought at Priam's side (4.5.197–98). With mock veneration, Ulysses hails Achilles as "great Thetis' son!" (3.3.94), but otherwise divine lineages are dropped: there is no mention of Helen as the daughter of Jupiter and Leda, for example, or of Aeneas as the son of Venus and Anchises. There is no Homeric or Virgilian interaction between gods and mortals, between their myths and human history. The gods are invoked for purposes of swearing—"by Jove multipotent" (4.5.130), "by great Mars" (199)—or as ground for analogy—Hector moves through the carnage "Like Perseus' horse" (1.3.42); Helenus takes flight from battle "like chidden Mercury from Jove" (2.2.45); Menelaus, like Jove, is transformed by love to a horned bull (5.1.52–53); Cressida's vow of fidelity is as "strong as Pluto's gates" (5.2.160).

Despite its modern orientation, the play remains alert to the extreme antiquity of its Homeric provenance. As in any plot that follows well-known events from the past, the audience knows in advance how they will turn out, for they took place long ago and have been recited and recorded throughout the intervening ages in history, epic, romance, drama, and ballad, in ancient tongues and modern. The characters, however, have not read or heard of them.[97] They do not know that Patroclus will die, that Achilles will be stirred to battle by his death, that Hector will be ignominiously slaughtered, that Cressida will betray Troilus, or even that Troy will be destroyed in fire. Cressida imagines that Troy will end by gradual erosion, "when waterdrops have worn the stones of Troy" (3.2.181). Achilles presumes to "prenominate" the body part where Hector will be mortally wounded, not knowing that his own name will attach to a fatally vulnerable anatomical spot (4.5.250). The irony that "Queen Hecuba laughed that her eyes ran o'er" (1.2.137–38) escapes characters who have no inkling that she will be remembered for her profuse weeping at the loss of her husband, children, and city. Thersites cannot know that in a much later vernacular Ajax's name will be phonetically indistinguishable from the flush toilet, *a jakes*; so only Shakespeare's audience would get Thersites's joke when he describes the incontinent Ajax going "up and down the field asking for himself" (3.3.246–47). The Trojans dismiss all intimations of the future as fear-inducing rant and madness. When Hector and Achilles "prophesy" the outcome of the war, it is mere warrior's boast. Andromache's ominous dreams, Hecuba's visions, Hellenus's premonitions, Cassandra's divinations, and of course Calchas's prophecy all go unheeded. Only the audience hears the irony in Ulysses's lecture to Achilles. The "good deeds" that he insists cannot outlive their performance—"Devoured as fast as they are made, forgot / As soon as done" (3.3.150–51)—are, of course, those that Homer has immortalized.

The characters' ignorance regarding the future is matched by their lack of knowledge about the past: "What's past and what's to come is strewed with husks" (4.5.167). Situated at the beginning of historical time, there is scarcely any past to remember. True to epic form, the play's action "Leaps o'er the vaunt and firstlings of those broils" (Prol.27) to begin in medias res, but unlike the great epics, it does not loop back to recall what came before, as the *Aeneid* does when Aeneas narrates the fall of Troy. Nestor, the oldest Greek, having outlived three generations (he "was a man / When Hector's grandsire sucked" [1.3.292–93]), is hailed as a "good old chronicle, / That hast so long walked hand in hand with time" (4.5.203–4), yet as counselor, he has little wisdom to show for his "stretched-out life" (1.3.61). In the Greek council meeting, instead of imparting sage advice, he simply seconds what has been proposed already, first by Agamemnon and then by Ulysses. And there is no other "old chronicle" for Greece. Agamemnon's reference to "every action that hath gone before, / Whereof we have record" pertains only to the recent past of the "seven years' siege" (1.3.13–14). The meeting with Ulysses that Hector remembers—"in Ilium, on your Greekish embassy" (4.5.216)—falls within the same time frame. Before Helen's abduction, the historical record is obscure. In the Trojan council, while arguing to keep Helen, Troilus asks, "Why keep we her?," and answers his own question: "The Grecians keep our aunt" (2.2.80). A few lines earlier he had alluded to this aunt's exchange as a quid pro quo to Trojan advantage: "And for an old aunt whom the Greeks held captive / He brought a Grecian queen" (77–78). She is mentioned again when Hector refuses to fight Ajax because the latter's mother is the former's "sacred aunt" (4.5.135):

> Thou art, great lord, my father's sister's son,
> A cousin-german to great Priam's seed.
> The obligation of our blood forbids
> A gory emulation 'twixt us twain.
>
> (4.5.121–24)

But who is this aunt who motivates this armistice? No history is given to account for her captivity or the Greeks' refusal to return her to Priam. She remains nameless and without a story.[98]

In the Troy of *Troilus*, there appears to be no writing from the past. The epics of Homer, Virgil, and their modern translators and imitators will not be written until long after Troy's destruction. Likewise, the great Attic tragedies of Aeschylus, Euripides,

and Sophocles that follow the fortunes of both the victorious
and the vanquished postdate the sack of Troy by over six centuries. Without a past of great deeds, mimesis has only the present from which to draw its subject matter: satire is the genre of
the day. In *Troilus*, the Greeks are entertained with impromptu
impersonations of Agamemnon. Patroclus "pageants" the Greek
king as well as his old counselor to Achilles's sidesplitting laugh-
ter and applause (1.3.151–84). Thersites observes others in order
to convert their deeds to entertainment for Ajax and for Achilles as well as for his offstage audience. In the wings he watches
the little melodrama of Cressida's yielding to Diomed with relish (see fig. 1.4), knowing how amused Achilles will be by his
burlesque of it. Satire needs no departed heroes and heroics: it
thrives on present folly and corruption.

Backed up against mythical time, the world of the play has
no cultural legacy. The Trojan debate on Helen's worth (2.2)
is the origin of what will become a long rhetorical tradition of
debating her value, from Gorgias's *Encomium on Helen* to the
Elizabethan schoolroom.[99] Ulysses's speech on degree (1.3.78–
137) has yet to become a political commonplace, as it would after its formulation in Homer and Plato and their medieval and
early modern redactors.[100] In the twentieth century, his theory
is upgraded to a worldview—*The Elizabethan World Picture*—
"common to all Elizabethans of even modest intelligence."[101] In
Troilus, however, Ulysses appears to have devised "the specialty
of rule" speech himself to address the crisis at hand: the emulous
disarray of the Grecian ranks.

And of course, the story of Troilus and Cressida has not yet
been written. The two lovers and their go-between make of
themselves the examples that are not yet available. In the play's
epilogue, Pandarus, having been slapped and cursed by Troilus,
looks for a precedent for his thankless service. "What verse for
it? What instance for it?" (5.11.39–40), he asks, as if forgetting
that by his own earlier dictum he will become that instance, his
own name a byword for *procurer*: "let all pitiful goers-between be
called to the world's end after my name: call them all panders"

(3.2.195–97). Troilus in love speaks in clichés, but only the audience hears them as such, for he knows nothing of the conventions of courtly love. Petrarchism, the English sonnet tradition, Romeo and Juliet, even Dido and Aeneas are beyond him. Lacking "similes" and "comparisons" for constancy, he makes himself into one: "'As true as Troilus' shall crown up the verse," to be cited "in the world to come" (3.2.177). Cressida does the same, promising that should she prove unfaithful, she'll be a byword for inconstancy: "'As false as Cressid'" (191). And Pandarus ratifies both "instances": "Let all constant men be Troiluses, all false women Cressids" (197–98). After witnessing Cressida with her new lover Diomed, Troilus fears that not just false women, but *all* women, "the general sex," will be seen through her example, "Cressid's rule," "a theme / For depravation" (5.2.137–39).

With no past examples, the characters make precedents of themselves, anticipating their own legendary literary status. But theirs is not yet a literary culture. Troilus imagines that the Trojans will be canonized for their defense of Helen (2.2.202). But how? Perhaps it is in the telling rather than in the writing, as Hector assumes when he intrepidly heads for what will be his last battle: "We'll forth and fight, / Do deeds of praise and tell you them at night" (5.3.92–93). Communication tends to take place orally, by messenger, between armies as well as lovers. The one letter Cressida writes to Troilus ends up in shreds. When writing is mentioned, it takes the form of flesh incised with wounds rather than parchment inscribed with letters. Hector catches Achilles perusing him as if he were reading a hunting manual on the best way to stalk and kill an animal: "O, like a book of sport thou'lt read me o'er" (4.5.239). Troilus, enraged by Cressida's betrayal, vows on the battlefield to divulge his passion in bloody red "characters" on Diomed's body (5.2.171). Ulysses finds Cressida's meaning encoded all over her body—eye, cheek, lip, foot—as openly legible as an unclasped book (4.5.55–61). Pandarus concludes the play with the promise of a written document: "Some two months hence my will shall here be made" (5.11.52). His bequest is his own diseased body, marked with the pocks and boils of syphilis—a modern disease, unheard of in the time of Pandarus but known to his audience. This is writing that perishes with the body rather than surviving it.

>>><<<

When Ulysses appears with a proleptic codex in hand, Achilles asks, "What are you reading?" Ulysses responds evasively, "a strange fellow" (3.3.95–96). Later commentators have attempted to supply an author, with candidates including Plato, Aristotle, Seneca, and Montaigne, thereby themselves committing anachronisms akin to Hector's.[102] But before the fall of Troy, there are no authors to cite. Hector names Aristotle not because Shakespeare thought Hector knew Aristotle but to exploit the fact that he could not possibly have known him. The context of the citation is key: reason itself is in the balance. A council has convened to advise Priam on what action Troy should take: should the abducted Helen be held or returned? Hector advises, "Let Helen go," asking what "reason" would deny her return (2.2.17, 23). Troilus responds by offhandedly dismissing reason from their deliberations. Helenus points out the absurdity of its exclusion from a meeting intended to advise the king. Troilus insists that reason conduces to cowardice and in the process repeats the word seven times. Then follows a debate over whether Helen is worth keeping. Troilus argues that since all agreed "'twas wisdom" to abduct Helen ("you all cried 'Go, go!'" [84–85]), there should be no regress now. After Cassandra's raving entrance, prophesying doom unless Helen is released ("Troy burns, or else let Helen go" [112]), Paris reiterates Troilus's argument: the Trojans gave "full consent" to take Helen (132), and their honor as well as Helen's depends on their defending her. And now, after facetiously commending the oratory of his two younger brothers—"Paris and Troilus, you have both said well"—Hector reprimands them for having "glozed— but superficially"; with their rash and shallow arguments they have borne out Aristotle's dictum that "young men" are "Unfit to hear moral philosophy" (163–67). He then proves both his own maturity and his capacity for philosophy by evincing principles of right, the laws both "of nature and of nations" (185). To keep Helen only extenuates the wrong of having taken her in the first place. Yet he then inexplicably does a complete about-face and defers to his little brothers: "yet ne'ertheless, / My sprightly brethren, I propend to you" (189–90), and again, "I am yours, / You valiant offspring of great Priamus" (206–7). He concludes by capitulating to their impulsive advice, proving himself as "unfit for moral philosophy" as he has just charged them with being. Aristotle signals what the Trojan council lacks: a basis for action in reason. The council concludes with Hector's "roisting challenge" (208), one befitting young Troilus, a mere "youth" (5.3.31), but not Priam's seasoned eldest son.

This is a play in which characters are trying hard to think, but with little consequence. It has been called Shakespeare's "most self-consciously philosophical play"[103] because so much of the dialogue takes the form of debate, disputation, reflection, and argument. And yet these cerebral set pieces notably fail to bear on the action. In the Greek council scene, as in the Trojan, reasoned discourse is voiced only to be cast aside. Ulysses analyzes the Greek failure to end the war in terms of the principle of degree: because hierarchy is not recognized, the Greeks are in disarray. And yet by the end of council, his high-minded exposition has given way to a cunning ruse: to stir Achilles from his proud intransigence by promoting Ajax. In the end, Achilles is roused not by Ulysses's philosophical reflections on the need to keep glory alive through constant action but by Patroclus's death. Universals like justice, virtue, and hierarchy, even where they are articulated, have no purchase on action. Instead it is the "universal wolf" of "appetite" (1.3.121) that prevails: Hector's for glory, Paris's for Helen, Troilus's first for Cressida, then, at the inconclusive close of the play, for revenge.

Aristotle is named for the same reason that *reason* is repeated twenty-one times, more often than in any other of Shakespeare's plays:[104] for its absence rather than its presence. Its absence is also underscored by Thersites's tirades against the stupidity of his superiors, "beef-witted" Ajax (2.1.12), "mouldy"-witted Nestor

(2.1.102), Agamemnon with "not so much brain as earwax" (5.1.51–52), Achilles and Patroclus of "too much blood and too little brain" (5.1.47). The characters have a hard time thinking, and not only because thought is antithetical to the passions stirred by the plot's twinned actions of love and war.

As both Trojans and Greeks are shown debating in council, so, too, are both Troilus and Cressida given occasions to think aloud. Cressida's monologue at the end of 1.2 is formally set off from her preceding loose prose banter with Pandarus. Her thoughts are expressed in two forms associated with introspection: the soliloquy (she is alone on stage) and the sonnet (she speaks fourteen lines of rhymed couplets). But her deliberation consists of nothing but a stockpile of truisms. The 1609 quarto typographically flags it as such by marginal inverted commas, the mark of sententiae or wise sayings that are worthy to be copied and redeployed (fig. 1.5).[105]

"Women are angels, wooing." "Things won are done." "Joy's soul lies in the doing." "Men prize the thing ungained more than it is." "Love got [is not] so sweet as when desire did sue" (1.2.277–82). The gist of all five maxims is the same: the object of desire, once obtained, ceases to be desired. Cressida concludes the list with still another: "Therefore this maxim out of love I teach: / '*Achievement is command; ungained beseech*'" (283–84, italics added). In the quarto, it is signaled by italics as well as inverted commas, as if to doubly affirm its import.[106] So, too, the couplet's culminating connective "Therefore" would seem to promise a resolution or conclusion, a logical deduction, perhaps, or (after five trial runs) a perfectly polished formulation. Instead, we get only another maxim, and one of such contorted and elliptic syntax that some editors have suspected textual corruption. Thus, Cressida's attempt at thinking culminates in a rough rehash of what in any case is a given, what every woman in love knows, if she knows anything at all: "That she beloved knows nought that knows not this" (279). It might be called the woman's cogito: the single thought (hold off!) on which her being is precariously predicated.

> *of Troylus and Cresseida.*
>
> Yet hold I off: women are angels woing,
> „Things woone are done,ioyes foule lies in the dooing.
> That shee belou'd,knows naughtthat knows not this,
> „Men price the thing vngaind more then it is,
> That she was neuer yet that euer knew
> Loue got so sweet,as when desire did sue,
> Therefore this *maxim* out of loue I teach,
> "*Atchiuement is command;vngaind beseech,*
> Then though my hearts content firme loue doth beare,
> Nothing of that shall from mine eyes appeare. *Exit.*

FIGURE 1.5. Cressida's commonplaces. *The famous historie of Troylus and Cres-seid* (1609), B3r. From *Troilus and Cressida: First quarto, 1609 / with introductory note by W. W. Greg* (London, 1952)

Yet for Cressida, this knowledge is of no avail. She has framed her sententiae at both ends by her resolution to resist desire: "Yet hold I off," she begins, and concludes with, "Then, though my heart's contents firm love doth bear, / Nothing of that shall from mine eyes appear" (277, 285–86). All the same, she yields to Troilus at the first chance and sees the cardinal knowledge of her sex confirmed when, after their first night together, Troilus takes his leave of her: "O foolish Cressid, I might have still held off, / And then you would have tarried!" (4.2.18–19). Her experience, rather than averting the truism, only confirms it, as it will again when she falls into the hands of the Greek camp.

The play also stages Troilus in thought, indeed, Troilus lost in thought—"You flow to great distraction," observes Ulysses (5.2.43). He thinks aloud as he tries to take in what he cannot believe but has just witnessed: Diomed taking postcoital leave of a besotted Cressida, his own surety of love now in Diomed's hand (fig. 1.4). What is remarkable here is how sexual jealousy, hardly contained during the protracted period of his witnessing the betrayal, breaks out not in inchoate passion but in quasi-methodical analysis of the rationally untenable proposition that something both "is" and "is not." The formulation is at first so contradictory that it requires two speakers stichomythically dividing two verse lines between them to articulate the conflict.

> Troilus. Was Cressid here?
> Ulysses.   I cannot conjure, Trojan.
> Troilus. She was not, sure.
> Ulysses.   Most sure she was.
>   (5.2.131–32)

But then Troilus makes it entirely his own paradox in a single hemistich: "This is and is not Cressid" (153). He internalizes the conflict and then analyzes it within himself: "Within my soul there doth conduce a fight" (154). It isn't a matter of "is" *or* "is not" (like Hamlet's more manageable "to be *or* not to be") but both at once, "is" *and* "is not." He names this proposition "Bifold authority" (151), raising paradox to the dignity of an a priori truth and one that flies in the face of the law of noncontradiction. Is it an accident that the climax of Troilus's thought is the antithesis of Aristotle's first principle, formulated in his *Metaphysics*: "it is impossible for any one to believe the same thing to be and not to be."[107] Without this first principle, nothing could be known.

>>><<<

Despite its ancient setting, *Troilus and Cressida* has been termed "the most modern of Shakespeare's works."[108] Its perceived modernity has been used to explain the fact that, both on stage and in criticism, it was appreciated only belatedly. As Kiernan Ryan has argued, the play's delayed recognition is the result of "its being not merely out of sync with its time, but so far ahead of its time that it took three centuries for the theatre and for critics to catch up with it."[109] In its precocity it has been seen to anticipate twentieth-century critiques of epistemology or metaphysics. Joyce Carol Oates proposed that the play was "one of the earliest expressions of what is now called the 'existential vision.'"[110] David Hillman saw in Troilus after Cressida's betrayal an anticipation of modern post-Cartesian skepticism, an early registering of the loss of any solid epistemological ground on which to stand or to know the other.[111] J. Hillis Miller maintained that the play challenges Western monological metaphysics by refusing absolute terms and values, anticipating the Derridean critique of logocentrism.[112] When, after a long hiatus, the play is revived in the twentieth century, its problematic acts of thinking, knowing, and acting are blamed on an expiring epistemology rather than on the utter absence of one. Its characters are imagined in the aftermath of a philosophical tradition when they are barely on its threshold.

In a time before the wisdom of the ancients (and of those who will subsequently stand on their shoulders), the past is something of a tabula rasa. The salient feature of modernity, "a desire to wipe out whatever came earlier," according to Paul de Man, is unthinkable in archaic Troy, where there is nothing yet to be wiped away.[113] By locating its action at the outermost back reach of history, the play removes its characters from the support of any possible precedents: tradition, experience, authority, and history. Troy's age is like that of "the youngest son of Priam, / Not yet mature," by Troilus's own self-estimation, "simpler than the infancy of truth"; even after suffering betrayal, he remains "young Troilus," "youth," "brave boy." Like Troilus, Troy might be said to be, as the saying goes, born only yesterday. Francis Bacon's famous apothegm might serve as the play's motto: *Antiquitas seculi Iuuentus Mundi*, the age of antiquity is the youth of the world.[114] By this retrograde logic, it is those who live in modern times who have been around for ages. The moderns are the hoary epigones, and the ancients the naive novices.

>>><<<

The action of *Troilus and Cressida* is set as far back in Greco-Roman history as possible. To world chronologers, the date of the fall of Troy was the fixed point from which subsequent dates were computed and coordinated with the calendars of other civilizations. The date's cardinal importance in world chronology may well explain why the charge of anachronism first alights in Shakespeare on the Trojan's mention of Aristotle. But Aristotle is not out of place in the play's contemporary idiom. There is nothing untimely, therefore, about dropping his name during a dramatization of the Trojan War any more than there is about any of the dialogue's many other modern references: all fall within the play's discursive purview.

Yet *Aristotle* is not quite like *potatoes*, *plackets*, and *table books*, and not simply because it is a proper name. *Aristotle* is synonymous with *authority*. The name is the source of what is accepted (or challenged) as knowledge; the prefix "as Aristotle saith" instantiates a proposition's claim to truth.[115] Certainly, there is much in Aristotle that might be pertinent to the deliberations of the Trojan council. The *Nicomachean Ethics* from which the citation is cribbed says much, for example, about right and wrong conduct. But why appeal to Aristotle in support of the claim that young men have no aptitude for moral philosophy? And why after discrediting their judgment does Hector join ranks with the "two young men," his little brothers, as if reverting to their fledgling state? While incidental to the council proceedings, Bacon's dictum applies to the world of the play at large: *Antiquitas seculi Iuuentus Mundi.*

Hector's citing of Aristotle becomes an anachronism in the eighteenth century when an alien computational standard devised by the likes of Scaliger and Newton is drawn into commentary on Shakespeare. Once the standard is introduced, the citation becomes an irregularity to be noted by editors and commentators. Further examples in the plays are checked as slips or glitches. But they can only be that when the play's semantics are assumed to be in sync with the historical time of the action. By stigmatizing such features as errors, commentators risk perpetuating a larger error: that a play represents the past rather than addressing the present via the past. It is a categorical error that takes a living play for a historical record.

The Trojan War in *Troilus and Cressida* does not signify 1184/1183 BC; it signifies a time too early to have a past. This makes for a highly artificial scenario: it puts characters on stage who think and act without precedents in front of an audience for whom they *are* the precedents. The words and deeds that are new to the characters are legendary to the audience. The play's extreme anteriority is not a historical fact, to be observed or transgressed by details. It is a dramatic postulate that enlarges the scope of irony by situating characters and audience at opposite ends of a tradition of almost three millennia.

Shakespeare in Chronological Order

Shakspere must be studied chronologically, and as a whole.
Founder's Prospectus for the New Shakspere Society (1874)

There is something gratifying about seeing Shakespeare's works listed in chronological order. Over the span of a page (or two), it appears to capture Shakespeare's entire literary output as it issued from his pen, one play after another, in the order of time (fig. 2.1). When editions of the complete works are ordered chronologically, our progress through them parallels the course of his development: we encounter the changes in his style and thought as he experienced them. Even if we do not in fact read the plays chronologically (and does anyone?), we can nonetheless imagine that we have in hand the order in which he wrote them, the program by which, through the course of his working life, Shakespeare became, as is often said, *Shakespeare*.

The chronology is also of great practical value. Our critical practices depend on it. It defines the object of our study: it gives us a discrete whole, from first work to last, differentiated on a temporal continuum. Complete unto itself, it appears autonomous, possessing an integrity and momentum of its own. While

PLAYS

1588–93	The Comedy of Errors
1588–92	2 Henry VI
1588–92	3 Henry VI
1588–92	1 Henry VI
1592–93	Richard III
1592–94	Titus Andronicus
1593–94	The Taming of the Shrew
1593–94	The Two Gentlemen of Verona
1588–95	Love's Labor's Lost
1594–96	Romeo and Juliet
1595	Richard II
1594–96	A Midsummer Night's Dream
1590–97	King John
1596–97	The Merchant of Venice
1597	1 Henry IV
1597–98	2 Henry IV
1598–1600	Much Ado About Nothing
1598–99	Henry V
1599	Julius Caesar
1599–1600	As You Like It
1600–02	Twelfth Night
1600–01	Hamlet
1597–1601	The Merry Wives of Windsor
1601–02	Troilus and Cressida
1602–04	All's Well That Ends Well
1603–04	Othello
1604	Measure for Measure
1604–09	Timon of Athens
1605–06	King Lear
1605–06	Macbeth
1606–07	Antony and Cleopatra
1607–09	Coriolanus
1608–09	Pericles
1609–10	Cymbeline
1610–11	The Winter's Tale
1611	The Tempest
1612–13	Henry VIII
1613	The Two Noble Kinsmen

FIGURE 2.1. Chronology at a glance. "The Canon of Plays," from *The Complete Signet Classic Shakespeare*, ed. Sylvan Barnet (New York: Harcourt Brace Jovanovich, 1972), 5. © 1972 South-Western, a part of Cengage, Inc. Reproduced by permission (www.cengage.com/permissions)

isolating the works from the world, it can also put them in contact with the world of both Shakespeare's life and his times. Chronology thus performs a double critical function: it shuts the canon off from the world as a timeless self-contained literary object, but it also opens it up to biography and history. As such, it has proven fundamental to formalist as well as to biographical and historicist criticism. No wonder editions of Shakespeare's complete works tend to be published in chronological order. And no wonder generations of scholars have applied themselves so assiduously to devising that order.

It seems indispensable now, but for a good century and a half after Shakespeare's death, no chronology existed for his works. They were reproduced, read, and discussed with no consideration for when they were written. In the case of the plays, the focus of this chapter, another order prevailed: the generic order of the first collection of Shakespeare's plays, announced in its very title, *Mr. William Shakespeares Comedies, Histories, & Tragedies* (1623). Indeed, in the four-hundred-year history of the canon's reproduction, the plays have been ordered more often by genre than by chronology. The chronological arrangement is a late innovation, first attempted in 1821 and not standard practice until the second half of the twentieth century. Since then, scholars have applied themselves with remarkable assiduity to the settling of that chronology. But the chronological order remains, as it was from the start, merely conjectural. The hard fact is that we do not know when Shakespeare wrote his plays. We might know the date when a play was performed by the acting company or when it was published by the stationer, but neither date should be mistaken for the one we have most wanted: the date when it was written by Shakespeare.

>>><<<

Edmond Malone, the father of modern Shakespeare studies, boldly dismantled the order in which Shakespeare's plays had been reproduced for almost two centuries and replaced it with a radically new one of his own devising.[1] By his editorial fiat, Shakespeare's plays were to be removed from the 1623 folio's generic arrangement and published in the order in which Shakespeare wrote them—or rather, in the carefully phrased proposal to his final edition (1821), in "the order in which they are supposed by Mr. Malone to have been written."[2] As Malone repeatedly stressed, despite the records he had amassed and the tests he had devised, his chronology was only speculative. As he concluded, "This is a subject on which conviction at this day cannot be obtained."[3] Even the modest title he assigned his essay on chronology admitted its uncertainty: "An Attempt to Ascertain the Order in which the Plays Attributed to Shakspeare were Written."[4] So, too, did the essay's two epigraphs. In the first, from Statius's *Thebaid*, Amphion takes aim in darkness at a moving specter. In the second, from Dante's *Purgatory*, the shade of Statius attempts to embrace the shade of Virgil.[5] All the same, before his death in 1812, Malone left instructions to his coeditor that the plays in *The Plays and Poems of William Shakspeare* be printed in the order of his suppositions, thereby giving fixity to what he knew to be merely notional.[6] When lined up on a shelf, the multiple volumes of Shakespeare's plays were to replicate the order in which Shakespeare had written them—as ascertained by Malone.

It is now standard for editions of Shakespeare's complete works to be ordered chronologically. It is, we might say, the received order. *The Complete Signet Classic Shakespeare*, *The Oxford Shakespeare*, *The New Oxford Shakespeare*, and *The Norton Shakespeare* are all so arranged. Even when the plays are grouped by genre, as is the case for *The Riverside Shakespeare* and David Bevington's *The Complete Works of Shakespeare*, chronology is at work. The four dramatic genres are taken to suggest four advancing phases of Shakespeare's working life: the youthful comedies mature into the histories and tragedies before mellowing into the romances. And the plays within each generic group are listed chronologically. *The Complete Pelican Shakespeare* organizes the plays into three genres, reverting to the tripartite classification of the 1623 first folio, but here, too, the order is chronological within each generic unit. Thus, whether the plays are listed chronologically or divided into genres, their placement replicates the putative order of their writing by Shakespeare. When serving as the table of contents, that order need not be explained, and it often is not;

its rationale is assumed to be self-evident. How else should a canon be organized except as a continuum unfolding in time, extending from Shakespeare's first work to his last?

And yet, arranging the complete works in chronological order is hardly a given of Shakespeare studies. It is the result of generations of prodigious labor against daunting odds. To begin, there is not a single extant example of what is ostensibly being chronologized: a playscript in Shakespeare's own hand. We have instead printed texts with their dates of publication. But how long an interval separated a play's writing from its publication? Half of Shakespeare's plays were published seven years after his death, in the 1623 folio volume that came to define his canon. As a result, *The Two Gentlemen of Verona* and *The Taming of the Shrew*, for example, were first published at least a quarter of a century after the conjectured time of their writing. Entries in the Stationers' Register granting the right to print are not always reliable, sometimes postdating the publication of the plays whose publication they are meant to authorize: *Love's Labor's Lost* was published in 1598 and *Romeo and Juliet* in 1597, but there is no entry for either play until 1607.[7] The date of publication or of registration reveals only the *latest* date of a play's existence, when what we want is the date that brings us closest to the time when Shakespeare set ink to paper.

In that interval between composition and registration or publication, we assume the playscript was held by the acting company. A dated record of a play's performance should then bring us closer to its composition, but only if it is of the play's first performance. The astrologer Simon Forman records in his diary having attended several plays at the Globe between 1610 and 1611, among them *Macbeth*, which is now thought to have been first performed at court in 1606.[8] Payment for a play should bring us closer still to the time of its authorship. The entrepreneur Philip Henslowe notes in his theatrical accounts payment for a "ne" play called "Harey the vj" in 1592.[9] Scholars generally agree that "ne" is an abbreviation for "new," but not on what it is intended to modify: a new play about Henry VI? A newly revised version of a previous one? A newly licensed one? Or is it an abbreviation, as one scholar has argued, for Newington Butts, a village where Henslowe may have once owned a theater?[10] Of one thing we can be sure: "ne" does not refer to a play newly penned by Shakespeare in 1592.

For court performances, we have the office book of the Master of the Revels for the financial year 1604/1605, but its records, too, are of limited use.[11] Of the seven Shakespeare plays performed at court in 1604/1605, five are thought to have been written before 1600. Thus, while the dates we have might tell us about the publication and performance of a play, all they reveal about the writing is its outer limit. For the repertory of the Lord Admiral's Men, we can come closer. We have the company's account book for the years 1592 to 1597 with dated entries of payment to the dramatists upon delivery of their play manuscripts.[12] But no such resource has surfaced for either the Lord Chamberlain's or the King's Men, the two companies to which Shakespeare belonged.

In addition to documents and records, the plays themselves have been mined for clues to their dating. The closest the canon comes to specifying a date is hardly precise: King Henry IV gives the time as "fourteen hundred years" since the Crucifixion.[13] Allusions tend to be identified with phenomena unusual enough to have been recorded. Usually these are disturbances either of nature or of state: for example, the double eclipses witnessed in London in 1605 are tallied with the "late eclipses in the sun and moon" mentioned in *King Lear*,[14] the Midland Insurrections of 1607 with the uprising at the start of *Coriolanus*. But because such events tend to recur (there were also double eclipses in 1601 as well as rioting in 1595), their dates are hardly conclusive. In addition, they may have been inserted after a play's composition in order to update a play with a topical reference. Even the allusion that enables the most precise fixing of a play's date might have been inserted later. In *Henry V*, the Chorus anticipates the return of Henry V from Agincourt, which is assumed to be an allusion to the return of the Earl of Essex from Ireland. The play, it is argued, had to be written within the six-month interval between Essex's departure for Ireland (March 27, 1599) and his return (September 28, 1599).[15] But such references are as easily inserted as removed—like the role of the Chorus itself, which features in the folio text of *Henry V* but not in the three previously published quartos.

Another strategy for dating plays looks for clues within the plays themselves. Certain metrical, stylistic, and linguistic features are seen to vary over the course of Shakespeare's career, among them feminine rhymes, hendiadys, rare words, colloquialisms, and most recently, function words and word adjacencies.[16] With the recent introduction of increasingly sophisticated digital technologies, such tests continue to multiply.[17] Of course, the data for such tallies is drawn not from autograph manuscripts but from surviving printed texts, so once again the object of our analysis remains at a distance from what we would calibrate. While digital analysis may be new, its anticipated outcome remains the same: "the movement of a mind and the evolution of a style," "the detail and maturing of Shakespeare's art."[18] Yet as analysts of such statistics readily allow, the results cannot be used to date the composition of a play, only to support or reject a prior chronological placement.

The fact remains that there is no Shakespeare play whose writing can be dated with absolute certainty.[19] Even the end points of the corpus are variable, stretched out in either direction, beginning as early as 1586 and ending, if collaborative plays are included (*Cardenio, Henry VIII*, and *Two Noble Kinsmen*), as late as 1614.[20] Among the candidates for Shakespeare's first play are *The Two Gentlemen of Verona, The Comedy of Errors, 2 Henry VI*, and *Titus Andronicus*; his last play, if the collaborative plays are excluded, is almost invariably considered to be the valedictory *Tempest*, though *The Winter's Tale* and *Cymbeline* are close contenders.[21] We have, then, a continuum without fixed termini. And this is not for want of more data or the skills by which to analyze them. It is because what we long for does not exist: the plays as Shakespeare penned them, in manuscript, directly from the source, before the distancing mediations of performance and publication. We lack even a single specimen of such a manuscript, as the New Oxford editors acknowledge: "there are no manuscripts of any of his undisputed works in his own undisputed handwriting."[22] One might go further: even were one miraculously to turn up, chances are it would not have been dated, at least not by Shakespeare. Of the eighteen playhouse manuscripts that have survived, only eight are dated, though not by the author with the date of composition but by the Master of the Revels or his deputy with the date of licensing.[23]

All we have, or believe we have, in Shakespeare's hand is three folio pages of an undated and anonymous theatrical manuscript, "The Booke of Sir Thomas Moore," now in the British Library, Harleian 7368. But this manuscript hardly gives us what we seek. Its seventeen other pages are written in several other hands and at several different times.[24] Unlike every other play in whole or in part attributed to Shakespeare, "Sir Thomas Moore" was never published in the seventeenth century. It was first printed in 1844 as a work "written in several hands."[25] It did not attract attention, however, until three of its pages, or 147 lines, were attributed to Shakespeare, first on the basis of paleography and subsequently through the drawing of parallels, mainly orthographic and stylistic, with the canonical plays.[26] But even if these pages could definitively be attributed to Shakespeare,[27] where in the chronologically arranged complete works editions should the new arrival be placed? When the Shakespearean passages were relegated to an appendix, as they initially were, there was no need for a date.[28] But once incorporated into the canon proper, as the fragment has been by both Oxford (1986) and Norton (1997), it has to be situated on the time line: it was inserted between the Sonnets and *Measure for Measure*. When the revised Oxford (2005) included the full play, its placement shifted to between *Troilus and Cressida* and *Measure for Measure*, as it did again in the New Oxford (2016), where it appears between *Hamlet* and *Othello*.

But it is not a question of *where* the play belongs in Shakespeare's chronology but rather whether it belongs at all on a time line devised to demonstrate the course of his individual authorship. John Jowett in his edition of *Sir Thomas More* (2011) concludes that seven different hands worked on the manuscript at no fewer than five distinct times.[29] First, the "original" was drafted (by Anthony Munday, perhaps with a collaborator), then it was transcribed (by Munday), to be subsequently censored (by the Master of the Revels, Henry Tilney) and shelved (by the theatrical company). Some years later, revisions were added (by four different playwrights—Chettle, Heywood, Shakespeare, and Dekker—and not necessarily concurrently). Finally, an attempt was made to coordinate their contributions (by an anonymous playhouse functionary). The New Oxford assigns Munday's "Original play" as early a date as 1590, with the additions dated as late as 1606, so that the play's composition might have spanned a decade and a half.[30] How, then, can the full play be slotted between any two works of Shakespeare?

We want the canon to be open to compositional practices of this complexity, but the single-author chronological lineup cannot accommodate them: the work of several authors appears as the work of one alone, and a process that might have occurred over a decade appears to have taken place in a single year. A many-handed compositional process involving the contributions over time of several playwrights, a scribe, a censor, and a playhouse agent is made to look like a stage in Shakespeare's development.

Thus, the manuscript that allegedly brings us closest to Shakespeare's playwriting might well shake our confidence in an arrangement purporting to follow Shakespeare's development. It is possible, of course, that Shakespeare's contribution to "The Booke of Sir Thomas Moore" is a one-off affair, a "red herring," as the transcript's first editor termed it, that should not be taken as representative.[31] If so, it is our bad luck that our one possible autograph specimen happens to be the exception to the rule. But perhaps, as other scholars have maintained, the manuscript *is* the rule to how playscripts, including Shakespeare's, were produced.[32] Suppose "The Booke of Sir Thomas Moore" had been printed and the manuscript subsequently trashed or lost rather than archived in the British Library. Would the printed copy look so very different from the early printed quartos of Shakespeare's plays? If it had survived only in printed form, we would have been hard pressed to imagine the heterogeneous and protracted compositional activity preserved in Harleian 7368. The date of publication on its title page would have only misled us further, compressing the protracted and interrupted time of writing into a single year.

As with Malone's 1821 precedent, the publication of the complete works in chronological order has given material fixity to what perforce remains indefinite. Yet the chronological format functions as an implicit directive, indicating the order in which the plays should be encountered. This was the aim of the first edition to be so arranged in 1821: "the reader might be thus enabled to trace the progress of the author's powers, from his first and imperfect essays, to those more finished performances."[33] The motive still holds, as is evident in what the Oxford Shakespeare editors intend: "we try to discover what Shakespeare wrote, and when he wrote it, in order to influence what readers read, and the order in which they read."[34] As the editors allow, readers can choose whether to follow or ignore "the guide's advice." Shakespeareans, it would seem, have largely chosen to follow it.

Almost invariably, monographs discussing the Shakespearean corpus follow the order of the complete works edition they are using. Harold Bloom prefaces his readings of thirty-six plays with a "Chronology" based on the Riverside edition, noting a few points of dissent; his thirty-six chapters follow that order, within generic groupings.[35] Marjorie Garber follows the Norton Shakespeare's chronology with a few minor deviations in her discussion of thirty-eight plays.[36] Derek Traversi, whose monographs on Shakespeare range from the *Early Comedies* to the *Late Phase*, insists that masterpieces must be studied in relation to the poet's chronological career.[37] Even when focusing on a particular genre, monographs discuss the plays within that genre in the supposed order of their writing. A. C. Bradley delivered his monumental lectures on the four great tragedies of "Shakespeare's Tragic Period" ("from about 1601 to about 1608") in their received order.[38] E. M. W. Tillyard's *Shakespeare's History Plays* does not follow

the course of regnal succession from *King John* to *Henry VIII* but
rather the order of the plays' writing by Shakespeare.[39] Studies of
the romances, like Sarah Beckwith's *Shakespeare and the Grammar of Forgiveness*, largely follow the favored (though hardly certain) ordering of the three roughly contemporaneous romances.[40]
Whatever the subject—Shakespeare's imagery (Wolfgang Clemen), his style (Russ McDonald), the development of his characters (Janet Adelman), his contemporary cultural and political
networks (Stephen Greenblatt), his use of acting techniques and
practices (Simon Palfrey and Tiffany Stern), his contextualized
verbal interplay (Patricia Parker)—critical discussions of Shakespeare tend to run parallel to the supposed schedule of his writing.[41] Even when disavowing interest in authorial development,
studies nonetheless tend to conform to the conjectured order of
composition.

Collected essays on Shakespeare also almost invariably follow
the order of composition, though sometimes it is that of the critic
rather than of Shakespeare. Stanley Cavell discusses Shakespeare's
incipient skepticism in seven plays in the order of Shakespeare's
authorship with one exception: the collection's first essay is on
King Lear, the essay that Cavell himself wrote first.[42] In Harry
Berger's collection of essays on Shakespeare, the editor supplants
the order of Shakespeare's writing with Berger's, arranging the
plays to foreground the "ongoing developments" of Berger's critical method.[43] Despite its persistent uncertainty, chronology remains the bedrock of critical work. And though it has little more
solidity now than it had at the turn of Malone's nineteenth century, it carries a great deal more authority.

>>><<<

To the frustration of editors from the late eighteenth century on,
the folio volume that collected and preserved the thirty-six plays
that defined the Shakespeare canon—*Mr. William Shakespeares
Comedies, Histories, & Tragedies*—recorded dates for none of them.
Its compilers, Shakespeare's colleagues, are often charged with

having neglected to record the dates of the plays they had so solicitously gathered. Indeed, their folio does not even record the date of the event on which the collection is premised. The volume casts itself as both tomb and tome, enclosing the author's literary remains within its monumental folio covers and prefacing them with elegiac tributes. The date of his death, however, is never mentioned. The volume gives one date alone, at the foot of its title page: "Printed by Isaac Iaggard, and Ed. Blount. 1623." The folio compilers had no interest in when Shakespeare wrote his works. They organized the plays they had gathered by another logic: that of literary kinds, two of them ancient and the third modern. The title of the 1623 folio announces that order; so, too, does its table of contents, "A Catalogue of the severall Comedies, Histories, and Tragedies contained in this Volume" (fig. 2.2). The Catalogue's typography stresses the generic dispensation, encasing each genre in its own rectangle and paginating it separately.

The 1623 folio's precedent, *The Workes of Beniamin Jonson* (1616), is also organized by genre. In keeping with its classicized title page, the contents belong to ancient literary forms: tragedies, comedies, satires, and epigrams.[44] It also includes court masques, which, while modern in form, are antiquated by their mythological subjects and costumes. Dates are given before each of the tragedies and comedies, but they tell when each "was first acted" by the acting company that is also named. In the earliest listing of Shakespeare's plays, genre is also the organizing rubric. In *Palladis Tamia. Wits Treasury* (1598), Francis Meres takes inventory of Shakespeare's plays, claiming that English poets can rival the excellence of the ancients. While the Roman Plautus excelled in comedy and the Roman Seneca in tragedy, the English Shakespeare has distinguished himself in both genres: "As *Plautus* and *Seneca* are accounted the best for Comedy and Tragedy among the Latines: so *Shakespeare* among the English is the most excellent in both kinds."[45] He names twelve plays by Shakespeare, six from each genre:

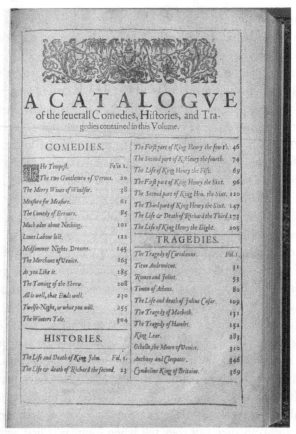

A CATALOGVE
of the feuerall Comedies, Histories, and Tragedies contained in this Volume.

COMEDIES.

The Tempest.	Folio 1.
The two Gentlemen of Verona.	20
The Merry Wiues of Windsor.	38
Measure for Measure.	61
The Comedy of Errours.	85
Much adoo about Nothing.	101
Loues Labour lost.	122
Midsommer Nights Dreame.	145
The Merchant of Venice.	163
As you Like it.	185
The Taming of the Shrew.	208
All is well, that Ends well.	230
Twelfe-Night, or what you will.	255
The Winters Tale.	304

HISTORIES.

The Life and Death of King John.	Fol. 1.
The Life & death of Richard the second.	23

The First part of King Henry the fourt'.	46
The Second part of K. Henry the fourth.	74
The Life of King Henry the Fift.	69
The First part of King Henry the Sixt.	96
The Second part of King Hen. the Sixt.	120
The Third part of King Henry the Sixt.	147
The Life & Death of Richard the Third.	173
The Life of King Henry the Eight.	205

TRAGEDIES.

The Tragedy of Coriolanus.	Fol. 1.
Titus Andronicus.	31
Romeo and Juliet.	53
Timon of Athens.	80
The Life and death of Julius Cæsar.	109
The Tragedy of Macbeth.	131
The Tragedy of Hamlet.	152
King Lear.	283
Othello, the Moore of Venice.	310
Anthony and Cleopatra.	346
Cymbeline King of Britaine.	369

FIGURE 2.2. "A Catalogue," *Mr. William Shakespeares Comedies, Histories, &*
Tragedies (London, 1623). Used by Permission of the Folger Library (093005)

for Comedy, witnes his *Gentlemen of Verona*, his *Errors*, his Loue
labors lost, his *Loue labours wonne*, his *Midsummers night dreame*, &
his *Merchant of Venice*: for Tragedy, his *Richard the 2. Richard the 3.*
Henry the 4. King Iohn, Titus Andronicus and his *Romeo* and *Iuliet*.

Though this passage has been key to Shakespeare's chronology,
providing 1598 as the terminus ad quem for twelve of the plays,
Meres himself has no interest in dates. The entry is organized
rhetorically, with its nicely balanced analogues ("As Plautus and

Seneca . . . so Shakespeare") and examples ("for Comedy . . . for Tragedy"). In his overall survey of English authors, Meres observes another nonchronological order besides genre: social rank. Titled authors come first. Sir Phillip Sidney heads the list of poets, Lord Buckhurst is the first of fourteen comedians, and Edward de Vere, Earl of Oxford, leads the seventeen tragedians. The lyric poets begin with the Earl of Surrey before descending to knights—Sir Thomas Wyatt the elder, Sir Francis Bryan, Sir Philip Sidney, Sir Walter Raleigh, Sir Edward Dyer—and then dropping lower still to the untitled Spenser, Daniel, Drayton, Shakespeare, Whetstone, Gascoigne, and Samuel Page.

Four of the six plays Meres classifies as tragedies—*Richard II*, *Richard III*, *Henry IV*, and *King John*—the folio would group under a new dramatic rubric. Lodged between the two ancient dramatic genres of comedies and tragedies is the modern newcomer, histories. Here, too, there is symmetry in the layout: thirteen plays on either side of the histories. While the comedies and tragedies observe no discernible order, the ten histories are in the order of regnal succession, from King John to Henry VIII. Each bears the title of an English monarch who ruled after the great watershed of the 1066 Conquest.[46] The Conquest is the cutoff point for the folio histories as it is for their source: Holinshed's *The Chronicles of England* (1587) begins "William the Norman, commonlie called the Conqueror and descending by degrees of yeeres to all kings and queenes of England in their orderlie successions."[47] The plays of monarchs who reigned *before* 1066—*King Lear*, *Cymbeline*, and *Macbeth*—fall on the tragic side of the epochal and generic divide.

The 1623 folio's generic arrangement survived its three seventeenth-century reprintings in 1632, 1663/1664, and 1685. It remained intact even when the second impression of the 1664 folio was enlarged to include seven plays that had previously been associated in print with Shakespeare's name or initials.[48] Instead of being incorporated into the "Catalogue"'s generic divisions, the seven new titles are listed (in no discernible order) on the title page and printed at the end of the original folio plays, after

Cymbeline. But the original thirty-six plays continue to be arranged generically even when the folio monolith breaks into multiple octavo volumes: six at the start of century and up to twenty-one at its end.[49]

The first of the eighteenth-century multivolume editions, edited by Nicholas Rowe, replaces the genre-specific title of the 1623 folio—*Mr. William Shakespeares Comedies, Histories, & Tragedies*—with the more economical *The Works of Mr. William Shakespear* (1709). The folio "Catalogue" is also dropped, but not its generic assignments. Indeed their importance is heightened. On the title page of every comedy and tragedy, the play's genre is in bolder and bigger print than its title:

TITUS

ANDRONICUS.

A

TRAGEDY

The engraved frontispiece printed before all six of the edition's volumes also foregrounds genre: Shakespeare is being crowned by Comedy and Tragedy, with winged Fame aloft, trumpeting the poet's glory, while dark Ignorance lies writhing beneath Comedy's right foot (fig. 2.3).[50]

The composition is distinctly awkward: the modern oval portrait rests incongruously on an ancient stone pedestal, precariously supported by Comedy's elongated forearm. And indeed, the classicizing frame was not designed for Shakespeare. It was lifted from the frontispiece of *Le Théâtre de P. Corneille*, printed in Rouen in 1664 (fig. 2.4). In the original, a bust of Corneille sits securely on the stone plinth, as is appropriate for the author celebrated as the most neoclassical of the French dramatists. It is the project of Rowe's 1709 edition, as prescribed by his publisher Jacob Tonson, to raise Shakespeare to the level of the ancients, a singularly challenging task when for over a century Shakespeare had been relentlessly identified with his neglect or ignorance of them.[51]

FIGURE 2.3. Shakespeare as classic. Gerard van der Gucht, frontispiece to each volume of *The Works of Mr. William Shakspear*, ed. Nicholas Rowe, 6 vols. (London, 1709). Used by permission of the Folger Shakespeare Library (56340)

Rowe does his best. In the edition's prefatory essay, "Some Account of the Life, &c. of Mr. *William Shakespear*," in keeping with the frontispiece engraving, he reduces the folio's three genres to the classical two, collapsing the histories into the tragedies: "His Plays are properly to be distinguish'd only into Comedies and Tragedies. Those which are called Histories . . . are really Tragedies, with a run or mixture of Comedy amongst 'em."[52] But he is hard pressed to find plays that readily fit into either

FIGURE 2.4. Corneille as classic. Guillaume Vallet after Antoine Paillet. Frontispiece to *Le Théâtre de P. Corneille* (Rouen, 1664). Private Collection/Bridgeman Images

prescribed genre. Only three comedies are "all pure comedy"—*The Merry Wives of Windsor, The Comedy of Errors,* and *The Taming of the Shrew*—"the rest, however they are call'd, have something of both Kinds" (xvii). *The Merchant of Venice,* for example, while "Receiv'd and Acted as a Comedy," Rowe believes to have been "design'd Tragically by the Author": Shylock's fierce and bloody vindictiveness "cannot agree either with the Stile or Characters of Comedy" (xix–xx). While the "generality" is content to receive such impure comedies as "Trage-Comedy," "the severer Critiques among us cannot bear it" (xvii). The tragedies are equally resistant to classification. Only three, according to Rowe, conform to the Aristotelian prescript that the "the Fable is founded upon one Action only": *Romeo and Juliet*, *Hamlet*, and *Othello*. The action of the rest, as with the so-called histories, is dispersed, tracking "the several Fortunes and Accidents of [great men's] lives" rather than concentrating on "any single great Action" (xxxi).

For Rowe, there is good reason why so few of Shakespeare's plays satisfy the classical requirements. As Ben Jonson famously remarked, and as was stressed by every commentator after him, Shakespeare had scant knowledge of the ancients: "It is without Controversie, that he had no knowledge of the Writings of the Antient Poets."[53] Rowe's first critical observation "from his Works themselves" confirms the same: "we find no traces of any thing that looks like an Imitation of [the ancients]" (iii). As a result, in his defense, Rowe warns against judging him by rules he could not know: "But as *Shakespear* liv'd under a kind of mere Light of Nature, and had never been made acquainted with the Regularity of those written Precepts, so it would be hard to judge him by a Law he knew nothing of" (xxvi).

Rowe cannot fault him, for example, for favoring character over plot, though Aristotle, following "the Model of the Grecian Stage," urged the opposite (xxvi). Nor can he commend him when one of his plays, *The Tempest*, happens to satisfy Aristotle's precepts: "One may observe, that the Unities are kept here with an Exactness uncommon to the Liberties of his Writing." For Shakespeare's genius lay elsewhere: "certainly the greatness of this Author's Genius do's no where so much appear, as where he gives his Imagination an entire loose, and raises his Fancy to a flight above Mankind and the limits of the visible World." So even when the unities are observed, Shakespeare ends up violating another Aristotelian requirement: probability: "He do's, in this Play, depart too much from that likeness to Truth which ought to be observ'd in these sort of Writings" (xxiii). Nevertheless, Rowe's "Some Account of the Life" raises Shakespeare's status by holding his plays to the same generic expectations that had been redacted from the ancients. Even when Shakespeare fails to meet those standards, the discussion lifts him into the ranks of Sophocles, Plautus, and Aristotle as well as of their modern neoclassical successors Rapin, Dacier, Scudery, Racine, and Corneille. For such a project, dates are unnecessary. Rowe gives only one: "*April* 1564" (ii).

Subsequent eighteenth-century editions continue to follow the folio's generic dispensation. When alterations are introduced, they still observe the generic order instated by the folio, as is nicely illustrated by Alexander Pope's six-volume edition (1725). Pope, returning to the folio thirty-six play canon, gives two volumes to each of the three genres. The two volumes of tragedies are separated into subgenres on the basis of their sources. Volume 5 contains "Tragedies from History":

PLAYS *contain'd in this Volume.*

TIMON of *ATHENS.*

CORIOLANUS.

JULIUS CÆSAR.

ANTONY and *CLEOPATRA.*

TITUS ANDRONICUS.

MACBETH.

Volume 6 groups together "Tragedies from Fable":

PLAYS *contain'd in this Volume.*

TROILUS and *CRESSIDA.*

CYMBELINE.

ROMEO and *JULIET.*

HAMLET.

OTHELLO.

The first group issues primarily from ancient Plutarch, while the second derives from modern novels or romances: *Troilus* from

Chaucer, *Cymbeline* from Boccaccio, *Romeo and Juliet* from Bandello, *Hamlet* from Belleforest, and *Othello* from Cinthio. Source is also the unifying principle of Pope's "Historical Plays," each of them drawing on Holinshed's *Chronicles*. On that same basis, Pope reclassifies *King Lear*, placing it first on his list of "Historical Plays":

PLAYS **contain'd in this Volume.**

King *L E A R.*

King *J O H N.*

King *R I C H A R D II.*

King *H E N R Y IV.* Part I.

King *H E N R Y IV.* Part II.

King *H E N R Y V.*

Pope further secures *Lear*'s new generic assignment by renaming it. On its individual title page, *King Lear* is retitled *The Life and Death of King Lear*. In the folios, the biographical designation "Life and Death" was inserted to distinguish the single-play histories from the comedies and tragedies, with the exception of the two single plays in which the king survives the end of the play: *The Life of King Henry the Fift* and *The Life of King Henry the Eight* (fig. 2.2). Pope also sets right the one instance in the folio where the biographical prefix has strayed into the list of tragedies: *The Life and death of Julius Caesar* is relabeled *The Tragedy of Julius Caesar* in conformance with the other tragedies.

By the same rationale, *Macbeth* might have been transferred to the histories. Perhaps Pope, or his publishers, at the time of the Jacobite uprisings, wished to avoid inserting "the Scottish play" into the history of the succession of English kings. Or perhaps he, or they, wished to observe the generically contrived symmetry of twelve "Historical Plays" and twelve Tragedies. Source also determines Pope's only change to the comedies: after *The Tempest* comes not *The Two Gentlemen of Verona*, as in the folio, but

A Midsummer Night's Dream, uniting the two plays believed to be without sources and therefore "original."

Pope also introduces refinement to the folio tragedies based on the "Historical Plays": within each of the volumes, he orders the tragedies chronologically by the time not of their writing but of the action they dramatize as specified in their sources. Thus, the "Tragedies from History" mainly follow the order of historical events as registered in Plutarch: *Timon of Athens'* Peloponnesian war, *Coriolanus's* republic, *Julius Caesar's* dictatorship, Octavius's pending empire in *Antony and Cleopatra*, and finally Rome's decline in *Titus Andronicus*. The "Tragedies from Fable" follow the same temporal rationale: from *Troilus and Cressida's* archaic Troy and *Lear's* ancient Albion to the three modern plays: *Hamlet*, *Romeo and Juliet*, and the most modern of all, *Othello*, set within mere decades of its first performance. While no subsequent edition reproduces Pope's schema in its entirety, two of his chronologically ordered subsets become standard: all the major editions up through the end of the century unite the three Roman plays and the three modern tragedies.

Like the engraving and critical commentary in Rowe, the modified order for the plays in Pope attests to the desire to make Shakespeare answerable to the category of genre.[54] By affiliating the tragedies with their sources, Pope attempts to rationalize and refine that order. His divisions, of course, are hardly unproblematic: *Titus* is only notionally sourced in ancient history; if *Lear* is a "Historical Play," *Macbeth* should be one as well; *Love's Labor's Lost* belongs with the comedies without known sources. More fundamentally, the alignment of genre with source material blurs the distinction between comedy and tragedy. Almost half the tragedies derive from the same source as the comedies: modern novels and romances. All these incoherencies bear witness to the challenge of the eighteenth-century editorial project of elevating Shakespeare to the ranks of the ancients by observing generic classifications. That the dramatic "kinds" were, as Stephen Orgel has demonstrated repeatedly, entirely fluid in early modern English drama made their determination all the more urgent in an age intent on aligning Shakespeare with the Augustans.[55]

However imperfect, the folio's generic taxonomy, like our current chronological arrangement, set the terms of critical discussion and debate. Do the plays satisfy generic requirements? Is history a proper genre? How do these plays compare with ancient works of the same genre or with other modern ones, in English as well as Italian and Spanish and later in French and German? What was the degree of Shakespeare's familiarity with the ancients? Was he the better or the worse for not having mastered them? Should genius and the imagination be bound to the ancient rules or allowed to follow their own impulses? These are the kinds of questions that precipitated critical discussion of the plays well into the eighteenth century. Even when the folio's generic assignments were disputed and rejected, genre remained the key critical category that affixed Shakespeare, however tenuously, to the classical tradition. When chronology replaced genre as the canon's organizing principle, the works were primed for a different attachment: not to a classical tradition but to Shakespeare's chronologized life and times.

>>><<<

Malone's first contribution to Shakespeare scholarship is "An Attempt to Ascertain the Order in which the Plays Attributed to Shakspeare were Written" (1778), and he would continue to work on Shakespeare's chronology throughout the three decades of his career. The project, he allowed, was a "new and curious enquiry," so much so that in his private correspondence, he feared it would be met with derision.[56] His correspondent, however, assured him of the supreme value of his "lucubrations": "what is your chronological account of the writings of Shakspeare other than the history of the progress of the greatest genius that ever honoured and delighted human nature?"[57] Malone appealed to the same defense at the start of "An Attempt": "Yet surely it is no incurious speculation, to mark the gradations by which [Shakespeare] rose from mediocrity to the summit of excellence; from artless and sometimes uninteresting dialogues, to those unparalleled compositions."[58] Malone expected that the value of his essay, crammed with dates, documents, and inferences, would be apparent in the novelty it produced: a numbered, dated list of plays attributed to Shakespeare, revealing at a glance the growth of Shakespeare's genius from lackluster mediocrity to dazzling efflorescence: "how the genius of the great poet gradually expanded itself, till, like his own Ariel, *it flamed amazement* in every quarter."[59]

Yet that fiery path of genius might have been difficult to discern in Malone's 1778 chronology, the first published chronology of Shakespeare's works (fig. 2.5). It consists of forty-three plays: the first folio's thirty-six plus the seven appended by the third and fourth folios. Along with *Titus*, whose authorship by Shakespeare Malone denied, these plays are in italics to indicate their uncertain status. By the time of his last chronology, in his posthumous 1821 edition of *The Plays and Poems*, he had ejected all the italicized plays.[60] For he had by then produced the first edition of the appended plays, a task undertaken, he explained, for the purpose of addressing the hundred-and-fifty-year controversy over their authenticity.[61] His verdict was conclusive: of them, only *Pericles* was by Shakespeare.[62] Malone also challenged the authenticity of three of the plays included in the first folio. In his *A Dissertation on the three parts of King Henry VI* (1787), he denied Shakespeare's authorship of the first part and argued that he had merely reworked the second and third.[63] If the chronology's purpose was to demonstrate Shakespeare's signature development, Shakespeare's exclusive authorship had to be established first.

Malone's project was predicated on the expectation that his research would produce a mounting gradient in which advancing years correlated with higher literary merit. The later the work, the better the work. A play's chronological position would indicate its literary value. Indispensable to the project, then as now, were the few lines of Francis Meres's 1598 survey listing twelve plays as Shakespeare's. Those plays, especially the comedies, formed the basis for Malone's classification of the early plays. Their distinguishing features of an early play were negative: "almost continual rhyme, the poverty of the fable, and want

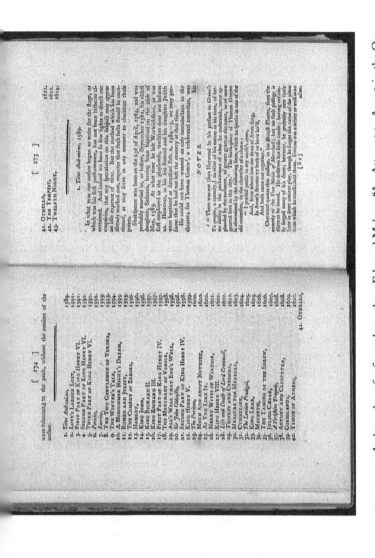

FIGURE 2.5. A chronology for forty-three plays. Edmond Malone, "An Attempt to Ascertain the Order in which the Plays Attributed to Shakspeare Were Written," in *The Plays of William Shakspeare*, ed. Samuel Johnson and George Steevens, 10 vols. (London, 1778), 1:274–75. PHOTOGRAPH: James Marshall and Marie-Louise Osborn Collection, Beinecke Rare Book and Manuscript Library, Yale University (Osborn pc270)

of discrimination among the higher personages"; "its imperfect versification, its artless and desultory dialogue, and the irregularity of the composition"; "hastening too abruptly and without preparation to the denouëment."[64] He believed that the plays not published until the 1623 folio, with only two exceptions, were late plays and correspondingly of higher literary quality. It was incumbent on those who disagreed "to enumerate . . . among the plays produced before 1600, compositions of equal merit with Othello, King Lear, Macbeth, the Tempest, and Twelfth Night" (2:291). Shakespeare, Malone assumed, wrote the plays more or less regularly over the course of his twenty-year career, about ten years on either side of 1600. If no sound evidence had surfaced for the dating of a play, he looked for empty slots on the continuum. The years 1609 and 1610 were blank, so they became the dates of *Coriolanus* and *Timon of Athens*, respectively: "it seems reasonable to ascribe them to that period to which we are not led by any particular circumstance to attribute any other of his works" (2:454).

For the purpose of his chronology, Malone gathered what remain the key documents for its devising: Meres's 1598 citation, most of the quartos printed in Shakespeare's lifetime, the Stationers' Register entries, the Master of the Revels office book, and finally, Henslowe's papers, though he makes little use of the latter, discovered just as his history of the stage was about to go to press.[65] Yet the dates he culled from official documents, then as now, needed supplementation. With considerable ingenuity, Malone turned the plays themselves into a secondary archive. He assumed that like documents, they, too, were dated, only their dates were encoded in allusions that required deciphering. Confident that "Shakspeare is fond of alluding to events occurring at the time when he wrote" (2:331), he scoured the plays for what he took to be references to events momentous enough to have been recorded elsewhere. Some of them were biographical, like births, deaths, and business transactions. From the Stratford parish register, Malone knew that Shakespeare's twelve-year old son had died in 1596, so Lady Constance's "pathetick lamentations" (2:353) over the death of her boy Arthur in *King John* led him to suppose "that this tragedy was written at or soon after that period": he dates the play 1596. Other allusions were historical, like those to wars, coronations, and state visits. He was inclined to think *The Merchant of Venice* was written in 1594 on the assumption that Portia's expectation that her victorious suitor would be greeted with the reverence due "To a new crowned monarch" referred to the coronation of Henry IV of France in Chartres in that year, as recorded in an English pamphlet (2:331–32). For Malone, little or no time elapsed between such events and Shakespeare's dramatization of them. Similarly, Malone sometimes allows no interval between the writing of a play and its registration and publication: "*Much Ado about Nothing* was written, we may presume, early in the year 1600; for it was entered at Stationers' Hall, August 23, 1600, and printed in that year" (2:369).

But Malone's most innovative strategy for dating required no outside materials whatsoever. Once the plays were classified as early and late, he observed that Shakespeare's rhymes tended to become less frequent as his career advanced. Shakespeare, he assumed, after having completed so many stanzas of alternating rhyme and couplets in *Venus and Adonis* and *The Rape of Lucrece*, was left "much addicted to rhyming; a practice from which he gradually departed, though he never wholly deserted it" (2:344). Rhyming, for Malone, was a sign of an immaturity that Shakespeare eventually outgrew, either because he found it too constricting or because he thought it inappropriate for dramatic dialogue (2:327n5). That the three *Henry VI* plays at the start of Shakespeare's career did not rhyme only confirmed his thesis that they were largely the work of others. Malone's rhyme test turned out to be the most generative of his dating techniques, having in the two centuries since its devising branched out to include the quantification of any number of metrical, stylistic, and linguistic features assumed to be solely and exclusively Shakespeare's.

Before his death, Malone instructed his coeditor, James Boswell the younger, to have the plays printed "according to the order in which [Malone] supposed them to be written."[66] Boswell agreed that such an arrangement would enable the reader "to trace the progress of the author's powers," but he could not bring himself to fully satisfy his mentor's directive:[67]

> In compliance with the general opinion of those whom I have con-
> sulted on the subject, I have ventured to deviate from his plan in the
> arrangement of those dramas which are founded on English history.
> Dr. Johnson has observed . . . that most of them were designed by
> Shakspeare to be read in regular connection; and I have therefore
> thought it more for the reader's convenience, not to break the his-
> torical chain.[68]

In the twenty-one-volume Malone-Boswell Variorum of 1821, only the comedies and tragedies are reproduced in Malone's chronological order.[69] The histories are cordoned off in five volumes (15–19), where they remain in the order of regnal succession, preserving the "historical chain" of English rule. With the removal of the ten histories, the chronological arrangement intended to display "the progress of the author's powers"—from mediocrity to sublimity, from his earliest work to his latest—is hardly comprehensive.

>>><<<

Shortly after the publication of Malone's revised chronological essay in his 1790 edition of Shakespeare, a monograph responded directly to it: *Cursory remarks upon the arrangement of the plays of Shakespear occasioned by reading Mr. Malone's essay on the chronological order of those celebrated pieces* (1792), by the poet and playwright James Hurdis. Hurdis regrets that Malone, rather than ordering his edition according to the chronology he had devised, followed instead a "series very little different from the first published by Heming and Condel." As he admits, his reaction to that customary order was almost visceral.

> From the days in which I first became a reader of the plays of Shake-
> spear, I have always been offended at the improper manner in which

those pieces are arranged. As they now stand in *every* edition . . .
the reader is continually surprised by a sudden transition from a
production of little merit to one of great excellence, or disgusted by
a change as instantaneous, from a performance in every respect ad-
mirable to one altogether as rude and contemptible. This, therefore,
we may with the greatest safety affirm, was not the order in which
these plays were originally written by their Author.[70]

If the plays could be ordered as "originally written by their Author," building up from those of "little merit" to those of "great excellence," they would lose their offending unevenness. To that end,
Hurdis runs through Malone's dates and inferences, play by play,
holding them up not to documentary data but to his own literary
standards: regularity of verse, discrimination of character, ingenuity of plot (particularly the denouement), and moral sentiment.
Dates are negligible. When Malone's dating is at variance with
his appraisal, he discounts it even when based on documentary
evidence. By his judgment, ten of the plays listed by Meres in 1598
were written *after* 1598. *The Merchant of Venice*, for example, "one
of the most ingenious and highly finished of all our author's performances," must be later than 1598: "This play Mr. Malone, upon
the authority of Meres, has attributed to the year 1598. I would
willingly give it a later date" (18). So, too, he considers those plays
printed posthumously in the 1623 folio to be Shakespeare's earliest.
He is certain that *Antony and Cleopatra* is Shakespeare's very first
play: he finds the play "most abounding in faulty lines" and deems
every scene "dull and tedious" (40). Almost as bad and therefore
early is *Coriolanus*, with its "many anachronisms, many broken and
ill managed lines, and a dissolute mixture of verse and prose" (39).
He considers *Henry VIII* fault ridden enough to be the first of the
history plays (22), though he refrains from commenting on the
order of the rest of the history plays, believing they should be read
"according to the chain of history": "I would not wish to see the
present arrangement of them disturbed" (27).

Hurdis inverts Malone's end points largely on the basis of
the criterion Malone himself had introduced: the frequency of

rhyme. But for Hurdis, regular rhyme and meter signal poetic mastery rather than immaturity. On that basis, he determines that the metrically irregular *Tempest* belongs among Shakespeare's very early plays: "it contains many incontestable proofs of having proceeded from the pen of a writer that was not very skilled in the art of making blank verse. Some lines are so unmusical, harsh, and laboured that it is almost impossible to make them run in any metre at all" (7). He faults *The Winter's Tale* with the same metrical and linguistic irregularity, as "of a young poet who is scarce master of his numbers" (38). *As You Like It*, by contrast, bears all the metrical signs of mature prosody.

Hurdis was unnerved by his experience of Shakespeare's unevenness not only from one play to the next but also from one part of a play to another. To explain the presence of both good and bad writing in the same play, he entertains two possibilities: either Shakespeare wrote the play at two different stages or else another author contributed. *Romeo and Juliet*, for example, consisted of unpracticed dialogue at the start but a high-minded and "irresistibly affecting" conclusion. If Shakespeare wrote the entire play, he must have started it early and finished it late with an "interruption" in between. Or if a play of uneven quality had been written at one time, a more skilled dramatist must also have been working on it. He comes close to crediting Drayton for the unified plotting of *The Comedy of Errors*—"I have been upon the eve of ascribing it to Drayton"—but stops himself short with an alarming possibility: "if Drayton had a hand in this piece, he must be admitted as an assistant in others, and where his claims would end I know not" (13). Hurdis faces the same dilemma when pondering the consequences of denying Shakespeare's authorship of *The Two Gentleman of Verona*. "But if we reject it, there will be reason to question many other of the plays, which were evidently written by the hand which produced this" (9). Finally, to shocking effect, he flips Malone's logic in accepting a play as Shakespeare's if it resembles other plays by him. By Malone's logic, "if *one* of them belongs to Shakespear, they are *all* his" (10).

For Hurdis, however, it is precisely the opposite: "On the contrary, if *one* of them can be proved to be not his, the authenticity of *the whole* will be dubious."

Despite his alarming counterfactuals, Hurdis concludes his essay with his own time order: a "New Disposition of Plays" (fig. 2.6). As in his appraisals of the individual plays, he assigns no dates. Their relative literary merit is demonstrated by their position in the vertical lineup, with *Antony and Cleopatra* first and *Hamlet* last.

>>><<<

Hurdis was not the only poet and literary critic to take issue with Malone's dated chronology. Samuel Taylor Coleridge, like Malone, worked on the order of Shakespeare's composition for decades and in multiple versions. Three of his attempts were published together by his nephew shortly after his death in a section of *Literary Remains* titled "Order of Shakspeare's Plays" and are dated by his nephew 1802, 1810, and 1819.[71] They are little more than sketches, with only elliptical and sporadic glosses, several in the 1802 version in German and Italian. Based on Coleridge's own fragmentary notes, as well as the sometimes inconsistent lecture reports by auditors, the three sketches differ widely from one another, and inexplicably. For example, why did he replace the plays he had assigned in 1802 to Shakespeare's last period (or "Fifth epoch" or "Fifth and last Aera")—*The Tempest, The Winter's Tale,* and *Cymbeline*—with *Julius Caesar, Antony and Cleopatra,* and *Troilus and Cressida* in 1819?[72] While his logic is elusive, his expectation is familiar: "the probable order in which his several Dramas were composed" is expected to reveal "the gradual ascent and expansion of his Genius."[73] If Coleridge had indeed produced the edition of Shakespeare he is said to have contemplated, it would most likely have been arranged according to that "probable order": as he remarked to his nephew, "I think the chronological order the best for arranging a poet's works."[74]

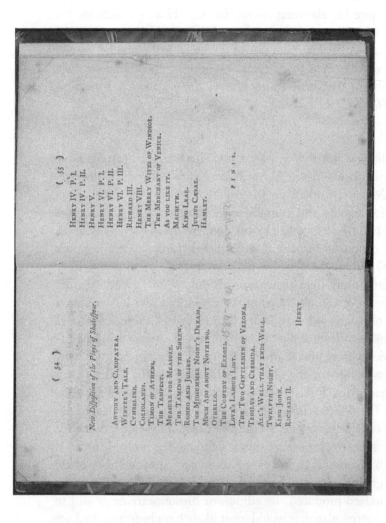

(54)

New Disposition of the Plays of Shakespear.

ANTONY AND CLEOPATRA.
WINTER'S TALE.
CYMBELINE.
CORIOLANUS.
TIMON OF ATHENS.
THE TEMPEST.
MEASURE FOR MEASURE.
THE TAMING OF THE SHREW.
ROMEO AND JULIET.
THE MIDSUMMER NIGHT'S DREAM,
MUCH ADO ABOUT NOTHING.
OTHELLO.
THE COMEDY OF ERRORS,
LOVE'S LABOUR LOST.
THE TWO GENTLEMEN OF VERONA,
TROILUS AND CRESSIDA.
ALL'S WELL THAT ENDS WELL.
TWELFTH NIGHT,
KING JOHN,
RICHARD II.

HENRY

(55)

HENRY IV. P. I.
HENRY IV. P. II.
HENRY V.
HENRY VI. P. I.
HENRY VI. P. II.
HENRY VI. P. III.
RICHARD III.
HENRY VIII.
THE MERRY WIVES OF WINDSOR,
THE MERCHANT OF VENICE,
AS YOU LIKE IT.
MACBETH.
KING LEAR.
JULIUS CÆSAR.
HAMLET.

F I N I S.

FIGURE 2.6. An alternative chronology. James Hurdis, "New Disposition of the Plays of Shakespear," from *Cursory remarks upon the arrangement of the plays of Shakespear* (London, 1792). PHOTO-GRAPH: Beinecke Rare Book and Manuscript Library, Yale University (Ig 8h 792)

Yet Coleridge ridiculed Malone for his obsession with dated materials—"Registers, Memorandum Books"—dubbing him "that eternal Bricker-up of Shakespeare." For Malone, Coleridge states, mere contemporaneity constituted relevance: "Bill, Jack, and Harry, Tom, Walter, & Gregory, Charles . . . &c &c lived at that time, but . . . nothing more is known of them."[75] Coleridge questioned not only the accuracy of the dates of publication but also their relevance to the time of composition, doubting that "the Priority of Publication [could] prove any thing in favor of prior composition."[76] Deeming "outward documents" misleading, he turned instead to "internal evidences, furnished by the writings themselves."[77] Inwardly sourced, Shakespeare's works "came out of the unfathomable depths of his own oceanic mind."[78] Whether experienced directly or through reading, externals supplied Shakespeare only "with the drapery of the figures"; their inner being or psychological core came from introspection.[79] Minor characters, like Juliet's nurse, may have been drawn from outside impressions. Commanding figures like Iago, Richard III, Othello, and Lear issued "rather from meditation than from observation."[80]

To follow the gradients of Shakespeare's internal growth, Coleridge dispensed with dates. They were appropriate to documents that fixed persons and events in time but not to Shakespeare's creative process. According to one of his reporters, Coleridge announced before lecturing on Shakespeare that he would pursue a "psychological, rather than a historical mode of reasoning" so that his discussion of the works would follow the order of Shakespeare's composition: "He should take them as they seemed naturally to flow from the progress & order of his mind."[81] He replaced dates with the more capacious and momentous units conventionally used to organize world history: epochs and eras. While the plays he grouped in each period varied from one series to the other, the underlying trajectory was the same: the growth or progress of Shakespeare's creative powers. In the early plays, Shakespeare progresses through collaboration but also through the reworking of his own drafts as he comes closer to approaching in his final epoch "the self-sufficing power of absolute Genius." In the 1802 order, Coleridge includes the plays appended to the last two folios, believing them written during Shakespeare's apprenticeship under the aegis of other playwrights. These he terms "<u>transition-works</u>, *Ubergangswerke*; not his, yet of him." In the second epoch, Coleridge sees Shakespeare beginning to come into his own with a "draft" of *Romeo and Juliet*, a "sketch" of *The Two Gentlemen of Verona*, and a version of *All's Well* "afterwards worked up afresh (*umgearbeitet*)." So, too, do *King John*, *The Merry Wives of Windsor*, and *Henry VI* all undergo a remaking or "*rifaciamento*." In the third period, according to the 1810 order, there is "a greater energy" but also "growing pains, and the awkwardness of growth." In the fourth, he is in "full possession" of his creative energies, which in the 1819 order reach their "very point of culmination" in the four great tragedies. In the final and fifth era, the intellect overcomes the "passion" of the fourth era in the densely cerebral Greek and Roman Plays (and *Measure for Measure*). In these plays, Shakespeare goes beyond the "culmination" of his powers: they are realized to a degree so absolute that Coleridge coins a new term to describe their form: "potenziated."[82]

Dismissing documentary evidence, Coleridge relies on a wavering sympathetic intuition deeply informed by German transcendental idealism. As he thinks through Shakespeare's creative development, he also has his own in mind, the subject of his *Biographia Literaria; or Biographical Sketches of My Literary Life and Opinions* (1817). It has been described by Coleridgeans as an "endless maze," a "strange medley," a "rubble-heap" "put together with a pitchfork."[83] But it might be fairer to say that, like his unmethodical orderings of Shakespeare's plays, it subscribes to a "psychological order" and "flow[s] from the progress & order of his mind." Certainly dates are not paramount, not even his own, as is apparent in the first sentence of his *Biographia Literaria*: "In 1794, when I had barely passed the verge of manhood, I published a small volume of juvenile poems."[84] His first book of poems, *Poems on Various Subjects*, was published in 1796.

>>><<<

Malone with documents and dates, Hurdis with literary taste, Coleridge with intuition inflected by philosophical idealism: all three worked toward the same end of ordering Shakespeare's works chronologically to reveal his development on a rising gradient. But their efforts were of little consequence. Coleridge's several fragmentary epochal orders were published posthumously and remain inscrutable. Hurdis's "New Disposition" has only rarely been remembered, and then only to be derided.[85] Malone's chronology, faulted by Hurdis and Coleridge, was foiled even by his own coeditor, who declined to bring the histories in alignment. It is no surprise, then, that subsequent editions did not follow the precedent of the Malone-Boswell 1821 edition. A number of major nineteenth-century editors worked on Shakespeare's chronology, but their editions followed the original and customary order of the folio template.[86] As one editor explained, "we should not do better than adopt the course pursued in 1623, so near to the time when Shakespeare was living."[87] The edition that came to dominate the later nineteenth century, the authoritative nine-volume Cambridge Shakespeare, reverted to the folio listing (1863–1866). So, too, did its single-volume derivative, the Globe Shakespeare (1865), the standard text well into the twentieth century in part because it was the first to establish line numbers for the plays and poems.[88]

>>><<<

But then came a change. In 1873, the New Shakspere Society was founded by F. J. Furnivall with the express purpose of establishing Shakespeare's chronology and thereby ascertaining his development "to do honour to Shakspere, to mark out the succession of his plays, and thereby the growth of his mind and art."[89] For Furnivall, the chronology was preliminary to any study of Shakespeare: "Unless a man's works are studied in the order in which he wrote them, you *cannot* get a right understanding of his mind, you cannot follow the growth of it."[90] He complained of what he perceived as the random order in which the plays had continued to be published. They were set "higgledy-piggledy," as they had been in the 1623 folio, "beginning with Shakspere's almost-last play, the *Tempest* and then putting his (probably third), the *Two Gentlemen of Verona*, next it." With the works so scrambled, "No wonder readers are all in a maze."[91] To Furnivall's dismay, Germany had anticipated the society's priorities. It was a "great disgrace" that the society's model was a German critic, Georg Gottfried Gervinus, a member of the Deutsche Shakespeare-Gesellschaft, the Shakspere Society's German counterpart. In his *Shakespeare Commentaries*, published in Bonn in 1849–1850 and translated into English in 1863, Gervinus had discussed the entire corpus in chronological order, from *Titus Andronicus* to *Henry VIII*. And his purpose was clear: "Let this genius of the poet be watched in its development, be discerned and traced out in its imperfect embryo, in its growth, and in its finished form."[92] Germany was also credited with the publication of the works in that order in an English edition with German commentary by Nicolaus Delius. Furnivall's mandate was urgent: "Do all you can to further the study of Shakspere, chronologically and as a whole, throughout the nation."[93]

Furnivall certainly did his part. Within a few years of the society's founding, he wrote the introduction to the English publication of Delius's 1874 edition, *The Leopold Shakspere* (1877), described on the title page as "The Poet's Works in Chronological Order, from the text of Professor Delius . . . and an Introduction by F. J. Furnivall."[94] He also wrote the introduction to the second edition of the English translation of Gervinus's *Shakespeare Commentaries* (1874)[95] and published it as a monograph in the same year, *The Succession of Shakspere's Works and the Use of Metrical Tests in Settling It.* Only the first half of that title rightly pertains to Gervinus's work: "the Use of the Metrical Tests" in settling the chronology was the signature preoccupation of Furnivall's English society.[96]

From the start, the society was committed to settling Shakespeare's chronology through the study of his versification. The results would compensate for the lack of documents: "Fortunately for us, Shakspere has left us the most satisfactory—because un-designed—evidence of the growth in the mechanism of his art, in the gradual changes in his versification during his life."[97] Once obtained and processed, the statistics would enable the society's members "to get [the works] as nearly as possible into the order in which [Shakespeare] wrote them," and that, in turn, would reveal "the progress and meaning of Shakspere's mind."[98] There was a notable precedent for this approach: a monograph by Charles Bathurst, *Remarks on the Differences in Shakespeare's Versification in Different Periods of His Life* (1857).[99] With Malone's final chronology at hand, Bathurst noticed that Shakespeare's versification over the course of his career altered "very nearly regularly and gradually, always in the same direction."[100] Had the plays been arranged "according to their order in time," readers would have noticed the development. He analyzes the plays in that order, from *Titus* to *The Tempest*, marking "four classes of periods," from adherence to the end-stopped line to "interruption of the verse carried to extreme." As Bathurst succinctly put it, the structure of Shakespeare's verse line "depends on the time of his life":[101] meter is a function of biography.

From Bathurst, the society derived its focus on verse tests as well as the division of their results into four periods: "On the basis of the verse test, with Bathurst (whom I follow) we make Four, and define the Characteristics of each Period."[102] Members of the society submitted reports tracking the development of other metrical features, like feminine endings and alexandrines, and grouping them in four progressing periods. Once the "me-chanical tests" were completed, it would then be possible, Furni-vall opined, to see whether or not they coincided with the higher authority of aesthetic criteria of "characterization, knowledge of life, music of line, dramatic development, and imagination."[103]

F. G. Fleay, the most passionate and numerate of the society's members, dismissed qualitative criteria altogether: "our analysis, which has hitherto been qualitative, must become quantitative."[104]

In the first of his many papers to the society, he insisted that scientific computation must obviate critical opinion: "If you cannot weigh, measure, number your results . . . you are merely a guesser, a propounder of hypotheses."[105] He took heart from Malone's seminal rhyme test. It might seem ludicrous, he granted, "to speak even of the application of mathematics to such a subject," but in its defense, he pointed out that the order he derived from numbers for Shakespeare's early plays accorded exactly with Meres's 1598 roundup. This, he calculated, could not be mere coincidence: "Now, the doctrine of chances gives us as the odds . . . more than 20 millions to one: in exact numbers, one chance only out of 20,030,010 would hit on this exact selection of plays." However reliant on statistics, Fleay held the same assumption as all the Shakespearean chronologers: the chronology, however devised, would display an upward trend in Shakespeare's writing.

Yet Fleay's determination to see a progression in Shakespeare's versification led to unexpected results. Passages and even entire plays could not be brought in alignment with the climb he set out to quantify. His metrical analyses confirmed prior doubts that *Henry VI* and *Titus* were not "in the main bulk" by Shakespeare, but more alarmingly, they introduced new ones: "These metrical tests made me suspect the genuineness of the *Taming of the Shrew*, parts of *Timon*, *Pericles*, and *Henry VIII*."[106] Middleton's revisions in *Macbeth* had already been proposed, but Fleay believed *Julius Caesar* in its entirety to be by Ben Jonson. As E. K. Chambers noted in his radical critique of statistic-driven chronology, the plays repeatedly frustrated Fleay's expectation of continuity: "There are eccentricities and dislocations, evidence of recension, wholesale borrowing, bad writing next to good, weak integrations, abrupt beginnings suddenly discontinued."[107] Thus, the attempt to create an evenly advancing trajectory led not to the consolidation of the corpus but to its undoing.

Another response to the society's mandate to "study Shakespeare chronologically, and as a whole" proved more constructive and enduring: a monograph titled *Shakspere: A Critical Study of His Mind and Art* by the Society's vice president, Edward Dowden, first published in 1875. The Society's influence is unmistakable.[108] Dowden reproduces Furnivall's "Trial Table of the Order of Shakspere's Plays" divided into four periods in his preface and frequently cites papers by the society's members, including Fleay, as well as their German counterparts.[109] Adhering to "the chronological method" in his discussion of Shakespeare's plays, he shares the Society's conviction that the succession of the plays is the "essential prerequisite" for observing "the growth of Shakspere's mind and art" (336). But while Fleay's statistics led to the dismantling of the canon, Dowden's criticism left a foundation so solid that the canon still rests on its cornerstones.

The subject of Dowden's critical study is less Shakespeare's "mind and art" than his mind *in* art. It is through the formal aspects of his plays that Dowden perceives "the growth of Shakspere's art" (xv), a spiritual movement apparent even in the society's metrical counts: "For, in truth, such an apparently mechanical thing as the stopping of a passage or verse is not mechanical, but in its essence spiritual" (54).[110] Shakespeare's plots and characters are also drawn toward release, and invariably, like the society's metrical counts, in four stages. His early "geometrical" plots have a static symmetry, as in *Love's Labor's Lost*, in which a king and three courtiers are mirrored by a princess and her three ladies; in his later plays, no longer fearing "the weight of too much liberty" (53), he loosens and complicates his plots. His characters, too, become less subject to accident and contingency as they advance toward a higher spiritual stage, from the errant Proteus to the impulsive Romeo and introspective Hamlet and culminating in the self-possessed Prospero. Even Shakespeare's clowns develop teleologically, and through the genres, from the comic Lance who "blunders into mirthful matter" (320) to the historical Falstaff in "whom humor has acquired clear consciousness of itself and become free" (321) to the tragic delicacy of the Fool's antics in *Lear* (243) to the pastoral abandon or "gay defiance" of Autolycus (335).

Dowden's *Shakspere: A Critical Study of His Mind and Art* is the first work in English to discuss all the plays, from *Titus* to

The Tempest, not in disconnected and discrete comments but as a developing, multifaceted but coherent whole—precisely what the society's founding document had mandated. Although his discussion of the plays mainly follows the order of Furnivall's chronological table (xv–xvi), Dowden has reservations about its ultimate importance: "Whether Macbeth preceded Othello or Othello Macbeth, need not greatly concern us." Dating the plays is significant only as it enables "us to trace with confidence the succession of Shakespeare's epochs of spiritual alteration and development." In this respect, the two tragedies are coterminous: "both plays belong equally to one and the same period in the history of Shakspere's mind and art." In Shakespeare's "history," as in world history, periods and not dates mark the advance toward spiritual ascendance. Indeed, Shakespeare's four "epochs of spiritual alteration and development" have quite a lot in common with the four eras of Hegelian world history: both move increasingly toward a freedom that entails submission to higher principles. As in Hegel's philosophy of world history, each period marks a stage of heightened self-consciousness, what Dowden terms "self-possession and self-mastery" (337). In Shakespeare's final period, that self-regulating freedom is achieved: "The style . . . becomes free and daring" and his art "as free as the winds . . . that is to say in complete, noble, and glad subjection" (55). In the Hegelian trajectory, the Reformation is the agent of change that precipitates the liberational break from medieval to modern. Shakespeare, for Dowden, benefits from its inspirational zeitgeist: "the spirit of Protestantism—of Protestantism considered a portion of a great movement of humanity,—animates and breathes through his writing" (33).[111]

Had Dowden's Shakespeare criticism been limited to his *Shakspere: His Mind and Art*, it might have faded into obscurity, like the publications of the other society members. Its long and abiding influence is the result of his primer, *Shakspere*, a slim octavo distillation of his critical study published two years later. Here Dowden marshals the lofty abstractions and generalizations of his critical study into a simplified schema. A chapter on the "Evidence of the Chronology of Shakspere's Writings" is followed by "Periods of Shakspere's Career" divided, predictably, into four.[112] The chronology breaks at 1600: "Now the division of the centuries marks roughly a division in the career of Shakspeare"; "ten years and upwards lie in the 16th century, ten years and upwards in the 17th." As the century turns, so, too, does Shakespeare change: "his genius began to seek new ways." Those ten-year units are themselves "clearly divisible into two shorter periods," each referencing his "supposed condition and state of mind." Their tags reflect his growth from his apprenticeship ("In the Workshop") to his involvement in business ("In the World") to his psychological descent ("In the Depths") to his final spiritual ascendancy in retirement ("On the Heights"). From the time of his apprenticeship, he writes in all three of the folio genres, so that comedy, history, and tragedy each develop through an "early," "middle," and "later" period. But in the first edition of *Shakspere: A Critical Study of His Mind and Art* (1875), following the third period, dominated by tragedy "In the Depths", there is no fourth genre for "On the Heights": only the generically unspecific "Last Plays."[113]

It is the masterstroke of his 1877 primer, *Shakspere*, to supply a genre for the last period. By one of criticism's most durable fiats, Dowden proclaims, "Let us, then, name this group, consisting of four plays, Romances."[114] *Pericles*, a play that Malone had dropped from his final chronology, is reinstated as "the first of the group of plays which I have named Romances," followed by *Cymbeline, The Winter's Tale* and *The Tempest*. With this dictum, each of the four periods of Shakespeare's mind and of his art has its own generic counterpart. All subsequent editions of *Shakspere: His Mind and Art* are revised accordingly, from 1879 up to the present.[115] Thus, the genres, formerly phased out by chronology, now return, not as literary categories but as stages of Shakespeare's psychological and aesthetic development: early, middle, later, and last.

In his critical study, Dowden discusses each of the plays individually in numbered and titled entries. Even thus individuated, they are linked by repeated references to their dated or periodized position in the course of Shakespeare's development. No special exemption is made for the histories. Dowden, like Malone, born and educated in Ireland, has none of Hurdis's or Boswell's qualms about breaking the "historical chain" of English sovereignty. Authorial development seamlessly assimilates the rules of English royal succession. Nor is Dowden bothered by the specter of joint authorship glimpsed by Hurdis, noted by Coleridge, and raised by Fleay. The debates over *Timon*'s authorship, for example, "do not essentially concern us." *Timon* belongs in the canon because Timon's sufferance of injury is "the ideal expression" of the tragic period and makes way for the conciliatory romances: it is "the decuman wave which sets shoreward" toward the final auspicious period of *The Tempest*.[116] A position in the sequencing or periodizing of the whole secures a play's authenticity. The two time orders not only interlock the plays to one another but also fasten them to their author whose development they make manifest. It was only after Dowden's foursquare schematization that totality was predicated to editions: editions once titled *The Works of Shakespeare* were retitled *The Complete Works of Shakespeare*. They hold together now, not just as a collection but as a whole, complete unto itself.[117]

>>><<<

Just two years after the publication of Dowden's *Shakspere*, the authoritative Cambridge edition, first published in 1863–1866, became available in a new format: *The complete works of William Shakespear: arranged in their chronological order . . . with an introduction to each play, adapted from the Shakespearean primer of Professor Dowden* (1879).[118] Both Dowden's *Primer* and his *A Critical Study of His Mind and Art* went through numerous editions; the latter remained continuously in print for almost a century, and has been reprinted repeatedly into the twenty-first.[119] Several major reference and critical works adopted his schema, beginning with Sidney Lee's *Life of Shakespeare* (1898), its abridgement, *Shakspeare's Life and Work*, his long entry on "William

Shakespeare" in the *Dictionary of National Biography*, as well his introduction to the Caxton complete works. E. K. Chambers's *William Shakespeare: A Study of Facts and Problems* (1930) endorses Dowden's four periods before discussing the plays in chronological order; Geoffrey Bullough's discussion in *Narrative and Dramatic Sources of Shakespeare* follows Chambers (1957). *The Alexander Shakespeare* (1951), Britain's most popular twentieth-century edition of Shakespeare, reproduces the works in the folio order, but Peter Alexander's introduction follows Dowden's "chronological method" and discusses the plays in four periods with an emphasis on their theatrical coordinates, as does Alexander's *A Shakespeare Primer*.[120] In time, introductory essays like those of Furnivall, Dowden, and Alexander would no longer be needed to justify the arrangement. Embedded in the format of the canon's reproduction, the rationale goes without saying.

It is not only Shakespeare's canon that now calls for chronological ordering. The plots of individual plays are expected to conform not to the neoclassical unity of time but to linear extension. In 1850 what has recently been termed "the greatest crux in Shakespeare" is brought to light: the inconsistent time scheme of *Othello*.[121] Its action in Cyprus, it is maintained, takes place on two different time lines: one as short as thirty-six hours (the time it takes for Iago to drive Othello to murder Desdemona), and the other as long as many weeks (the length of time of Desdemona's imputed adultery, Cassio's slighting of Bianca, Roderigo's emptying of his purse, etc.). According to the theory, in "short time," the audience feels the urgency of Othello's passion; in "long time," it accepts the play's events as probable. The expectation that action, whether enacted or reported, should advance uniformly is extended to other plays as well, so that the New Variorum edition, begun in 1871, includes not only a fourteen-page note on "double time" in *Othello* but also introduces "Duration of Action" as one of the critical categories of its commentary along with date, characters, plot, and criticism. All time references in a given play are tallied (in weeks, days, hours, even minutes), and irregularities are noted, which—like those other violations of chronological time, anachronisms—call out for critical attention.

At the turn of the twenty-first century, the new New Variorum Shakespeare drops "Duration" from its commentary, but the crux of "double time" in *Othello* remains a critical challenge, as is evidenced not only in the introductions to most editions of the play but also in a number of recent essays. There have been attempts to obviate the need for double time by extending the single time line in Venice back by weeks before the play begins.[122] Or to give historical specificity to the play's "two clocks" by establishing the copresence of two calendars in the sixteenth-century, the Julian in Venice and the Gregorian in Cyprus.[123] Or to see the slippage as a structural problem incurred when Shakespeare attempted to convert his narrative source, Giraldi Cinthio's novella, into dramatic form.[124] Or to identify the irregularity with a poststructural "palimpsested time" that in breaching the standard of homogenous time throws the ideologies it sustains into disarray.[125] Or to align it with developments in jurisprudence, in which jurors, like spectators, are confronted with two types of evidence: one of rhetorical force and the other of forensic proof. The expectation still lingers that plot, not to mention character, develop on a single time line, like that which has been devised to organize the canon itself.

>>><<<

There are now signs that chronology's grip on the Shakespeare corpus is slackening. The Arden complete works has abandoned chronology in favor of a more trusted schema: the alphabet. Arden's table of contents thus doubles as an index, facilitating the location of a play in the volume rather than embedding the plays in a theory of development. The *RSC Shakespeare* has also steered clear of it, reverting to the generic order of the 1623 folio's catalog. Tucked away in an appendix is a tabular "Conjectural Chronology" of "Probable Dates" in which the evidence for dates is repeatedly qualified as "apparent," "suggested," "assumed," or downright nonexistent: there is "No firm evidence for the date" of *All's Well*, *Timon of Athens*, or *Coriolanus*.[126]

Norton and Oxford continue to reproduce the plays in chronological order while at the same time raising issues that militate against its viability. A chronology devised to accommodate Shakespeare's works as written by him alone, each play finished once and for all, is thus being asked to accommodate the work of other hands—George Wilkins's in *Pericles*, for example, or Thomas Middleton's in *Macbeth*. So, too, the postulate of revised or alternate versions of the same play—three *Hamlet*s, for example, or two *Othello*s—requires that multiple dates be given for a single or ostensibly single play. How can we list the plays in a chronological order keyed to Shakespeare alone when so many are now deemed collaborative, certainly at the start and end of his career, but perhaps in the middle as well? How can we assign each play a single date when by some estimates Shakespeare revised after publication as many as sixteen of the plays ascribed to him?

One solution here is to replace or supplement the shaky chronology of composition with the solid one of dates of first (known) publication. The Norton digital edition introduces such a list for the plays and poems it reproduces, though it follows the chronological arrangement of the print edition. The New Oxford goes further in its two-volume old-spelling edition.[127] It divides the plays into two units by date of publication and accords a separate volume to each: volume 1 contains works published in Shakespeare's lifetime, and volume 2 works published posthumously. There can be no disputing this dispensation. Nor can there be any hope of charting Shakespeare's development when sixteen of the plays converge on a single date, 1623, the date of the first folio's publication, seven years after his death.

Yet the modernized New Oxford remains faithful to authorial chronology, claiming to present the works "in the order in which Shakespeare wrote them, so that readers can follow the development of his imagination, his engagement with a rapidly evolving culture and theatre, and his relationship to his literary contemporaries."[128] In doing so, it adapts a new dating layout in order to accommodate the complexities it acknowledges: a table for each play consisting of a "Date Range" (from as little as a year for *Henry V* to as many as twelve years for *The Two Gentlemen of Verona*) followed by a single date called "Most Likely."[129] In the case where coauthorship, additions, or revisions are assumed, a separate "Date Range" and "Most Likely" are added for each category of composition. The tabular unit tacitly acknowledges not only the variability of the chronology but also the impossibility of compressing the time of a play's making to a single date by a single hand.

But there is more. Each "Date Range" and "Most Likely" date concludes in an even hazier rubric: "Best Guess." As the editors explain, "our Best Guess represents *the period of the year* in which we think the work was most likely written." Having enlarged the single dates to a flexible "Date Range," they proceed to shrink it, calendaring each work to a period *within* a year: to a season or term or month. With this degree of flexibility, the projection of a dated continuum—a time line for Shakespeare's writing of his plays—is hard, if not impossible to imagine.

>>><<<

As we have seen, chronology was late to be entertained as the system for organizing Shakespeare's plays. Not until about 150 years after the publication of the first folio was a chronology attempted, and not until the passing of another 150 years did it become the standard order of the complete works editions. Work on the chronology still continues, spurred on by new databases and quantitative analyses, still undaunted by what is often admitted: that the order remains only conjectural, perhaps no better than a "best guess." But this is not for lack of evidence—or the technology and ingenuity by which to analyze the evidence we have. The problem is more fundamental. For as this chapter has worked to demonstrate, the desire to ascertain the authorial chronology has always been driven by the need to track

Shakespeare's singular development—the highly personalized course of his art, his life, and his times—on an advancing trajectory. But the plays are no longer thought to issue from one mind and in one hand at one sitting, one play after another, *ad seriatim*. Their composition is now seen as more of a durative process than a punctual event. Under the strain of coauthorship and revision, the chronological throughline that has so effectively organized both the reproduction of Shakespeare's plays and their critical discussion can only buckle. It may, then, be outlasting its service as the heuristic by which to understand "how Shakespeare became *Shakespeare*."

Period Drama in the Age of World Pictures

The fact that the world becomes picture at all is what distinguishes the essence of the modern age.
M. HEIDEGGER, "The Age of the World Picture"

Two engravings (figs. 3.1 and 3.2) depict the same climactic moment in *Coriolanus*: Coriolanus entreated by his mother and wife to spare Rome. The first is Coriolanus *à la Romaine*, a theatrical confection (ca. 1750).[1] The second is Coriolanus the Roman, a historical representation (ca. 1800).[2] In the former, clothing, scenery, and props are modern; in the latter, they are all ancient. The histrionic Coriolanus comes toward the end of long theatrical tradition largely indifferent to the time of a play's setting, in this instance the early history of Rome. By contrast, the historical one marks the start of a new tradition in which the time of the setting prescribes all aspects of what is on view. The latter marks the beginning of what would become the norm in staging Shakespeare: Shakespeare performed *in period*.

The first play staged in period was John Philip Kemble's production of *Coriolanus* at Covent Garden in around 1800. Why did it take two centuries before this play—indeed *any* play by

FIGURE 3.1. Coriolanus *à la Romaine. Mr. Quin in the Character of Coriolanus* (ca. 1750). Photograph: © The Trustees of the British Museum

Shakespeare—was staged uniformly in its historical setting? Theater historians once accounted for the long lag with a narrative in which the theater from the start was headed toward a more realistic representation of the past.[3] Little by little, the resources necessary for the desired end were acquired: a larger budget, movable sets, archaeological and antiquarian sources, and a manager with control over all aspects of a production. Once Kemble took over the management of Covent Garden, all these conditions were finally fulfilled so that a coherent historical picture could be displayed within the picture-frame stage of his theater. At last, after two hundred years, a play set in the historical past could be enacted in true with that past, just as Shakespeare, it was assumed, would have wanted it.

But as that narrative moves toward Kemble's achievement, it stumbles badly when it hits the historical abandon of the 1750 Coriolanus. Only half a century separates James Quin's spectacle of 1750 in Covent Garden from Kemble's representation in 1800 at the same theater. During that interval, there is no sudden advance toward period representation. Indeed, during those decades the stage was dominated by the celebrated actor David Garrick who preferred to wear suits with jackets, breeches, and

FIGURE 3.2. Roman Coriolanus. James Caldwall after Gavin Hamilton, *"Coriolanus." Act V. Scene III*. Josiah Boydell, *A Collection of Prints, from Pictures Painted for the Purpose of Illustrating the Dramatic Works of Shakspeare* (London, 1803), vol. 1, plate 29. Photograph: © The British Library Board (Tab.599.c)

FIGURE 3.3. Roman Titus Andronicus. Henry Peacham [?], drawing from *Titus Andronicus* (ca. 1600). Longleat Portland Papers (I f. 159v). Reproduced by kind permission of the Marquess of Bath, Longleat. Photograph: © The Marquess of Bath, Longleat House, Warminster, Wiltshire, UK

hose even when portraying historical characters.[4] In their disregard for period realism, both Garrick and Quin are closer to the staging practices of 1600 than of 1800. In the earliest illustration we have of a Shakespeare play, a sketch of *Titus Andronicus* (fig. 3.3), the figures are also in varieties of modern dress. There is, however, one salient exception: Titus, the central and titular character, togaed and laureated, is recognizable as an ancient Roman.[5] We might then go further still in troubling the assumption that the stage was advancing toward historical realism by suggesting that the 1600 sketch, with its one token Roman, comes closer to representing ancient Rome than the 1750 engraving.

Rather than tracking a gradual development toward a prescribed end, this chapter dwells on the change from one depiction of Coriolanus to the other: from a blithe indifference to history (fig. 3.1) to a strict adherence to it (fig. 3.2). Period coherence, it argues, is not the ultimate achievement of a realism that was always desired. Rather, it is a new priority in keeping with the period to which it belongs, the wide turn of the nineteenth century, a span now periodized as Romanticism. During that span, novels, painting, history, and even philosophy also represented the past in self-contained synchronic period units. It is not only the outward features of a given age that must conform but all aspects of a period's culture. To designate this more comprehensive framework, the concept of a "world picture" emerges from German idealist philosophy to individuate one period unit from another: *Weltanschauung*, a way of looking at the world, cognitive, affective, and evaluative.[6] Its English translation as "world picture" invites comparison to the period drama within the picture-frame stage: the one a complex of thoughts, beliefs, and feelings; the other a mise-en-scène of costume, props, and settings.

It might then be said, indeed it *has* been said, that the distinctive feature of the period centering on 1800 is its consciousness of itself as a period, the recognition of its own "spirit of the age" as well as those of earlier ages.[7] Of course, such a claim itself depends on period logic, and so too does this chapter in identifying the rise of period drama with Romanticism. In this respect, the chapter might serve to confirm the maxim put forth by Fredric Jameson, the great theorist of the modern and postmodern periods: "We cannot not periodize." In his extended essay on the ontology of the modern period, he concedes that periods, while "intolerable and unacceptable," are all the same indispensable.[8] Yet this chapter, while relying on period logic, argues for an exception: before 1800, on the English stage, periods *were* dispensable.

>>><<<

In the engraving of Coriolanus *à la Romaine* (fig. 3.1), every feature puts the production's artifice on display, beginning with the billowy stage curtain drawn to the left.[9] Clearly this is a performance, played for and before an audience. Costumes are designed to catch the eye by exaggerating and embellishing the actors' stage presence: for Coriolanus, this is accomplished with bouffant plumes, full-bottomed periwig, wide brocaded bodice, and balletic skirt or *tonnelet*; for the suppliant women, with volumizing gowns, flounced sleeves, and oversized handkerchiefs. The dais is clearly a stage prop, a movable ramp from which Coriolanus has descended from his "chayer of state," as it is called in Shakespeare's source, North's translation of Plutarch,[10] but here a fauteuil or armchair in the style of Louis XIV, a touch of Versailles. On the scenic backdrop appears the Rome Coriolanus is threatening to destroy. But what Rome? The crenellated walls with banner flying from the keep are medieval; within the walls, the Roman Forum is recognizable by Trajan's column but is dominated by the baroque dome of Saints Martin and Luke. The scene represents no prior time in history. Temporally afloat, it does not represent anything at all. It is pure show. The action is a pretext for spectacle: farfetched African feathers, French finery and furnishings, a bodice of Chinese brocaded silk, a panorama of the Eternal City. Where else but on stage could such wonders appear? (Unless perhaps on a mid-eighteenth-century Chinese porcelain punch bowl commemorating Quin's performance [fig. 3.4].).[11]

In the engraving of Roman Coriolanus, no looped curtain announces the theatricality of the depicted event: the confrontation appears to be taking place in historical time. The engraving accurately illustrates the ten lines spoken by Coriolanus's mother Volumnia that are printed in the caption below the engraving:[12] Coriolanus glances down ("He turns away"), the women have dropped to their knees ("Down, ladies"), Coriolanus's son kneels with his arms raised ("kneels and holds up hands for fellowship").[13] Yet Shakespeare's scene is represented not as it might be staged but as it is imagined to have happened, outside the gate of Rome, in the early days of the Roman republic. Volumnia's exaggerated size and gesture are intended less to attract the viewer's attention than to give weight to her momentous role in saving Rome from destruction. Coriolanus's attire is not theatrical

FIGURE 3.4. Mr. Quin in the character of Coriolanus, Quinlong period (1755–1765). Chinese export porcelain punch bowl. From William Motley, *Baroque & Roll* (Reigate: Cohen & Cohen, 2015), no. 67, p. 106. Photograph: Cohen & Cohen, reproduced by courtesy of the author

costume but authentic Roman gear (or its simulation): anatomic breastplate (*lorica musculata*) with military skirt (*pteruges*), sandals, and sword (*gladius*); his crested helmet (*galea*) is held by his nearby page, while the plumed helmet of the Volscian general, Aufidius, seated to the left, lies on the ground to the right. Women are appareled in loose stoles (*stolae*) and mantles (*pallae*). The suppliant wife and son are pleading in Roman fashion, with hands extended, *manus tendentes*.[14] At the gates, ROMA is chiseled in Roman letters on Doric columns.

Every attempt has been made to Romanize the scene so that it appears to depict the past event itself rather than a latter-day theatricalization. Costumes have been modeled on Roman statuary (as has Coriolanus's contrapposto stance) or else on the classical revivals of both Renaissance and neoclassical art. The women's drapery derives from Raphael's Vatican frescoes, and Volumnia's plane-defying outstretched arms rival those in Poussin's painting of the encounter as narrated by Livy.[15] But the picture admits no mediation: its disparate sources have been lost to period conformity. Instead of the eclectic theatrical mock-up of 1750, we have a synthesized realization of the event itself. Self-contained and self-enclosed, the scene acknowledges no spectator: any notice of the contemporary world would spoil the period illusion.

The sketch of what is assumed to be a staging of *Titus Andronicus* from around 1600 also depicts a scene of supplication in Rome (fig. 3.3 above): the queen of the Goths pleads to the Roman conqueror for the lives of her sons. The costumes are indexical.[16] They identify the two rulers (the Roman general, laureated and bearing the staff of office; the coronated Goth queen), differentiate male from female, distinguish conquerors (armed and overdressed soldiers) from conquered (bound, unarmed, and sparsely dressed prisoners), and single out the ethnic other (in black stockings, gloves, and face makeup) from the rest. But the costumes are not historical. The Roman soldiers on the left are in modern breeches, holding modern halberds; the queen is in a modern gown (and kneeling with hands clasped in Christian prayer); the puff sleeves of the Moor's doublet are distinctly Elizabethan, though his lower garment and that of Tamora's sons might indicate either Roman pleated skirts (*pteruges*) or Elizabethan trunk hose. The one figure not part of the focal action, the menacing Moor, may be the drawing's acknowledgment of its theatrical provenance. His position at the downstage edge of the focal action as well as his weapon reference the Vice figure of the medieval and Tudor morality plays. Like the Vice, he stands between the characters and the notional audience in order to comment on the scene to which he is pointing with what has been identified as a "sword of lath," a wooden prop associated with the Vice.[17]

While commentators might disagree about the attire of the Moor and the two Goth captives, all agree that Titus is in Roman dress. Yet even his costume is makeshift rather than historical: the "toga" is cobbled from a rusticated, low cut, sleeveless undergarment with a sheet tied at the shoulder like a baldric, a theatrical expedient for transforming modern dress to ancient.[18]

The longsword hanging to the floor from his side is modern, as is his tasseled ceremonial spear.[19] The staging sketched in 1600 displays the same eclecticism or indifference to period accuracy as that engraved in 1750. It, too, exploits the variety and rarity of costume: a Roman conqueror, a queen in full regalia, and a Moor, all impersonated by ordinary players. What need to signal antiquity visually when the play's title and dramatis personae are sufficient to situate the play in the ancient Roman past? Given the choice, why opt for players in plain uniform togas? One early witness, a French tutor in Sir John Harington's household who saw *Titus* performed there in 1596, possibly by Shakespeare's Chamberlain's Men, reported to being more taken by the spectacle of the play than its content: "la monstre a plus valu que le sujet."[20]

That the attire worn on the early modern stage was intended to be eye-catching is confirmed by our primary theatrical source: the account books and inventories of Philip Henslowe, owner of the Rose Theatre and manager of the Admiral's Men. His itemized lists of the company's wardrobe reveal that dress on stage consisted primarily of clothes that had been recently worn off stage and acquired by the acting company from previous owners through purchase, loan, or gift. As Susan Cerasano has noted in her study of Henslowe's inventory, the clothes were predominantly of superior quality, like those worn at court or in civic processions, and they were expensive: the worth of the Admiral's Men's wardrobe, she estimates, was in excess of the playhouse itself.[21] The fabrics were sumptuous (damask, velvet, satin) and of bright colors (scarlet, purple, yellow). Ornamentation added further sheen and luster: lace, fringes, spangles, and buttons—in gold, silver, and copper.[22] The spectacle was enhanced further by the costumes that could only be had by making: for gods, monsters, devils, and exotic others like Persians and Turks. In sum, the apparel, whether second hand or bespoke, was selected to make a strong visual impression. One might say that through the opulence and diversity of costume, the stage strove not to imitate reality, historical or contemporary, but to upstage it.

Such costuming practices do not, however, preclude the presence of a token toga, as in the Longleat drawing, signaling the ancient past and adding to the production's pageantry. One theater historian has categorically ruled out togas on stage before the closing of the theaters in 1642, maintaining that "No play performed in the Early Modern English professional playhouses references the toga."[23] But the absence of the Latin word is a sign not of the nonexistence of the garment but of the unfamiliarity of the term. In both North's Plutarch and Holland's Livy, when the Latin word is retained, it is followed by an English translation, "gowne" or "robe." This might also account for the absence of "togas" in Henslowe's accounts of theatrical apparel. But it is also possible that togas were itemized not as articles of clothing but as measurements of linen—"Itm iiij elles qter of fine holland" or "ix elles of cowrse lawne"[24]—the few yards of cloth needed to drape over the shoulder and wrap around the body of the actor. As in the Longleat drawing, the lead role might have stood out in his plain ancient garb against the backdrop of flashier modern dress.

Sixteenth-century academic productions appear to have followed the same practice despite the greater knowledge of ancient history and literature of both their actors and their audiences. Surviving records indicate that the ancient Greeks and Romans in the neo-Latin plays performed at Cambridge and Oxford also performed in contemporary dress.[25] The same kind of garments were kept in the "chests" of St. John's College, Cambridge, as in the wardrobe of the Admiral's Men.[26] One list from Magdalen College, Oxford, does itemize "Antique fashions" for a performance on the occasion of a visit from King James and his queen, among them "Syxe antique suites of cloth of gold" and "14. Antique vizards."[27] But gold cloth and masks suggest that the performance was striving to reproduce for the royal audience not ancient history but the extravagant theatricality of a court masque.

Nor were court entertainments, infamous for the lavish sums spent on their costuming, interested in evoking a historically correct antiquity. Inigo Jones, the great designer of masque sets and costumes, had studied classical sculpture in Italy and advised Lord Arundel on his collection of Roman statues known as the Arundel Marbles.[28] While his costume drawings were certainly influenced by the ancient models he knew first hand, he by no means attempted their accurate reproduction. We have a sketch he made in Rome of a Roman statue (fig. 3.5) as well as of the costume he based on that statue for Albanactus, the Romano-British king in the masque of *Albion's Triumph* (fig. 3.6).[29] The Roman statue has been transformed for the royal entertainment: its cropped hair is shoulder length and crowned with plumes, its pleated Roman skirt altered to Renaissance trunk hose, its bare feet shod in balletic buskins, and the hand that

FIGURE 3.5. Inigo Jones, a Roman figure, in *Roman Sketchbook* (1614). Photograph: © The Devonshire Collections, Chatsworth (I, flr 5v 6r). Reproduced by permission of Chatsworth Settlement Trustees

FIGURE 3.6. Inigo Jones, costume design for the Romano-British king Alba-nactus, *Albion's Triumph*, in *Roman Sketchbook* (1634). Photograph: © The Devonshire Collections, Chatsworth (O&S 203). Reproduced by permission of Chatsworth Settlement Trustees

would have rested on a sword opened as if to receive a partner in dance.

When the London theaters reopened after their closure of almost twenty years, much was altered: the open platform stage was replaced by an enclosed proscenium, a mainly bare stage was backed with scenic flats, female parts formerly given to males were played by actresses. In addition, the wardrobe needed to be replenished, with generous sponsorship from the crown. But dress remained primarily contemporary, sometimes belonging to the actors themselves. If new costumes were acquired, it would have been with an eye to updating dress rather than to historicizing it. Costume *à la Romaine* was an exception, made exclusively for the stage and suggesting a faraway time and place, but this was to the end of varying and enhancing spectacle. Samuel Pepys, an avid theatergoer, was struck by the opening scene of a performance of the tragedy *Heraclius, Emperor of the East*, featuring the ruler and his entourage "standing in their fixed and different postures in their Roman habits."[30] But those costumes would have been drawn from the theater's conventional *à la Romaine* stock, evoking nothing more specific than antiquity and certainly nothing of Heraclius's seventh-century Byzantium. In staging Shakespeare's plays, the same "Roman shapes," as they were also called, would have been used for both his Greek and Roman plays, from the Trojan War of *Troilus and Cressida* to the declining Roman empire of *Titus Andronicus*. So, too, with the other class of noncontemporary attire: the "old English shapes," or Tudor dress that would have outfitted the principal characters in Shakespeare's histories, from the early thirteenth-century reign of King John to the mid-sixteenth-century death of Henry VIII. Even when the Roman or Tudor costumes did appear on stage, they were worn selectively rather than by the entire dramatis personae. Women's costume, whatever the date of a play's setting, was always contemporary, preferably modeled on the latest French fashions, like the handsome mourning gowns of the two women appealing to Quin's Coriolanus in figure 3.1.

We now call stage garments "costumes," but according to the *OED*, *costume* did not signify "a set of clothes worn by an actor or performer for a particular role" until 1829.[31] In theatrical documents before the nineteenth century, the variety of terms used for what actors wear on stage are generic—clothes, garments, habits, attire, outfits for example—but not "costumes." The several inventories included among Henslowe's papers itemize his company's "goods," "sewtes," and "apparell."[32] Edmond Malone, in the *Historical Account of the English Stage* published in both his 1790 and 1821 editions of Shakespeare, refers to "stage-habiliment," "stage dresses," and "stage-habits"—but never "costume."[33] The word existed, but it overlapped phonetically and orthographically with *custom* as well as also deriving from the French *coutume*. The earliest costume books are not of theatrical dress but of dress customarily worn in a given country or at an earlier time. At the end of the eighteenth century, *costume* comes to specify apparel exclusively for the stage. This reflects stage practice. Bespoke apparel that was in Shakespeare's day an exception is after the Kembles the rule. A play performed uniformly in dress of a particular historical period is now called either "costume drama" or "period drama."

>>><<<

At the end of the eighteenth century, the tradition of performing Shakespeare's plays primarily in contemporary dress came to a halt. In Stephen Orgel's wide-ranging essay on how history has been theatricalized in the performance of Shakespeare, the change was sudden and momentous: "All at once, in 1786, Shakespeare stopped being our contemporary and became history."[34] Orgel overdramatizes here, as he himself allows, to stress what he holds to be "a radical and unprecedented" shift in the staging of Shakespeare. In 1786 the engraver and publisher John Boydell announced to his colleagues his intention to foster a school of British historical painting to counter the opinion abroad that England had "no genius for historical painting."[35] The problem, according to Boydell, was that the English lacked not talent but "a proper subject." That subject was sought not, as we might expect, in eighteenth-century historical writing, such as Edward Gibbon's *The History of the Decline and Fall of the Roman Empire* for ancient history or David Hume's *History of England* for English history. Rather, as Boydell announced and as his colleagues unanimously agreed, it was to be located in Shakespeare: "no subjects seem so proper to form an English School of Historical Painting, as the scenes of the immortal Shakespeare." The playwright's "characters and scenes" were to stand in for the actual agents and events of history itself. The theater, as we will see, would adopt this same standard, performing his plays as if they were history, synchronizing all visual elements on stage to the time of a play's action. Historical truth thus came to be identified with Shakespeare's plays set in the historical past, sometimes, as Orgel observes, overriding both the historical record and Shakespeare's text.[36]

Three pictorial projects issued from Boydell's initiative: the Boydell Gallery that exhibited some 167 paintings of historical subjects from Shakespeare (1790), an illustrated edition of the *Dramatic Works of Shakespeare* (1801), and a two-volume elephant folio of engravings, *A Collection of Prints, from Pictures Painted for the Purpose of Illustrating the Dramatic Works of Shakspeare, by the Artists of Great-Britain* (1803). Not all the illustrations Boydell commissioned strove for historical accuracy. In the paintings by Henry Fuseli and William Blake, for example, historical events melded into dreams, nightmares, and reveries. But the paintings that had an immediate influence on the stage were those committed to a historical exactitude based on materials from as close as possible to the illustrated event. For ancient history, the materials were archaeological: statues, vases, bas-reliefs, and medallions. For the English histories, they were antiquarian: manuscript illuminations, effigies, and seals. The textual sources Shakespeare was known to have used—for example, Plutarch for the Roman plays or Holinshed for the English histories—were neglected in favor of artifacts Shakespeare hardly could have known.

One of the paintings commissioned by Boydell was Gavin Hamilton's *"Coriolanus." Act V. Scene III*, now lost, but reproduced in figure 3.2 above. Kemble may well have seen Hamilton's painting when it was first exhibited in 1790, the year after his first performance as Coriolanus at Drury Lane. Its painter had a profound interest in Roman antiquity, having lived in Rome, excavated major sites of central Italy, and collected and sold ancient pieces throughout England and the Continent.[37] According to the art historian Roy Strong, his six paintings from Homer's *Iliad* "were seminal not only for the neoclassical style as such but also for the use of the most recent archaeological evidence."[38] A recent essay on the Boydell Gallery singles out Hamilton's painting *"Coriolanus." Act V. Scene III* as the painting that came closest to achieving the ideals of historical painting, including the use of classical models.[39] The painting was also admired in its own time. When viewers entered Boydell's Gallery, they were met by a bas-relief by Anne Seymour Damer modeled on Hamilton's *Coriolanus* painting. An engraving of the bas-relief also appeared as the title page vignette to Boydell's *A Collection of Prints* (fig. 3.7), the folio volume that included the engraving of Hamilton's painting.

Kemble certainly would have known Damer's bas-relief based on the painting if not the painting itself.[40] James Boaden, friend and biographer of both Kemble and his elder sister Sarah Siddons, notes Damer's influence on the two actors: "Mrs. Damer had led her friends into admiration of the forms which she had modelled"; both brother and sister "were instructed [by her] on ancient forms."[41] As a result, "antiquity became better known to Mrs Siddons; and Mr. Kemble also grew more completely Roman."[42] Siddons's exposure to statuary had a transformative effect on her stage presence, as Boaden emphasizes: "the antique . . . made a remarkable impression on her," so that on the stage she adapted a new style of "simplicity of attire and severity of attitude" that "remains in a great degree the standard of female costume to the present hour."[43] In her dramatic role as mother to her younger brother's Coriolanus, she was the first woman on the English stage to appear in Roman drapery. The reform, Boaden insists, was entirely the result of her "attention to sculpture," and indeed a direct line could be traced from the excavation of Roman statuary to Hamilton's neoclassical painting and its engraved reproduction to Damer's sculpted bas-relief and its engraved title page reproduction: all culminating in Siddons's

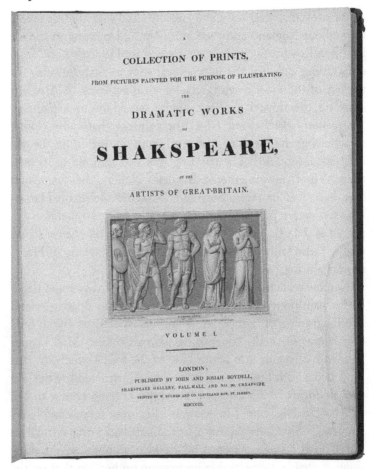

FIGURE 3.7. Vignette print of bas-relief by Anne Seymour Damer. Title page to Josiah Boydell, *A Collection of Prints, from Pictures Painted for the Purpose of Illustrating the Dramatic Works of Shakspeare* (London, 1803). Used by permission of the Folger Shakespeare Library (50966)

statuesque appearance on stage as Coriolanus's overbearing mother.

Kemble, too, brought archaeology to the stage with the sculpted Roman look he cultivated throughout his long career of performing Shakespeare's Coriolanus.[44] His features were said to excel the art fashioned by "the chisel of Greek sculptors," and Roman ones, it might be added, particularly in the aquiline contour of his nose. As one reviewer wittily put it, "His nose was large and of the true Roman arch."[45] For his production of *Coriolanus*, he cut a scene (4.1) from Shakespeare's text and added another to give him occasion to strike a statuesque pose in the presence of a mounted plaster statue.[46] In his modified promptbook, Coriolanus, after his banishment from Rome, arrives at the house of Aufidius, the Volscian general, but not, as in Shakespeare, concealed "in mean apparel"; nor is there a skirmish with the servants who rebuff him. Instead, the curtain opens on the house's interior to reveal what an officer, in Kemble's interpolation, has already prepared the audience to see:

> One of exalted port, his visage hid,
> Has plac'd himself beneath the statue of
> The mighty Mars, and there majestick stands
> In solemn silence.[47]

Kemble stands silent and still, like the statue on the plinth above him. Reviewing Kemble's performance at his retirement from the stage, William Hazlitt noted their interchangeability: "[Kemble as Coriolanus] stood at the foot of the statue of Mars, himself another Mars!"[48] By the time of his valedictory stage performance, antiquity seemed engrained in him, "so complete had he made the habits, manners, and mode of thinking of the ancients identically his own."[49]

Kemble's portrait was painted at least three times in the costume by which he entered Antium incognito.[50] In the most famous, Thomas Lawrence's full-length *John Philip Kemble as Coriolanus at the Hearth of Tullus Aufidius*, his Roman armor and sandals are just visible under the dark cloak.[51] In Peter Bourgeois's portrait, *A Scene in "Coriolanus,"—with a Portrait of the late J P Kemble as Coriolanus*, Kemble wears the same costume, but the painting's scope is enlarged to include more of the action (Aufidius and a guard have entered) and more of the interior space (the statue of Mars and two niches with urns).[52] When

FIGURE 3.8. Richard Earlom after Peter Francis Bourgeois, *Mr. Kemble in the Character of Coriolanus* (1798). Photograph: © The Trustees of the British Museum

this painting is engraved by Richard Earlom (fig. 3.8), the interior space is expanded further to display still more Roman artifacts: a stool with Ionic arm rests, a helmet, a beaked pitcher, weapons mounted on the wall but also scattered along the floor, two brass horns, and a stately arch opening out into a landscape. It is as if all of the production's props had been put on display, each of them a period piece establishing the veracity of the historical scene in an improbable household arrangement. Actor, props, and set are all in keeping with the antiquity of Coriolanus. Indeed, the image might be mistaken for a historical painting, a representation of an encounter in ancient Rome rather than an enactment of *Coriolanus*, act 4, scene 4.

Walter Scott applauded Kemble's effort to synchronize the various aspects of his production with the historical time of their setting, believing that in the theater, "the dresses ought to be suited to the time and country, the landscape and architecture should be equally coherent."[53] Before Kemble, he pointed out, "there was no such thing as regular costume observed in our theatres." The extent of Kemble's costume reform was spectacularly exhibited in his staging of an interpolated ovation procession honoring Martius's triumphant return from Corioli.[54] The highlights of the procession were transcribed shortly after Kemble's death from three pages of stage directions in his own hand and interleaved in his promptbook:

> No fewer than 240 persons marched, in stately procession, across the stage. In addition to the recognized dramatis personae, thirty-five in number, there were vestals, and lictors with their fasces, and soldiers with the spolia opima, and sword-bearers, and standard-bearers, and cupbearers, and senators, and silver eagle-bearers, with the S. P. Q. R. upon them, and trumpeters, and drummers, and priests, and dancing-girls, etc., etc.[55]

As Kemble's stage directions also specified, the entire procession was to remain on stage for the duration of the scene to form one of Kemble's celebrated *tableaux vivants*. Many of the figures (priests, lictors, officers in chains) and objects (SPQR banner, bier with trophies, silver and gold eagles) on his list can be seen in *The Triumphs of Caesar returning from the Gallic Wars*, a series of nine huge canvases painted by Andrea Mantegna and housed at Hampton Court since their acquisition by Charles I.[56] Kemble may have seen Mantegna's originals, but almost certainly he knew of their reproduction in the twelve engravings appended to a magnificent folio edition of *Commentaries of Caesar* (1753), a volume he might well have consulted in researching his production of *Julius Caesar* (fig. 3.9).[57] There could be no greater authority for his staging of ancient Rome than Mantegna, acclaimed from his own day for his exacting study and reproduction of Roman statuary as well as for his reliance on the Roman historians, Plutarch and Appian in particular.[58] For music to accompany the procession, however, Kemble had to drop his standard of authenticity. In the same interleaved stage directions,

FIGURE 3.9. C. Huyberts after Andrea Mantegna, "The Arms taken from the Enemy, consisting of helmets, shields, bucklers, coats of mail, bows, quivers: also plate and booty of the conquered nations and kings," from *The Commentaries of Caesar* (London, 1753). Photograph: © Beinecke Rare Book and Manuscript Library, Yale University (GGnc20 Ag753)

Kemble calls for a chorus, "See the Conquering Hero Comes," from Handel's oratorio *Judas Maccabeus*, composed in 1746, celebrating the victory of the Hebrew leader over the Seleucids in the second century BC.

Like costumes and props, scenery also had to be in sync with the times. Before Kemble, as Boaden reports, "The old scenery exhibited architecture of no period."[59] The scenic stock had been generic—depicting a garden, forest, chamber, or street—and suitable for any number of plays. Designs for the 1811 *Coriolanus* survive in a series of ten prints made in 1815, now in the British Museum.[60] They include "A Street in Rome," "Another Street in

Rome," "An Apartment in Caius Marcius' House," "A Triumphal Arch in Rome," and "The Capitol and The Forum." The sets are perspectival, so that the dramatis personae would have appeared to be standing not in front of a theatrical backdrop but lodged within a spatially defined enclosure. As Christopher Baugh observes, perspectival sets create a space that contains the period illusion: "The scenic artist's approach parallels the growing desire to conceive of the plays as being firmly bound within a period context illustrated by significant visual and architectural styles."[61]

Not only was Kemble's Roman mise-en-scène thought to embody "all his best ideas on the subject of Roman architecture, dress, habits, and manners"; it was admired for doing so "on a scale of great sculpturesque beauty."[62] The artistry of his production was widely acclaimed: "a matchless scenic exhibition . . . every movement an attitude for the painter . . . a panorama of patrician Rome," so accomplished as to instruct the most fashionable painter and sculptor of the day, "a lecture for Lawrence and Canova."[63] Performed in Covent Garden, his production was in stylistic harmony with its surrounds. When rebuilt after the fire of 1808, it was described by Leigh Hunt as "classical and magnificent throughout," with interior classicizing motifs and decor as well as a pedimented and porticoed facade.[64] The sight of Kemble appearing like a Roman in a Roman ambience, both based on archaeological models, simultaneously satisfied the desire for both historical coherence and aesthetic harmony. Indeed, the former risked being overwhelmed by the latter: Kemble's representation of Rome, said one reviewer, went beyond any Rome that had ever existed: "It was an epic painting—not of what Rome was, and still less of what *Coriolanus* was; but of the *beau ideal* of Rome and *Coriolanus*."[65]

>>><<<

With time, Kemble's "*beau ideal*" was held to a more exacting standard of period definition. His early productions of *Coriolanus* were criticized for allowing modern elements into the ancient setting. A reviewer of his 1792 Drury Lane *Coriolanus* complained of seeing his own London in Coriolanus's Rome: "a pretty exact representation of Hanover square, and some very nat [*sic*] Bond-street shops appeared two or three times, as parts of Rome."⁶⁶ By 1811 the sets at Covent Garden were uniformly classical, but as critics pointed out, they were not historically accurate. The time of Coriolanus was closer to the founding of Rome, *ab urbe condita*, than to its imperial glory days. Yet the sets reflected the Rome Augustus Caesar claimed to have left as his legacy, as Suetonius famously reported: "it was with justification that he boasted he had found it a city of brick and left it a city of marble."⁶⁷ Indeed the "grandeurs of Imperial Rome" represented on the scenery flats had been erected by later emperors still, "The arch of Severus or Constantine . . . the pillar of Trajan."⁶⁸

But what had Rome looked like several centuries before those imperial monuments? Robert Elliston, who directed Edmund Kean's *Coriolanus* after Kemble's retirement, raised the problem in the advertisement to his production: "Not even a fragment remains to us of the Roman building or dresses in the time of Coriolanus."⁶⁹ If brick was before marble, what was there before brick? Mud huts, he concluded. All the same, Elliston claimed that for his sets, he "drew on bas-relief and vase paintings," brazenly citing an unidentified bas-relief as his model: "The nearest approach to the time, is to be found in a *basso relievo* from Herculaneum, which represents Coriolanus receiving his wife and mother, as advocates of Rome."⁷⁰ For one scenic innovation, however, he did have verifiable textual and archaeological sources. The "gilded splendor of [his] scenery" was not, he insisted, a mere "stage effect" in violation of the ancients' "supposed purity of taste." Pausanius and other ancients, he pointed out, had written of painted and gilded statues, and marbles had recently been excavated "with sufficient vestiges of this barbarous habit."

In costuming, too, historical standards became stricter. The *toga alba*, based on Roman statuary, in which Kemble had clad his thronging crowds, was much admired in his time. As a nineteenth-century theater historian remarked, "his togas, then for the first time exhibited on the English stage, became a theme of universal admiration. They were pronounced faultless, minutely Classical . . . severely correct, and beautifully graceful beyond precedent."[71] But by the time his younger brother Charles succeeded him as manager of Covent Garden, a more precise pattern had come to light. The antiquary and dramatist James Robinson Planché recounts that an "ingenious foreigner," "the *costumier* to the Théatre Français," had discovered in "Dionysius of Halicarnassus that the toga was semi-circular . . . [and] practically demonstrated that, though not perfectly semi-circular, it was such as to be better described by that term than any other."[72] For his revival of *Julius Caesar*, Charles hired that *costumier*, who then "made the beautiful togas which have since been worn in all the Roman plays at that theatre." But here, too, the attempt to be archaeologically correct was met with a stricter standard. Elliston wondered whether togas, like marble architecture, belonged at all in such a primitive stage of civilization. In the absence of any models from that far back, he looked to "prototypes in the fashion of our modern world" and proposed as the closest analogue "the costume of the French peasants."[73] The clothing of the agrarian poor, he inferred, had remained unchanged for almost two millennia, since the first century BC when the Romans had taken control of southern France.

In his *Pictorial Edition of the Works of Shakspere*, Charles Knight attempts to illustrate Shakespeare's Roman plays with the same archaeological accuracy that Kemble sought to realize on stage. As he announces in the prospectus to the edition, his aim was to base his illustrations on "the realities upon which the imagination of the poet must have rested."[74] But in the case of *Coriolanus*, he has difficulty locating such realities: "It would be extremely difficult to represent the Rome of Coriolanus . . . without a violation of historical propriety."[75] Planché, who supplies notes for Knight's edition, recommends that he study earlier non-Roman sources: "For the habits of Romans during the commonwealth," one must look to the Greeks and Etruscans rather than "the columns and arches of emperors that are like monuments of another nation."[76] For the architecture, Knight has a more viable solution. To avoid the "impropriety" of inaccurate illustration, he provides "the nearest associations we can offer": engravings which show "the unchanging natural localities of Rome, and some of the remains of the ancient city." Among the ageless natural features of Rome are a grove of willows, a herd of grazing long-horned goats, and the steep cliff overlooking the Roman Forum. Among its architectural remains are the Forum itself, in ruins, and a stretch of crumbling Roman wall. With these images, Rome long before its rise is illustrated by Rome long after its fall—in ruin and given up to nature, looking not unlike the picturesque sketches of Rome travelers brought back from the eighteenth-century Grand Tour.

But Knight had to face the possibility that Coriolanus's Rome was not only archaic but legendary. He cites the recently translated *History of Rome* by the great German scholar of antiquity Barthold Georg Niebuhr, now considered the founder of modern German historiography. Niebuhr's chapter on Coriolanus casts doubt on the veracity of virtually everything that was known of Coriolanus, including his victory over the Corioli, his betrayal of Rome, his capitulation to his mother and wife, and his assassination by the Volscians: "The credible and the incredible parts of his pretended history are almost equally suspicious."[77] Yet Knight holds his ground. Plutarch and especially Shakespeare, he insists, have made it "almost impossible to believe that such Romans did not really live, and think, and talk, and act, as we see them."[78] Yet there was no archaeological or scholarly authority for his belief or for the play Kemble had placed at the vanguard of period drama, not because the action took place so early in Rome's history but because it may not have taken place at all. As the editor of the New Variorum edition concludes in his preface to the play, "Coriolanus really belongs to the legendary history of Rome, and by Niebuhr and Mommsen is classed as almost as shadowy a character as Romulus or Remus."[79] In an ironic turn, the first play that was staged as history, in period, lacked any historical record—either archaeological or literary.

>>><<<

Kemble played the part of Coriolanus more often than any other, from 1789 to his valedictory performance in 1817. The number of performances would have been greater still had the play not been removed from the stage for almost a decade, from 1797 to 1806. The playwright and theater critic Elizabeth Inchbald, in her remarks on the play, broadly attributes its withdrawal to "some reasons of state." It was advisable, she explains, to suppress *Coriolanus* during a time of political instability lest the "lower order of people" be offended by Coriolanus's insults: "poverty puts them out of humour at the slightest disrespect." In "times of repose," however, the underclass "will bear contempt with cheerfulness, and even with mirth." Inchbald took *Coriolanus*'s return to the stage in 1806 "as joyful evidence—that the multitude at present are content in their various stations."[80] There is little evidence, however, that 1806 was a time of "happy repose," much less one when the poor were cheered by insults. There were no bread riots like those of 1795–1796, but bad corn harvests compounded by the blockading of grain during the Napoleonic wars meant that food was still in short supply. It may have been less the political climate that had changed than the play itself. A number of Kemble's cuts to his 1811 promptbook weaken the grievances of the citizens.[81] He deleted some of Coriolanus's most toxic insults to the populace as well as two speeches charging the patricians with having starved the people by hoarding grain. He also removed Menenius's feeble attempt to justify that hoarding with "The Fable of the Belly."[82] John Ripley, in his examination of Kemble's promptbooks, concludes that "Kemble's radical depoliticization and aestheticization of Shakespeare's drama reduces the citizens to little more than theatrical furniture."[83] But Kemble's innovative mounting of the production may also have worked to distance the play from current events. The new period staging not only pulled the play's fractious class antagonism into the remote time of its ancient setting but also enframed it within a proscenium arch and ensconced it in a recessed perspectival stage, so that the conflict between patricians and plebeians appeared to be happening not only elsewhere and long ago but in a classicized painting—not unlike Gavin Hamilton's.

Certainly William Hazlitt, a critic and theater reviewer with strong democratic leanings, allows no topicality to disturb his appreciation of Kemble's performance. His reading of Shake-speare's play is another matter: his essay on *Coriolanus* begins by stressing its relevance to the volatile present: there is no need, he maintains, to study Edmund Burke's *Reflections on the French Revolution* or Thomas Paine's *Rights of Man*, for *Coriolanus* represents both by setting out "the arguments for and against . . . the privileges of the few and the claims of the many."[84] But nothing of that political conflict is registered in his review of Kemble's fare-well performance of Coriolanus in 1817. For him, Kemble's per-formances in the role over a near twenty-year interval collapsed into a still point: "Time has no effect on them." His abiding im-pression of Kemble's Coriolanus is of stability: "unshaken firm-ness" and "unbending sternness of temper."[85] It is as if Kemble's statuesque equilibrium in the role displaced any possible analo-gies with the current status quo: "He had all the regularity of art."

There were riots during and outside Kemble's productions, but at performances of *Macbeth* rather than *Coriolanus*, and pro-voked not by anything enacted on the stage but by a sudden spike in the price of admission.[86] Withdrawn from the stage for its factionalizing provocation, the play reemerged as a coherently depicted historical totality installed on a picture-frame stage for spectators to admire and ponder of a time and place distinct from their own here and now, both visually (by costume and sets) as well as spatially (by the raised, recessed, and enclosed prosce-nium stage). Suppression may have been unnecessary when the play's potential offense was neutralized by its withdrawal into a time and place far from the present, not only historicized but aestheticized.

>>><<<

While dedicated to the periodizing of ancient Rome, Kemble had little interest in researching the English histories. Planché noted the inconsistency: while Kemble's "classical mind revolted from the barbarisms which even a Garrick had tolerated," like the bag wig of Brutus and the gold-laced suit of Macbeth, he had done little to reform the costumes of plays founded on English history. While Kemble, according to Planché, had made the histories more visually pleasing or "picturesque," he had added "but little to their propriety" or historical correctness to their performance. Under Kemble's direction, "the whole series" of plays on the English monarchs—from *King Lear* to *Henry VIII*—was acted in the same Tudor dress, "in habits of the Elizabethan era," an era postdating the last rule to be dramatized by Shakespeare, that of Henry VIII, by three reigns, and, added Planché, "very inaccurately representing the costume even of that period." On the battlefield, the "impropriety" was particularly apparent: the same weapons and heraldry served in battles centuries apart: "It was not requisite to be an antiquary to see the absurdity of the soldiers before Angiers, at the beginning of the thirteenth century, being clothed precisely the same as those fighting at Bosworth at the end of fifteenth."[87]

It fell to the next manager of Covent Garden, Charles Kemble, John Philip's brother, to extend period stagecraft to the English histories.[88] His production of *King John* applied the same historical standard to the English history plays that his brother had to the Roman tragedy. As one reviewer notes, once Charles took over the management of Covent Garden, he followed his brother's precedent: "he endeavored to exhibit in the dresses and the scenery of every play a picture of the precise era in which the action was supposed to pass." The picture, he continues, was so compelling that "it carried back the imagination to the moment when the character of history really existed."[89]

For the English histories, the authority was antiquarian rather than archaeological, derived not from classical statuary and artifacts but from medieval tomb effigies, manuscript illuminations, and royal seals.[90] According to Planché, before Charles Kemble, the stage had relied on "make-shift scenery, and at the best, a new dress or two for the principal characters."[91] The younger Kemble, however, was determined "to commence the reformation he [had] long been anxious to introduce in dramatic costume, and military costume of every nation, at every period, down to the present century." His goal was most fully realized with his production of *King John*: "for the first time, one of Shakespeare's historical plays was staged with the utmost possible accuracy of costume, every detail." To prepare for the play's radically new look, Planché had published a collection of twenty-two designs, *The Costume of Shakespeare's Historical Tragedy of King John*, giving authoritative sources for each. The production's playbill announced that the play's "attention to costume" was unprecedented on the English stage: "Every character will appear in the precise habit of the period, the whole of the dresses and decorations being executed from indisputable authorities."[92] On the battlefield, King John's barons appeared wreathed in mail, with cylindrical helmets and correct armorial shields; at court, his courtiers wore the long tunics and mantles of the thirteenth century.[93] The production's showpiece was King John's costume, modeled on the effigy in Worcester Cathedral, but the minor roles were also the result of antiquarian research.

With their periodizing productions of *Coriolanus* and *King John*, both Kembles were credited with having reformed the theater. Their period stagings of ancient Rome and feudal England were seen to divide an enlightened and historically alert present from a backward theatrical past that had neglected the history it presumed to dramatize. For Planché, the change was precipitated by the younger Kemble's *King John*: "a complete reformation of dramatic costume became from that moment inevitable upon the English stage."[94] But for another contemporary antiquarian and theatrical consultant, Francis Douce, the reform was initiated by the elder Kemble, the great actor who also had managerial skill and judgment "to reform these follies and, by exhibiting to us times as they were, to render the stage what it should be, a true and perfect mirror of history and manners."[95] But both theatrical commentators would have agreed that the change was an expression of the times rather than of any individual agent.

The concept of an invisible force that courses through the age and impels its defining characteristics is itself a novelty of the very age in question.[96] In 1831, in an essay titled "The Spirit of the Age," John Stuart Mill observes that "spirit of the age" was a recent coinage:

> The "spirit of the age" is in some measure a novel expression. I do not believe that it is to be met with in any work exceeding fifty years in antiquity. The idea of comparing one's own age with former ages, or with our notion of those which are yet to come, had occurred to philosophers; but it never before *was* itself the dominant idea of any age.[97]

William Hazlitt also uses that "dominant idea" as the title and organizing rubric of his collection of twenty-five portraits of his own contemporaries, *The Spirit of the Age* (1825), repeating the phrase throughout the essays.[98] It is now so familiar that it is used quite casually, as by Stephen Orgel, who attributes Boydell's idea for historicizing Shakespeare not only to Boydell's colleagues but to the times: "the idea was doubtless somewhere in the air," "an idea whose time had come."[99] Planché, in the first sentence of his preface to *The Costume of Shakespeare's Historical Tragedy of King John*, identifies the pictorial aesthetic and the scholarly research informing Kemble's *King John* production with the spirit of the age: "The true spirit of the times is the desire for beauty and accuracy." His costume book, consisting of elegantly executed and carefully researched costume designs, embodied the same spirit. The same current was sweeping through the Continent as well as England: "The taste for correct conception of the arms and habits of our ancestors has of late years rapidly diffused itself throughout Europe."

And in England, its force is not exclusive to the stage: "The historian, the poet, the novelist, the painter and the actor, have discovered in attention to costume a new spring of information, and a fresh source of effect."[100] Douce praises Thomas Stothard's recently exhibited (and much reproduced) painting of Chaucer's pilgrims, *The Pilgrimage to Canterbury*, for its scrupulous attention to the historical detail that illustrators had been neglecting for centuries.[101] Planché finds the same attention to keenly observed period details in the novels of Walter Scott; their popularity is due to his genius, he grants, but also "as much to the learning."[102]

Yet Planché finds fault in Scott's "antiquarian details," detecting an inaccuracy of some four centuries: "his descriptions of ancient costume are not always to be relied upon. The armour of Richard Coeur de Lion in *Ivanhoe* is of the sixteenth rather than the twelfth century." He also reproves the artist Benjamin West, president of the Royal Academy, for his paintings of the Trojan War that depict Paris in Roman dress when he should, Planché insists, have been in Phrygian.[103] As in period theater, any breach of period accuracy damaged the integrity of the whole: "works of greatest intrinsic worth . . . [were] depreciated by the most absurd violations of historical accuracy and a want of adherence to the manners of the times they refer to."[104]

Such anachronisms are seen as lapses back into what, in the light of the historically conscious present, appears an oblivious "previous age." Douce identified evidence of earlier performances of Shakespeare in the engravings to Nicholas Rowe's 1709 *The Works of Mr. William Shakespear*, the first illustrated edition of Shakespeare, in which characters are depicted mainly in dress of contemporary style.[105] He valued the engravings not because they dignify the edition, as its publisher had hoped, or because they preserve an earlier tradition of performance, as we might think, but because of the "many pleasant absurdities that will not fail to excite a smile in the beholder." He is amused by Quin's having performed Othello in a flowing powdered periwig. Even David Garrick, the greatest actor of the century, Douce maintains, succumbed to such "follies" and "whimsicalities": "Many persons now recollect the state of the English stage in Garrick's time, when that excellent performer used to exhibit his Hamlet in a common French suit of black velvet and a cocked hat, and his Macbeth in a scarlet coat with broad gold lace like the uniform of a modern general." His own "readers will smile at the costume," but earlier audiences, he assumes, took them as actual representations of the past, and were thereby misled by "distortion of reality" and "impostures." Another reviewer is still more indignant in denouncing "the anomalous costume which has hitherto disgraced the stage"; after the Kemble reforms, he trusts, they "will not be permitted to continue."[106] The stage had deluded earlier audiences by not visually differentiating the past from the present. Such inattention to period features was a betrayal of what had become the stage's responsibility: "exhibiting to us times as they were."[107]

Douce has no interest in how Shakespeare's theater had staged "the times as they were." Shakespeare's stage had been no more faithful to the propriety of costume than were the productions of Quin or Garrick, as Douce acknowledges: "we have no reason to suppose that much propriety was manifested." For Shakespeare was a man of his times, even slightly behind them; Douce places him in the same age of endemic anachronism as Chaucer. Before King James I, he maintains, few authors could escape "the charge of uniting dissimilar manners and discordant periods." Jonson is an exception, but not Shakespeare. The great dramatist himself, like his theater, had attributed to "preceding ages . . . matter which had originated in subsequent periods." Douce compiles a "partial catalogue" of "The Anachronisms and Some Other Incongruities of Shakspeare," and to the same end as the engravings to Rowe's 1709 edition: "as an object of amusement." The list of incongruities include persons (the ubiquitous Aristotle named by Hector), events (the fall of Constantinople in the reign of Henry IV), currencies (groats and farthings), fashions (silk stockings and ribbons on pumps), inventions (cannons, clocks, and paper), and customs (dubbing, modern fencing). But the greatest number of amusing "incongruities" result from the presence of AD beliefs and practices in BC settings. "Antipholus calls himself a Christian" in "the ancient city of Ephesus"; "the unity of the Deity" is referenced in the "period a little antecedent to the Christian aera" of *Pericles*; *Hamlet* alludes to Christian mores "long before the introduction of Christianity into North of Europe," and in a play containing "a plentiful crop of blunders," Kent talks "like a good Protestant, of *eating no fish*" in pagan Albion.

Douce was neither the only critic concerned with periods and anachronism in the arts nor the most significant. During the same years that the Kembles were performing in London, G. W. F. Hegel was delivering his lectures on fine art in Heidelberg and Berlin. In discussing poetry, he notes that the work of art almost invariably looks to the remote past for its material. Homer, for example, was "separated by four centuries at least from the time of the Trojan War; and a twice greater period separated the great Grecian tragedians from the days of the ancient heroes."[108] As a result, when determining how the external world "is to be configurated" in the work of art, the writer experiences a "clash between different ages" (265). As a result of the difference between the "customs, outlooks, and ideas" of his own times and those of his distant subject, the artist is faced with a dilemma:

> Namely whether the artist should forget his own time and keep his eye only on the past and its actual existence, so that his work is a true picture of what has gone; or whether he is not only entitled but in duty bound to take account solely of his own nation and contemporaries, and fashion his work according to ideas which coincide with the particular circumstance of his own time. (265)

Hegel calls the first alternative "objective" for its staunch fidelity to its historical object; he terms the second "subjective" for its self-regarding bias in favor of its own present. Germans, he maintains, are intent on period or "objective" drama: "Therefore nowadays astonishing care is taken in the theatre [to observe period coherence], and the producers have kept carefully to historical truth in costume and scenery" (277). As a recent example in Berlin, he cites the performance of Schiller's *Maid of Orleans* famously featuring a coronation procession keyed to Joan of Arc's fifteenth century (277), an effort he regards as "wasted." By contrast, the French incline to a modernized or "subjective" drama, catering performances to their own fashion and taste. On stage, Racine's Achilles is hardly recognizable as an ancient Greek: "his hair was curled and powdered; his hips were broadened by pockets, and he had red spurs fastened to his shoes with coloured ribbons" (267).

Having set up the mutually exclusive alternatives (and in terms that recall the contrast between the Coriolanus of Kemble and Quin), Hegel strikes a dialectical compromise. Dramatists must choose a period in the past, "a determinate reality, something appropriately and intelligibly circumscribed," but must then assimilate it to the higher interests of their own more advanced times (279). Because, for Hegel, the content or "essential kernel of a period and a people" (278) is true throughout history, only the form and expression of that truth are advanced and elevated. In the process, anachronism is inevitable: earlier characters are given the ideas and speech of a later time. The anachronism, however, is not caused by ignorance or accident or even design—all of which might be avoided or redressed. Instead it is a *"necessary anachronism,"* driven beyond its own dated horizon by the inexorable forward momentum of Hegelian history: "the development of culture *makes necessary* a metamorphosis in its expression and form" (278, italics added).[109] The systematic avoidance of such anachronism in the Kemble productions and in the endorsements of commentators like Douce and Planché is, by Hegel's logic, hardly a reformation of the theater, a repudiation of the past that opens to the future, but just the opposite. For Hegel, it would inhibit progress by grounding the past in its own "period, level of civilization, religion, view of the world," and thereby foreclose its participation in history's forward movement.

>>><<<

This chapter began modestly by observing a shift in the costume of the London stage around 1800 from histrionic to historical. The change inaugurated a mode of staging the past that came to dominate performance: period drama. Enframed by the proscenium arch, the onstage periodized past arrogated to itself the autonomy of a picture, standing for a priori reality, self-enclosed and self-contained. The same attention to synchronous periods characterized contemporaneous painting and fiction, a phenomenon identified even at the time as an expression of the "spirit of the age." Hegel problematized the anachronistic clash between the past of a work's setting and the present of its realization and proposed a dialectical solution. In this context, period drama is cast as a period phenomenon of the period 1780–1830. The span it circumscribes might be called the "The Period of Periodization," echoing the tautology of the title of Martin Heidegger's essay, "The Age of the World Picture."[110] For, as we have seen, the world picture of an age could qualify as the defining concept of the age. In Heidegger's wake, the intellectual historian Hans Blumenberg exploits the same redundancy in a chapter of the *The Legitimacy of the Modern Age*, his great opus in defense of the period status of modernity: "The Epochs of the Concept of an Epoch."[111]

Heidegger's "Age" spans more than those few decades straddling 1800 that have been the focus of this chapter. For him, "the age of the age" is the last of the three divisions of the grand schema of world history. Believing that "metaphysics grounds an age" (115), Heidegger assigns to each age its own distinctive way of taking in the world: the ancient through direct encounter, the medieval through revelation, and the modern through representation, in which "the world [is] conceived and grasped as picture" (129). The medieval changes to the modern when Christian truth is "transformed into the certainty of representation" (127). In the new age, representation constitutes being itself: "whatever is comes into being in and through representedness" (130). Heidegger credits Descartes's cogito with the epoch-making break. Doubt is overcome when the object to be known is "set forth" in a certain way before the subject who would know for the purpose of its being known, as if it were a picture placed before and apart from the viewer so that it can be viewed as what it is. In Heidegger, the Cartesian cogito is a setup that objectifies what is to be known so that it can be known: "whatever is comes to a stand as object and in that way alone receives the seal of Being" (132). This objectification leads to an alarming claim: "The fundamental event of the modern age is the conquest of the world as picture" (134). The world formatted as picture, as representation, can then be mastered: thus, science takes control of nature, and history seizes possession of the past.[112]

As this chapter has argued, representation also conquers the world of the stage. What is the mise-en-scène of period drama but an instance of the Cartesian setup? For it sets forth the past in such a way that it can be conceived and grasped as such by its objectification on a raised, recessed, and enframed stage that is literally set over and against the audience, securing a clear-cut division between the onstage object and offstage subject. On the period stage, arranged as a uniform and synchronous whole, the period mise-en-scène stands in for the real past and receives the "seal of Being" by virtue of being represented as such. What Heidegger says of "what is" might also be said of *what was* as represented by period drama: it "stands before us—in all that belongs to it and all that stands together in it—as a system" (129).

The Kembles' representations of the ancient world in *Coriolanus* and the medieval in *King John* would seem to satisfy the criteria for modern world pictures. But in Heidegger, at least, a startling corollary militates against the existence of either representation. Heidegger asks, "Does every period of history have its world picture . . . ? Or is this, after all, only a modern kind of representing?" (128–29). For him, it is decidedly the latter. Only the modern period takes in the world as picture: "The world picture does not change from an earlier medieval one into a modern one, but rather, the fact that the world becomes picture at all is what distinguishes the essence of the modern age" (130). To assume a medieval world picture, for example, would be to transform medieval faith into modern representation and thereby betray its own constitutive metaphysical essence. By Heidegger's argument, the world views, mindsets, and epistemes we so freely attribute to the past—the mindset of the ancient Greeks, the medieval worldview, the Elizabethan world picture—are back projections of a world picturing possible only in the modern "Age of the World Picture." The world pictures that might have looked like a way of observing historical and cultural difference, by Heidegger's logic, pertain only to modernity's way of apprehending the world.

Fredric Jameson calls Heidegger "a thinker of periodization";[113] and Jameson might be called a rethinker of Heidegger's periodization. For Jameson, too, periods are intrinsic to the modern age. As he maintains in *A Singular Modernity*, his extended essay on the "ontology of the present," the one entails the other: "The terms 'modern' and 'modernity' always bring some form of periodizing logic with them, however implicit it may at first be" (28). If for Heidegger the modern age apprehends the past as periods, for Jameson it also periodizes its own present, and precipitously, before it has come to a definitive close. Indeed, in Jameson's account, there is something almost compulsive about modernity's need to bring itself into being, "its irrepressible search for the break, for the 'first time,' for the beginning" (145). Jameson catalogs and tallies fourteen such inceptions drawn from history, science, technology, politics, philosophy, and aesthetics, and discusses several more in the course of the essay, including Heidegger's interpretation of the Cartesian break. He also discusses other modern periodizing schemes: Foucault's epistemes, Althusser's "expressive totalities," Raymond Williams's "structures of feeling." Periodizing, then, would seem to be symptomatic of the modern age, and the prolific instances he cites confirm his startling generalization or "maxim of modernity": "We cannot not periodize" (29); "One cannot not periodize." (94).

Jameson resolutely abides by his own dictum, and nowhere more than in *Postmodernism, or, The Cultural Logic of Late Capitalism*, in which he offers "a periodizing hypothesis" about a later stage of modernity which has repudiated the recent impulse to periodize.[114] Faced with these critiques, he likens his project to "the effort to take the temperature of the age without instruments and in a situation in which we are not even sure there is so coherent a thing as an 'age,' or zeitgeist or 'system' or 'current situation' any longer."[115] He proceeds all the same, insisting that while periods are "intolerable and unacceptable," they are all the same ineluctable.[116] But what accounts for their indispensability? It is not, as for Heidegger, an epistemological necessity: at least, it is not only that. For Jameson, there is also an ethical or political imperative. Without periodization, history can deliver no change. It proceeds instead through a static succession of one chronological selfsame thing after another. "The dialectic of the break and the period" is, for him, like class conflict, the catalyst of future social transformation. For this reason, modernity's periodization of its own present "requires the relationship to the future fully as much as it involves the taking of a position on the past."[117] If modernity were to advance beyond its period status, it would not then find itself in a new and different period, yet unnamed, for the very fact of its periodization would betray its persistent modernity. In utopia there are no periods.

Meanwhile, on the Shakespearean stage, periods still flourish, and even when their defining proscenium frame has all but disappeared. In his rich survey of the production history of *Coriolanus*, John Ripley deems Kemble "the most influential figure in Coriolanus's stage history" and traces his influence up into the twentieth century.[118] In that century, period production ceased to be the norm it had been since the early 1800s. Yet even on the twenty-first-century stage, *Coriolanus* has continued to be performed in Roman costume and sets with the same attention to period consistency introduced by the Kembles. Now, however, other options are available. The play can be performed in Tudor costume, approximating that of Shakespeare's England. Or costume might be contemporary with the dress of the audience, to give it immediate relevance. Or the play can be staged to conform to any historical period, particularly one whose salient crisis can be mapped onto that of the play: the political protest in the wake of the French Revolution, for example, or the military dictatorship of Nazi Germany, or more recently in film, in the violent nationalism of the Balkans. But all these options remain under the sway of period logic—if not that of ancient Rome, then that of Jacobean England, the French Directoire, the Third Reich, or the modern present. Even when eschewing period categories, productions cannot altogether suppress their invocation. Mixing costumes from diverse periods, for example, risks multiplying period representation rather than dissolving it. Nondescript attire (neutral in color, shapeless in cut) might be intended to suggest the universality of the play's themes, but its challenge to the representational norm might also be taken as avant-garde modernism or futurism or even nihilism.

This chapter, too, could be taken as a demonstration of the persistence of period thinking. Its argument depends on the introduction of an epochal break. Its rhetoric abounds in periodizing terms: centuries, centurial turns, breaks and clusters, even the overused tropes of the "spirit of the age" and "world picture." Its concluding remarks draw on theoretical accounts that stress the foundational presence of periods in thinking about the past as well as the present (and the future). Yet this chapter has sought to challenge the necessity of period logic by drawing attention to its absence on the Shakespearean stage before 1800. Thus, even in this attempt to demonstrate their nonexistence, periods have proven indispensable, and Jameson's maxim is upheld. Yet not absolutely. "We cannot not periodize" is, after all, a maxim of *modernity*, drawn from and applicable to the modern age and its attenuations. On the other side of 1800, the maxim falters, at least on the Shakespearean stage. With no proscenium stage, no fourth wall, no synchronous costumes and sets, and no fidelity to a postulated prior reality, that stage could not represent the past in historically framed and historically informed coherent units. From the syncretic *Titus Andronicus* of the Longleat drawing to the confected Coriolanus *à la Romaine*, the stage did "not periodize."

4

Secularity before Revelation

Shakespeare never wishes his spectators to forget that the story takes place in a dreary and barbarous age.

A. W. VON SCHLEGEL, *Lectures on Dramatic Art and Literature*

Like *Troilus and Cressida*, *King Lear* features a famous anachronism.[1] As Hector cites Aristotle, so Lear's Fool names Merlin. In the throes of an apocalyptic storm, the Fool steps out alone before the audience, announces that he will deliver a prophecy ("I'll speak a prophecy ere I go"[2]), delivers it, and then ascribes it to a source who does not yet exist: "This prophecy Merlin shall make" (3.2.95).[3] There is no need for editors to identify the anachronism, as they continuously have for Hector. The Fool himself does: "I live before his time" (95–96). As we have seen, prolepsis is routine in Shakespearean plays. Whatever the time of a play's action, allusions freely index the time of its first audiences, as does costume. The prophecy's references to priests, heretics, and churches, for example, are clearly out of sync with heathen Britain. So, too, is the Fool himself, in motley and coxcomb. If they pass unremarked, why single out the Fool's antedating of Merlin?

Merlin is not the anachronism here. Prophecy is. The primary source for the Lear story, Geoffrey of Monmouth's *The History of*

the Kings of Britain (ca. 1138), situates Lear's rule in the age of the
Hebrew prophets, between Elijah and Isaiah.[4] But that is in Judaea. In Lear's backwater Albion, so distant from the Holy Land,
there are as yet no prophets. By a long tradition originating in the
same work, prophecy is introduced to Britain by Merlin, King Arthur's seer. In a chapter titled "Prophetia Merlini," Geoffrey col-
lects and translates into Latin some one hundred prophecies from
a fifth-century Welsh manuscript.[5] These prophecies and scores
of others attributed to him circulate in England deep into the
seventeenth century, in pamphlet form as well as in Geoffrey's
History, in manuscript and print, singly and in numbers, in English and in Latin, in prose and in verse, and sometimes in code.[6]
Objections to them only attest to their popularity: for example,
the complaint in an attack against them that they had been
"chained to the desks of many libraries in England with great
reverence and estimation."[7] It made no difference whether Merlin was a genuine prophet or a counterfeit, whether his prophecies were thought to be diabolically or divinely sourced, the result
of astrological calculations or sheer guesswork. Merlin was firmly
instated as Britain's first and foremost prophet.

In Albion, to prophesy before Merlin is to prophesy before
prophecy. The Fool pretends to see the future before the veil
has been parted to yield even a glimpse of the divine program.
Nothing has yet been revealed of the future that will in time be
disclosed, however obscurely and partially, first to the Hebrew
prophets, then to the apostles, and finally and most forcibly to
John of the Apocalypse in the prophecies of Revelation. But Albion has no access to these intimations yet to come, and this is by
hard-edged dramaturgical design. Their absence forms the play's
grounding postulate, making for what has always been perceived
as *King Lear*'s singular distinction: the extremity of its suffering.
Over the centuries, the play's programmatic suspension of revelation will be experienced as something quite different: not as
divinity withheld, but as no divinity at all. A world imagined as
before revelation will be taken for a world in which there never
was any to begin with: in sum, a secular and modern world.

>>><<<

When Lear's Fool professes to foresee the future, he is bluffing, and it shows. His prophecy is so garbled that for most of its textual history, it has been either rejected as spurious or broken into two discrete prophecies.[8] Its when-then structure is perfectly in keeping with the genre of prophecy: when certain conditions are fulfilled (the Fool lists ten), then the predicted outcome will occur (he ventures two). But there are two sets of conditions, each prefaced by "When," and they are contradictory:

> When priests are more in word than matter,
> When brewers mar their malt with water,
> When nobles are their tailors' tutors,
> No heretics burned but wenches' suitors,
> *When every case in law is right,*
> *No squire in debt, nor no poor knight,*
> *When slanders do not live in tongues,*
> *Nor cut-purses come not to throngs,*
> *When usurers tell their gold i' the field,*
> *And bawds and whores do churches build—*
> (3.3.81–90, italics added)

The first set of conditions signals an unjust world of hypocritical priests (81), swindling brewers (82), foppish nobles (83), and diseased prostitutes (84). But the second set points to a just world of no crime (85), no debt (86), no slander (87), no theft (88), no usury (89), and no prostitution (90). Nor are the prophecy's final two couplets particularly illuminating:

> Then shall the realm of Albion
> Come to great confusion.
> Then comes the time, who lives to see't,
> That going shall be used with feet.
> (91–94)

The future will bring either drastic change (the ruin of Albion) or more of the same (walking with feet).

The Fool's vision is necessarily muddled. In prophesying, he hasn't had the advantage that distinguishes prophecy from any other kind of statement about the future: a divine source. The Old Testament prophets were believed to have been divinely prompted, often in dreams or visions; both their Hebrew and Greek names (*na-vi, profetes*) designate a spokesman, one who speaks on behalf of God. In the last book of Scripture, titled Apocalypse in the Wycliffite Bible and Revelation in later English translations, John the Divine begins his book of prophecies with a disclosure of their provenance: an angel delivered them to him directly from God with the mandate that he make them known to the world (Rev. 1–2). Merlin's divining powers, too, are thought to be God-given despite his alleged conception by an incubus. But Lear's Fool lives in a preprophetic time, before the removal of the covering that is designated by both the Greek Apocalypse (*apo-* "un-" + *kaluptein* "to cover") and the Latin Revelation (*re-* "opposite of" + *velare* "to cover, veil"). Editorial glosses on the prophecy, in measuring the distance between the Fool and Merlin, place King Lear's reign in the eighth century BC and King Arthur's in the sixth century AD.[9] But in Shakespeare's sixteenth-century source, Holinshed's *Chronicles*, the two rules are dated from different starting points. Lear's rule is dated from the Creation: "Leir the sonne of Baldud was admitted ruler ouer the Britaines in the yeare of the world 3105."[10] But Arthur's is counted from the Incarnation: "[Merlin] was in the time of king Arthur, about the yeare fiue hundred and threescore."[11] Lear's Fool and Arthur's seer exist in different time zones, the latter in *Anno Domini* time and the former in a time so remote that it is reckoned from *Anno Mundi*, the Creation rather than the Incarnation. Lear's time is so very far from the AD time of the audience as to be hardly imaginable. Indeed, that is the challenge the play puts to the audience: to entertain, from its own much later vantage, a time in which the providential program is nowhere yet visible.[12]

One of the most widely circulating chronologies in the sixteenth century allotted a third of the world's history to such a godless time.[13] While originating in an obscure Rabbinical text, the Babylonian Talmud, where it took the form of a prophecy attributed to Elijah, the tripartite division was widely known throughout the sixteenth century, commented on by theologians (Melanchthon, Luther) and astronomers (Rheticus, Kepler, Copernicus) but also referenced in popular treatises and sermons.[14] According to Elijah's prophecy, the world was to last 6,000 years from its creation to its destruction, a span whose tripartite division is neatly summarized by the Latin *duo milia inane, duo milia lex, duo milia dies Messiae* and translated in a popular sixteenth-century treatise as "Two thousand Vaine, two thousand the Lawe, two thousand Christ."[15] The last two eras are familiar: the time when Moses received the Tablets of the Law and the time of Christ's redemptive promise, the two main events by which the divine program was disclosed in the Old and New Testaments, respectively. Quite unfamiliar, however, is the first era, *duo milia inane. Inane* echoes the start of the Vulgate, "Terra autem erat inanis et vacua" (Gen. 1:2), and is variously translated by the vernacular Bibles: as "idle and empty" by the Wycliffite, "formless and void" by the Geneva, and "void and empty" by the Douai-Rheims. Another rendering of the prophecy translates *inane* with a nominative that permeates the text of *Lear*. William Leigh, the tutor to King James's eldest son, in an apocalyptic sermon published in 1605 names the first millennial unit "nature": "two thousand yeares *nature*," to be followed by "two thousand yeares the Law, two thousand yeares grace."[16] Chronologically, Lear's rule belongs to *duo milia lex*, but Albion, as we have also seen in regard to the Fool's prophecy, lags behind Judaea.

Lear's favorite axiom, pronounced twice, might date him to the primordial period of vacuity or inanity, before there is any knowledge of creation ex nihilo. "Nothing will come of nothing" (1.1.90), he proclaims, in response to Cordelia's profession that she has "nothing" to say, and then again, "nothing can be made out of nothing" (1.4.130), when the Fool asks Lear whether he can't make something out of the "nothing" the Fool has just spoken. The dictum originates in the cosmogony of the ancients, particularly the materialist philosophers Epicurus and Lucretius, who both assume the necessary existence of some kind of primordial material, atoms or particles that conjoin not by any demiurgical design but by chance motion.[17] In a Christian context, the materialists' *ex nihilo nihil fit* is heresy, a denial of the miraculous creation of the world from nothing, a key tenet of Christian doctrine.[18] Shakespeare's audience might have heard a hint of atheism or skepticism in the maxim, but for Lear, it is simply a truism. In the dark times of his rule, he knows nothing of how the world began according to Church doctrine; nor does he seem to know, by the same doctrine, how it was to end, anticipating its destruction in the spouting of "cataracts and hurricanoes" (3.2.2), in ignorance of the covenant in Genesis, "never again will there be a flood to destroy the earth" (Gen. 9:11).

For Shakespeare's audience, the principal epochal divide was the event that introduced *duo milia dies Messiae*, the Incarnation. A few years after *King Lear* was first performed at Whitehall during the Christmas season,[19] Lancelot Andrewes, King James's favorite clergyman, gave a sermon explaining that the Incarnation draws a "partition of the two times," between *Olim* (formerly) and *Dies novissimi* (recently), between the time before the Incarnation and the time after. The Incarnation provides "the very *Kalends* of Christianitie, from whence, we begin our *Æra*."[20] Time comes to be counted from that day, its point of sacral origin affixed to every date, first spelled out as *Anno Domini*, Year of our Lord or Year of our Redemption, and later abbreviated to AD. Other epochal incipits slip into patterns of alternation: the building and destruction of cities, battles won and lost, the rise and fall of rulers and kingdoms, the captivity and emancipation of peoples, revolutions and restorations. But the incarnational event that marks the start of *Anno Domini* has the advantage of having occurred only once: never before and never again.

For this reason, Augustine takes issue with Solomon's famous proverb, "*there is* no new *thing* under the sun" (Eccles. 1:9). He identifies the principle with the philosophy of heathens like Plato and Cicero who believed in the recurrence of all things.

Like Solomon, they, too, would dismiss what appeared new—
"See, this is new"—as mere renewal: "it hath been already of old
time, which was before us."[21] Augustine acknowledges the truth
of the maxim in respect to nature: the orbit of the sun, the course
of rivers, and the life cycle of creatures. Even monsters and miracles are "no new thing under the sun"; however aberrant, they
belong to a category. But the proverb is not true absolutely, as
Augustine warns: "God forbid, I say, that we should believe this."
There is one great exception: "Christ died for our sins once." It is
from that unique exception that time is counted, an event both
unprecedented and not to be repeated. As the Hegelian philosopher Benedetto Croce has observed, in the West the Incarnation marked the epochal watershed: "Christian thinkers divided
history into that which preceded and that which followed the
redemption." Nor was this just an arbitrary imposition. Without
that divide separating the impossibility of redemption from its
possibility, Christianity was unthinkable: "this periodization was
not an addition to Christian thought, but Christian thought itself."[22] For another Hegelian thinker, Karl Jaspers, from Augustine through Hegel, the event has the same epochal status: "The
appearance of the Son of God is the axis of world history."[23] Only
once does Shakespeare situate a play chronologically, and it is in
relation to that BC-AD axis. A year into his reign, Henry IV,
with blood on his hands, gives the date in relation to the redemptive sacrifice he needs to cleanse him of that stain: "fourteen hundred years ago" when Christ's feet "were nailed / For our
advantage on the bitter cross."[24]

In the last century, in deference to the greater part of the world
that is not Christian, an attempt was made to detach what had
become the global dating standard from its messianic onset.[25]
Anno Domini was renamed the Common Era or the Current
Era, the AD abbreviation amended to CE. The sacral starting
point was thereby secularized, at least in theory, with the implica-
tion that the incarnational date had been arbitrarily selected and

made customary through use over time. No one better understood the degree to which Christianity is invested in the incarnational beginning than Friedrich Nietzsche. In his fierce polemic against Christianity, *The Anti-Christ*, he proposes a more
radical way of severing the dated continuum from its AD incipit.
Why count time from the first day of Christianity, he asks, "the
dies nefastus when this catastrophe began. . . . Why not rather
from its last?" For Nietzsche, Christianity's last day is the very
day when *The Anti-Christ* was delivered to the world. He gives
that date at the close of his manifesto as "30 September 1888,"
but that is "according to the false [AD] calculation of time." By
his true calculation, it is "the first day of the year one," marking
the revelation of a new system of values altogether antithetical
to those ushered in by *Anno Domini*.[26] From that point on, "the
revaluation of all Christian values" would prevail, deploying "all
means, all instincts, all genius to allow the opposite values [from
those of Christianity] to triumph."[27]

Modernity also turns on Christianity to clear the way for its
own installation—not to annul it, however, as in Nietzsche's *The
Anti-Christ*, but to cordon it off as a self-contained period, the
Christian or medieval era. Consigned to a period frame, what
had been held as divinely sanctioned truth is recast as a medieval
worldview, one among others, to be countered or superseded.
Before its periodization, the Christian era knew no end point
other than doomsday itself. Empires of world history and the
reigns of monarchs would end to be succeeded by others, but the
Christian era would outlast all but the final one, continuing until
the coming of "a new heaven, and a new earth" envisioned in
Revelation (Rev. 21:1). Once converted to a period unit, the age
of faith can be left behind. No longer an age that was to endure
until end-time, it becomes a thing of the past, defined by the
faith in the salvation now regarded as credulity.

With the Christian era sealed off, modernity could assert its
novelty, claiming to represent a new beginning, released from
the constraints of theological and ecclesiastical domination. It
marks its own onset—whether in the Renaissance, the Enlight-

enment, or the centuries straddling the two[28]—by proposing any number of innovations. Hans Blumenberg mounts his massive defense of modernity, *The Legitimacy of the Modern Age*, to counter the looming charge that modernity cannot lay claim to epochal autonomy because it does not innovate.[29] According to this imputation, its self-defining novelties are no more than tacit borrowings or appropriations from the Christian theology of the Middle Ages. To defend "the legitimacy" of modernity's period status against this secularization thesis, he critiques the thesis itself, demonstrating how virtually any modern phenomenon can be loosely cast as a transposition of some aspect of Christian dogma. He cites copious examples of "secularization 'run wild.'"[30] Some are serious, like modern epistemology as a secularization of the certainty of faith and the modern work ethic as a secularization of Protestant asceticism, and others less so, like the "dandy" as a secularized saint and the academic examination system as "the secularized Last Judgment."[31]

As an alternative mechanism or hermeneutic for accounting for the epochal shift, Blumenberg formulates a theory of "reoccupation" that assumes the perennial urgency of certain questions. When answers once secured by medieval theology ceased to satisfy, modernity proposed new ones in their place, originating in what he terms *self-assertion*, a positioning or grounding of the self that presupposes no divine dispensation or intervention and sets no limits on its powers and resources.[32] Thus, Blumenberg's modernity retains its epochal exclusivity, for no theological antecedent for "self-assertion" exists in a providentially governed cosmos. The concluding section of his great tome sets up the "threshold" for the new epoch with its own inaugural epochal figure and epochal event: Giordano Bruno in 1600 "averting his face from the crucifix that was held before him."[33]

But Solomon's question—"Is there *any* thing whereof it may be said, See, this *is* new?" (Eccles. 1:10, Authorized [King James] Version)—continues to loom over the modern era as it had over the Christian. Augustine answered confidently that Christ was the one new thing under the sun. Modernity claims to be new on the basis of its abnegation of that same incarnational novelty. But if, as the proponents of secularization maintain, modern novelty simply transfigures the theology of what came before, the epochal threshold dissolves: the medieval blurs into the modern, the sacral into the profane. There would then be only one continuous AD epoch, the Christian era, or *duo milia dies Messiae*, and with the same point of origin: the momentous theophanic event notched into the historical continuum.

>>><<<

To clear the way for the modern epoch, Christianity's end point as well as its incipit had to be dislodged. Christ, the Alpha and the Omega, introduces both termini: the former with his arrival, or Advent, bearing the promise of redemption, and the latter with his return, or Second Coming, bearing its fulfillment. The Gospels tell the story of his first coming; the Book of Revelation closes Scripture in anticipation of the second. While the first line of Revelation maintains that its prophecies are of "things which must shortly come to pass," it specifies no date for their fulfillment. For centuries, predictions were ventured despite caveats from the apostles: "But of that day and that hour knoweth no *man*" (Matt. 24:36; Mark 13:32). When a prophesied date came and went without incident, that particular date was disconfirmed, but not the apocalyptic event itself: it was merely deferred.

But these predictions did not continue indefinitely, as the conceptual historian Reinhart Koselleck maintains. Over time, during the long transitional interval between the medieval and the modern epochs, eschatological expectation foundered and, for Koselleck, to momentous effect: "It was only when Christian eschatology shed its constant expectation of the imminent arrival of doomsday that a temporality could be revealed that would be open for the new and without limit."[34] With the lifting of the providential cap, the future was no longer hemmed in by a preordained *finis*, always pending and always prorogued. Its removal resulted in a new temporality of enlarged and deepened horizons in which novelty, as something that had hitherto not existed, became possible and desirable. The world-without-end previously awaited in the next world thus became a feature of this one. In the familiar terms of the secularization thesis, the promise that was to be fulfilled imminently in the hereafter becomes immanent and achievable in the here and now. A new and better world was to be ushered in not by Last Things but by development and progress, concepts that Koselleck demonstrates to be themselves modern coinages.[35] With no millennial program in place, new skills were required in an attempt to predict or control the newly "*open future.*"[36] The future was now to be anticipated through rational prognosis requiring not biblical hermeneutics but technical expertise based on statistics and calculation.[37]

The waning of millenarian expectation also figures as a precondition of modernity in a work now considered a classic of literary criticism. In *The Sense of an Ending* (published in 1967 and reissued to coincide with the millennial in 2000), Frank Kermode assumes the eschaton's gradual discrediting: "the End grew harder and harder to think of as an imminent historical event . . . so that the duration and structure of time less and less supported the figures of apocalypse [*sic*]."[38] As belief in the providential end point receded, leaving a "world without end or beginning," modern fictive writing emerged, replacing the scripturally prescribed eschaton with endings devised by the imagination. No longer constrained by Last Things, our fictions "have become more 'open'" (6). In Kermode's theory of fiction, what he terms the "naïve apocalypticism" (9) of the devout Middle Ages is shaken by the "clerical scepticism" (109) of a nascent modernity.

But even a skeptical or secular age, Kermode maintains, needs endings that engage beginnings and thereby give form and sense to the interval between them, the time "in the midst" in which he situates the life of the individual. The break from the revealed eschaton is not therefore absolute: "the paradigms of the apocalypse continue to lie under our ways of making sense of the world" (28). For the "alpha and omega" of the Messiah's arrival and return (Rev. 21:6), Kermode substitutes a mechanical model, the "tick-tock" paradigm (192): "*Tick* is a humble genesis, *tock* a feeble apocalypse" (45).

But, as is typical of accounts of modernity, self-consciousness makes all the difference. In modernity, all termini are recognized as "apocalyptic postures," contrivances of the imagination rather than God-given truths. Scripture, for Kermode, is no less fictive than literature, but unlike literature, it fails to acknowledge itself as such. Medieval "naïve apocalypticism" takes as truth what is, for Kermode, "a fiction not consciously held to be fictive" (190). If theology is fiction passing for truth, then fiction is theology without professing to be true, as it famously is for Harold Bloom. For Bloom, Shakespeare's poetry goes even beyond theology: his *Hamlet*, for example, "seems to go beyond Christian belief into a purely secular transcendence."[39]

In his account of the emergence of fictive writing, Kermode positions Shakespeare at the forefront of the secularizing process, at a time "too late for apocalypse, too critical for prophecy" (88). Shakespearean tragedy, *King Lear* in particular, signals "the moment when the terrors of apocalypse were absorbed by tragedy" (27). The Last Things once expected to take place imminently and cosmically occur instead within the tragic experience of the protagonist: "The end is now a matter of immanence; tragedy assumes the figurations of apocalypse, of death and judgment, heaven and hell" (82). Tragedy ends in personal ruin rather than world extinction. Instead of conforming to "its obviously predestined end" (18), the tragedy fashions its own that in its unpredictability is, for Kermode, truer to the complexity and uncertainty of real life. Instead of satisfying expectation, Shakespearean tragedy reverses and falsifies it, and this for Kermode is the measure of a literary work's sophistication: "maximum peripeteia" (19) is the hallmark of the best modern literature.

Here, too, *Lear* signals the way forward. Audiences and readers would have expected Cordelia to survive, as she had in the many earlier versions of the Lear story. In addition, the tragedy sets up hope when Edmund countermands her execution. But instead comes the tragedy's notorious peripeteia: "Enter Lear with Cordelia in his arms." Her death is not merely unexpected: it is a shock. For Kermode, this is the kind of "maximum peripeteia" that in literature phases out eschatological expectation. *King Lear* may invoke the eschaton through its earth-shaking tremors, but only to leave it behind midway through the play, now a "broken apocalypse" (88), according to Kermode, like the many inoperative doomsday predictions. Albion endures in the aftermath, and indefinitely: "the world goes forward in the hands of exhausted survivors" (82). In Kermode's theory of fiction, as in Koselleck's modern world, the future, no longer capped by end-time, is open to unlimited duration. When bounds are set, they are the doings of not providence but human ingenuity, whether of Koselleck's scientific prognosis or Kermode's fictive projection, "human time in an eternal world" (88).

In *The Sense of an Ending*, Kermode discusses the endings of a wide range of twentieth-century authors, among them Wallace Stevens, Samuel Beckett, and William Burroughs. But he names no work from the premodern period that he identifies with "naïve apocalypticism." He alludes instead to the "Beatus tradition" (27), a cluster of illuminated commentaries on the Book of the Apocalypse, the earliest of which is an eighth-century Spanish codex that continued to be carefully copied up through the twelfth century. The omission is telling. According to Kermode's "theory of fiction," there can be no literature until the era in which, for him, the imagination is released from the constraints of theology. Nor can there be any literary criticism: in his "Beatus tradition," there is only commentary on Scripture.

An early work that Kermode might have used to demonstrate the modern shift from the apocalyptic to the fictive is one that has more recently received critical attention: a neo-Latin play by the Reformer John Foxe, *Christus Triumphans: Comœdia Apocalyptica*, published in 1556 and performed shortly thereafter by students at both Cambridge and Oxford.[40] In the Dedicatory Epistle, the author announces his intention: "to transfer [the events of Apocalypse] as far as possible from the sacred writings into the theater."[41] Modeled on the Apocalypse of John and freely quoting from it, the play's content is, as its Prologue attests, "totally apocalyptic," particularly its final act, where the course of the play takes a dramatic turn into the realm of Last Things.

The generic classification announced by the play's subtitle, *Comœdia Apocalyptica*, is contradictory only if, like Kermode, we limit *apocalypse* to its modern sense of world destruction. As a perusal of the early modern lexicons demonstrates, until the eighteenth century, *apocalypse* and *revelation* were synonymous.[42] As we have seen, both the Greek and the Latin derivatives signify the removal of a cover or the lifting of a veil. The New Testament's final book is named Apocalypsis in the Latin Vulgate and Revelation in the English Bibles; "Apocalypsis Iesu Christi" is the incipit of the former, and "The Revelation of Jesus Christ" of the latter. In Foxe's comedy, the apocalypse is not the dreaded doom that, according to Kermode, will be subsumed by Shakespearean tragedy. It is instead something imminent and deeply desired: the arrival of the titular *Christus Triumphans* returning victorious over sin and death. Foxe's apocalyptic comedy ends, as does John's Apocalypse (Rev. 22:17), in happy anticipation of a nuptial between Christ and the Church or Ecclesia: here both comedy and eschatology share the same end point.

The apocalyptic comedy is pitched from the start toward that foregone *finis*. As the protagonist Ecclesia understands, "We must consider not only those things which are, but the end of things, those things yet to come which the words of God promise soon" (293). The body of the play concerns those "things which are": the abuse Ecclesia suffers over the course of centuries and her resolution "to endure willingly whatever I endure since I endure it for the sake of Christ" (359). But the last act shifts to "those things yet to come," and through a marked peripeteia: the fulfillment of the prophecy that an imposter would substitute himself for Christ before the Second Coming (1 John 2:18, 4:3).[43] The Antichrist is discovered: he is the pope, disguised in the play as Pseudamnus. The play now moves unimpeded to its prophesied comedic end.

Antichrist's identity would come as no surprise to an audience of Reformed believers whose sovereign had within recent
memory broken from the authority of the pope.[44] (Indeed it is
at this turning point that the plot's long and uneven temporal
movement intersects with the recent present of the audience.)
On stage, the news changes the lives of the impious and pious
alike. "It is incredible," says Europus, one of Ecclesia's faithful
sons, accustomed to deceit and lies: "You say Pseudamnus is the
Antichrist?" (339) Suddenly truth is transparent: "A fig tree is not
more a fig tree."[45] Satan, in an aside, realizes, "I'm sunk." Pseudamnus, while scoffing at "the trivial news," is desperate to prove
that the symbolic beast of the prophecies (Rev. 13) is not him
but the "Mahommedan Turk" (353). His consort, the apocalyptic
Whore of Babylon, starts to faint ("I feel awful"). And one of
Satan's henchmen runs off to write an epitaph for his master and
his cohort (341). For the faithful, however, the discovery heralds
a marriage, the conventional ending of Roman comedy, as well
as (in Revelation) of the world.

To prepare for the imminent nuptial, the stage exploits all
possible resources: costume, props, special effects, and stage ma-
chinery. The play's only full stage direction calls for a curtain to
open on a spectacle:

> Here from the upper part of the theater, when the curtains open, are
> shown as if from heaven thrones with books placed upon them. At
> the same time garments are lowered in which Ecclesia is dressed and
> prepared for the wedding. (363)

Ecclesia's son provides the gloss to it when he reads aloud from
one of the heaven-sent books of the Bible, Apocalypse: "I saw
the new Jerusalem descending from heaven prepared by God as a
bride adorned for her husband" (365, from Rev. 21:2). Here Foxe's
intention to transfer the sacred writings to the theater is at its
most literal. Ecclesia's bloody and ragged garments, the stigma
of her persecution in this world, are removed and she is arrayed in the newly descended "silken robe" with various precious

accessories, including a small veil for her hand, betokening the upcoming unveiling (367). "Wondrous indeed . . . are the things I see" (365), exclaims Ecclesia, her vision enhanced by the shining lamps held by the attendant chorus of virgins. Her other senses are also overwhelmed: by the wafting of incense ("what wondrous fragrance of perfume suddenly breathes upon my senses?" 363), the shaking of the stage ("And now the very earth seems to tremble"), and the singing of an epithalamion (367). And if the production were successful, the faithful audience would also experience wonder, identifying with Ecclesia's moment of ecstasy as it had earlier with her suffering.

Ecclesia is now fully prepared for her groom: "Spectators, now you see the bride decked out and all things in readiness" (371). Her longing is passionate and urgent: "My bridegroom, my beloved, come, break through the heavens, that we may rush into your embraces" (363). All her attendants join in addressing the groom—"Come, oh bridegroom" (369)—as if he were within hearing distance, "now near the door" (363).

But something is missing, as the Chorus remarks: "the bridegroom himself" (371). The play stops short of satisfying the desire it has aroused. The withholding is inevitable, as the Prologue explains. The poet would have preferred to have ended with Christ's "coming from heaven, in triumph in the clouds" (229), just as Apocalypse envisions his arrival. This may have been what spectators expected from a play titled *Christus Triumphans*: Christ in majesty riding a covenantal rainbow (fig. 4.1), as depicted in church frescoes and stained-glass windows, as well as at the high point of the title page engraving of Foxe's illustrious *Actes and Monuments* (1563) and as performed, however ineptly, in the medieval mysteries.[46]

But as the Prologue admits, the play can deliver only the *promise* of Christ's return. Its fulfillment must await the event itself, when "God sends in actual fact what he now only promises" (229). Foxe has taken his comedy as close to that actuality as possible. "Nothing seems to remain except that apocalyptic voice soon to be heard from heaven. 'It is finished'"(207), he writes,

FIGURE 4.1. Christ triumphant. John Foxe, detail of title page from *Actes and monuments of matters most speciall and memorable* (London, 1596). Used by permission of the Folger Shakespeare Library (18583)

again quoting Apocalypse (21:6).[47] But here's the twist: the apocalyptic finish is itself a peripeteia, "the reversal of things, the overturning of the world as it was" (369). Foxe calls it a *catastrophe*, a technical term among the Latin dramatists, akin to the Aristotelean peripeteia, for the overturn that brings a play to its resolution.[48] It is also the planetary turn that astronomers are watching for as the sign that the world is coming to an end.[49] For Foxe, the eschaton is the "final catastrophe" (371), "the catastrophe of everything" (207), a "maximum peripeteia" indeed that brings about the consummational switch from this world to the next.

>>><<<

"Is this the promised end?" (5.3.261) might well have been a line from the close of *Comœdia Apocalyptica*. It comes instead in *King Lear* at the point when the tragedy attains its Kermodean "maximum peripeteia." The apocalyptic comedy and the apocalyptic tragedy turn on the same elusive promise of the end. The prospect belongs in a drama that ends with its imminence. But what is it doing in *King Lear*, set so long before the promise was even delivered? Like all the play's Christological references, the "promised end" is spoken for the audience, over the heads of the characters, suggesting that Shakespeare, at his most modern, has not quite left the "Beatus tradition" behind.

"Is this the promised end?" is the first response to the tragedy's great shock: "Enter Lear with Cordelia in his arms." Until then, the sight had stunned the onlookers into silence. They
stand transfixed as if themselves lifeless. "O, you are men of
stones" (5.3.255), Lear exclaims. When dialogue resumes, it takes
the form of a self-contained set piece. Each of the three principal onlookers, in tandem, chorus-like, react as if end-time or its
intimation were upon them.

> Kent.   Is this the promised end?
> Edgar. Or image of that horror?
> Albany.   Fall, and cease.
>   (5.3.261–62)

The apocalyptic outburst is triggered by the horrific spectacle
before them: their old king, after terrible suffering, broken by
the worst blow of all, the death of the one who was to have
redeemed his suffering. The blow is unendurable—literally, for
Lear will not survive it. Nor may the world itself, as Albany fears
in imploring that destruction from above be immediate and final: "Fall, and cease." The tragedy, it could be said, has taken the
tragic to its outermost limit. In no sense a "promised end," it is
an end devoid of promise.

In his sketch (fig. 4.2) of a possible early staging of this moment, C. Walter Hodges shows the onlookers standing spellbound before the tragic object. The spectators offstage share
their focal point, bracketed by the bodies of Regan and Goneril.
They, however, may see something more in the tableau. Hodges,
like countless artists, critics, and directors before and after him,
on the basis of the stage direction, imagines Lear with Cordelia
lying across his lap.[50] This is the familiar pose of the Pietà, or the
Pity, a popular devotional object in which the Virgin holds her
dead son after his deposition from the cross.[51] The effigy cap-
tures the bleak moment in the Passion between the deposition
and the entombment. It is the low point of the Passion, the *tene-
brae* or darkness when the promise of salvation is at its weakest.

FIGURE 4.2. C. Walter Hodges, possible staging of act 5, scene 3, *The Tragedy of King Lear*, ed. Jay L. Halio (Cambridge: Cambridge University Press, 1992), 30. © Cambridge University Press. Reproduced with permission of Cambridge University Press through PLSclear

An image of extreme sorrow, the Pietà elicits sorrow for both the desolate Virgin and her lifeless son, the savior who was to bring deliverance from death, now ready to be lowered into a tomb.

If in performance the Pietà pose were struck and recognized, it would draw out Cordelia's Christlike qualities, the compassionate and forgiving nature that impels her to come to her father's rescue. But, as so often in this play, prefigurations of Christianity tend to underscore difference rather than likeness. In the Passion narrative, Christ's death is followed by the resurrection, the ascension, and the promise of his redemptive return. In *Lear*, however, there will be no sequel to Cordelia's death. Lear's strained efforts to bring her back to life only stress the futility. Upon entering with her in his arms, he pronounces her dead: "She is dead as earth" (5.3.257). Several times he urges the finality of her death:

"she's gone for ever," "now she's gone for ever" (268), and "No, no, no life!" (304). This final pronouncement, the only one in the future tense, declares her not only gone but gone forever, irrevocably: "O thou'lt come no more, / Never, never, never, never, never" (306–7).

Yet Lear throughout this scene looks for evidence to the contrary. He strains to see life in Cordelia, looking for breath in the most fleeting of signs: in the misting of a mirror ("If that her breath will mist or stain the stone, / Why then, she lives," 5.3.260–61), or in the quivering of a feather ("This feather stirs, she lives," 263). He pins his hope of redemption on this fragile possibility: "if it be so, / It is a chance which does redeem all sorrows / That ever I have felt" (263–65). As the scene proceeds, while Kent arrives and Albany tends to state matters, Lear may still be straining for a sign that Cordelia breathes: "O, see, see!" (303). With this cue, once again action and dialogue stop, as eyes turn on the two, now more tightly focused: "Do you see this? / Look on her: look, her lips, / Look there, look there!" (309–10, 1623 folio only).

It is impossible to know what Lear sees on Cordelia's lips, or believes he sees, and wants others to see. Perhaps her lips have parted to breathe or to whisper. If so, both onlookers and audience would be at too great a distance to mark it. Whether there is anything "there" to see cannot be confirmed or disconfirmed.[52] Only Lear is close enough to detect a quiver, if there were one, and by his own admission, his vision is unreliable: "Mine eyes are not o'the best" (5.3.277). The return to life that "would redeem all sorrow's else" is either not "there" or "there" only to Lear's "dull sight" (280).

The folio version of these lines allows for even less possibility. Modern editions punctuate Lear's directive with as many as four exclamation points: "Look on her! look! her lips! / Look there, Look there!"[53] The folio punctuation is more subdued:[54]

> Do you see this? Looke on her? Looke her lips,
> Looke there, looke there.   *He dies*

Lear's four injunctions to look, as he points toward Cordelia's lips, raise the expectation that there is something extraordinary there to be seen. But the revelation may be the stillness of Cordelia's lips rather than their movement. If so, it would support what he has just conceded: "No, no, no life . . . no breath at all." His last words would then signal not a last-minute flash of hope but its ultimate extinction.

At Lear's death, as at Cordelia's, there is no mention of an afterlife, what the service for the "Buriall of the dead" refers to as the "sure and certein hope of resurrection to eternall lyfe."[55] Kent arrives with a last wish for Lear—"I am come / To bid my King and master aye good night" (5.3.233–34)—as if there were no better wish for the dying than a permanent sleep with no awakening. Lear's death is a departure—"let him pass" and "he is gone indeed"—but the euphemism implies no higher destination. Albany, in his momentary role as de facto king, declares his intention to address the "general woe," but his terms are notably vague: "What comfort to this great decay may come / Shall be applied" (296–97). Edgar, who assumes rule at the tragedy's end, does little better. In the play's final lines, his proffered "comfort" takes the form of a guarantee that no life will ever attain the extremity of Lear's, neither in degree of suffering nor in length of years: "we that are young, / Shall never see so much, nor live so long" (324–25, Folio 1623 only). Lear's experience has been unique, so exceptional that it will not happen again, except of course where it has just occurred: on stage.

At the tragedy's close, Lear is remembered for one thing alone: his phenomenally long endurance. As Kent remarks, in the closest the play comes to eulogizing Lear, "The wonder is he hath endured so long" (5.3.315). Even in his lifetime, his survival was deemed a wonder by Cordelia: "'Tis wonder that thy life and wits at once / Had not concluded all" (4.7.41–42). Like a miracle and a marvel, a wonder challenges credulity because no explanation for it can be found in nature or experience. "Fourscore and upward" (4.7.61), Lear has reached the furthest limit of a long life span, as Regan points out: "Nature in you stands on the very verge / Of her confine" (2.2.336–37). In the span before he dies, his suffering is so great that it catches up with his advanced years, so that the two end up commensurate, as Lear observes when he counts himself "as full of grief as age, wretched in both" (2.2.270). To survive extreme suffering in extreme old age is a preternatural feat. By keeping death so long at bay, Lear has, if not triumphed over death, at least momentarily overthrown its tyranny, as Kent concludes: "He but usurped his life" (5.3.316).

For his prodigious endurance, Lear has frequently been compared to all-suffering Job, but the analogy, like the striking of the Pietà pose, only draws out the difference. Job's affliction is sustained by his abiding faith: "For I am sure that my Redeemer liveth" (Job 19:25). In the world of Lear, when such certainty is never entertained, enduring is life's only objective, as Edgar affirms: "Men must endure / Their going hence even as their coming hither" (5.2.9–10). The maxim is intended to fortify the tragedy's other old and wretched man, but Gloucester is no wonder. Unlike Lear, he is unable to bear affliction and seeks to "beguile the tyrant's rage" (4.6.63) by violently ending his own life. After his suicide attempt, his survival is also hailed as a wonder, another death-defying event: "Thy life's a miracle" (4.6.55). But in his case, the wonder is the result not of endurance but of divine intervention, or rather what Edgar convinces his father is divine intervention: "the clearest gods . . . have preserved thee" (4.6.73–74). The miracle, if there is one, is the result of Edgar's showmanship that can create the illusion that the old blind man has survived a leap off the precipitous cliff of Dover. And its effect is only momentary. Though Gloucester first resolves to outlast his misery—"Henceforth I'll bear / Affliction till it do cry out iself / 'Enough, enough' and die" (4.6.75–77)—the news of the defeat of Cordelia's army throws him back into death-seeking despair: "a man may rot even here" (5.2.8).

In order to make a wonder of old Lear's long life, the tragedy sets him on a protracted course of injury. From the moment that his abdication leaves him vulnerable, the plot subjects him to one blow after another. We see the tragedy's tactic in miniature when his two daughters reduce the number of his retainers by halves until nothing remains to be divided: from 100 to 50 to 25 to 10 to 5, to "what need one?" (2.2.260). Edgar experiences a similar drop. Having already in his guise as madman and beggar been reduced to "the lowest and most dejected thing of fortune" (4.1.3), he expects an upturn. But the tragedy's action does not follow the rotational spin of Fortune's wheel. Instead, it keeps plummeting lower, and indefinitely, as Edgar instantly discovers when he sees his father led by an old peasant and then, still worse, that he is blind. The pejoratives fly fast and loose, unable to keep pace with the decline: "Who is't can say 'I am at the worst'? / I am worse than e'er I was. . . . And worse I may be yet" (4.1.27–28, 29). From his experience, Edgar formulates an axiom: "the worst is not / So long as we can say 'This is the worst'" (4.1.29–30). Lear's trajectory confirms its truth, ever worsening until it is halted by death. Any wish to prolong his torture would be sadistic, as Kent insists: "He hates him / That would upon the rack of this tough world / Stretch him out longer" (5.3.312–14). The tragedy has racked him long enough, turning the pulleys and tightening the ropes to stretch the old man out beyond the breaking point.

In the final act, with all survivors in attendance, Edgar delivers a long narrative that, like the tragedy, draws attention to its own unbearability. Just halfway through, he is interrupted by Albany, "almost ready to dissolve," who bids him stop: "If there be more, more woeful, hold it in" (5.3.201). Edgar concurs: "This would have seemed a period / To such as love not sorrow" (203–4). All the same, as if he himself relishes sorrow, he continues with "more, more woeful" in the form of another tale, "the most piteous tale of Lear" (213). He knows its effect. Already "too much," sorrow will increase to "much more," until it exceeds the utmost: "To amplify too much would make much more / And top extremity" (205–6). The tragedy follows the same course, amplifying sorrow with its double plot of two men debilitated by age and affliction. It also risks having the same shattering effect on its audience that Edgar's synopsis has on Albany. Indeed, the risk is greater, for the tragedy does not stop at the "period" of Edgar's narrative. The worst is yet to come: Cordelia's shocking death and Lear's agonized craving for her return. Kent's words at the play's conclusion sum up the tragedy's achievement. It has hit rock bottom: no hope, no light, no life: "All's cheerless, dark and deadly" (288).

>>><<<

One of the ironies of *King Lear* criticism is that the tragedy that makes a "wonder" of Lear's endurance should be faulted for being itself unendurable to its audiences and readers. The inordinate sorrow that the tragedy strains to achieve has been deemed offensive, in excess of what the audience should be asked to bear. The cause is not Lear's death but Cordelia's. Nothing requires it: neither the sources (in which she survives), the genre (tragedy requires the death only of the protagonist), the plot (there is hope of a reprieve), and certainly not poetic justice (which cries out for her to be spared). Indeed, the history of the tragedy's reception could be told in terms of the various attempts to cope with the shock of Cordelia's death. In 1681, the poet and playwright Nahum Tate devised the most long-lasting solution: in his adaptation of *King Lear*, he omits her death altogether. As Tate explains in the play's dedicatory epistle, one simple expedient resolves the play's difficulties.[56] By generating at the start a romance between Edgar and Cordelia, two characters who never encounter one another in Shakespeare's tragedy, the play could end with Cordelia's nuptial rather than her death. For an astonishing 150 years, his adaptation of *Lear* preempted Shakespeare's tragedy on stage. Nor was its popularity limited to audiences. Shakespeare's illustrious editor and critic, Samuel Johnson, admitted to agreeing with "the general sufferage": he, too, preferred Tate's version, in which Cordelia "retired with victory and felicity."[57] As he allows in the preface to his edition of Shakespeare's plays, before having to edit the play, he could only bring himself to reread Shakespeare's *Lear* by stopping short of her shocking death: "I was many years ago so shocked by Cordelia's death that I know not whether I ever endured to read again the last scenes of the play till I undertook to revise them as an editor."

The same impulse that led Tate to rewrite the play's last act and Johnson to avoid returning to it has prompted critics since the nineteenth century to read the play in the tradition of the medieval enactments of the Passion: as an allegory of Christian salvation. When Christianized, Cordelia's sacrifice is seen to be as necessary to Lear's redemption as Christ's was for the expiation of original sin. Her sole motive in returning is to save Lear, as she insists, "O dear father, / It is thy business that I go about" (4.4.23–24), in words paraphrasing those of Christ: "I must be about my father's business" (Luke 2:49). Pity is what impels her, as she manifests through her importunate weeping, lavishly reported by a Gentleman over the course of twenty-three lines (4.3.11–33): "There she shook / The holy water from her heavenly eyes" (4.3.30–31). She weeps as she reads letters describing her father's suffering, but in his presence, too, she is moved to tears by his contrition: "poor perdu" (4.7.35). Because Lear knows he is guilty, his "burning shame / Detains him from Cordelia" (4.3.47–48). He believes he deserves poison at her hands, but instead she extends forgiveness: "No cause, no cause" (4.7.75). If this typological strain is followed, a redemptive ending is almost overdetermined. The play ends with Cordelia's sacrificial fulfillment of "her father's business." Even if it is only in Lear's mind that "she lives," her return to life, like Christ's resurrection, is salvific: it "doth redeem all sorrows else."

No critic has been more preoccupied by the problem of Cordelia's death than A. C. Bradley in his singularly influential *Shakespearean Tragedy*. "Why does Cordelia die?," he asks, on the supposition that "no reader ever failed to ask that question."[58] His reading, too, looks outside the tragedy for a motive, but not to Christian sacrifice, for Bradley categorically excludes "theological interpretation" (209): "Requital, redemption, amends, equity, explanation, pity and mercy, are words without meaning here" (208). However, he cannot avoid investing supreme value in Cordelia, not as a Christ figure but as an ideal. Her destruction has the same devastating effect as Christ's crucifixion but without its expiatory consolation. Comfort comes instead from an idealist metaphysics that stipulates a realm other than the "wild and monstrous" one of the tragedy, "the most terrible picture that Shakespeare painted of the world" (205). Here, as in the world of Platonic forms or Kantian categorical imperatives, ideals are untouched by the chance phenomena that destroy Cordelia. The two realms remain distinct. Indeed, for Bradley, even the abrupt violence of her death—the "sudden blow out of the darkness" (203)—is necessary in order to sever her conclusively from the tragedy's brutal world. By Bradley's logic, the more crushing the blow, the clearer its irrelevance: "The more unmotived, unmerited, senseless, monstrous, her fate, the more do we feel that it does not concern her" (247). This "feeling" of a realm apart, unlike the belief in salvation, does not obviate Cordelia's death, but it does alleviate its agony by intimating a realm where moral value is inviolable. In the presence of that "feeling," Lear can die in a state not of insufferable sorrow but of "unbearable *joy*" (220), the reader can leave the tragedy not outraged by Cordelia's gratuitous death but fairly reconciled to it (246), and *The Tragedy of King Lear*, suggests Bradley, can with equal validity be titled *The Redemption of King Lear* (215).

But without a transcendent cause for Cordelia's death, either theological or metaphysical, the play ends not in the reaffirmation of belief but in its utter shattering. Without an appeal to some system of value extraneous to the tragedy, criticism finds in the tragedy's hard ending nothing but privation. This is what William R. Elton concludes in the last sentence of his monumental study of *Lear*'s philosophical and religious context: "No redemption stirs at this world's end; only suffering, tears, pity, and loss—*and* illusion."[59] For him, the play's only solace is the cruel illusion that Cordelia breathes. In the godless world of *Lear*, any appearance of providence is forged, like the miracle Edgar stages for his father. Prayers go unanswered, as when Albany's plea for Cordelia's survival, "The gods defend her," is followed by the notorious stage direction "Enter Lear with Cordelia in his arms" (5.3.254). The play's value is seen to reside in its refusal to conceal hard realities with Christian pieties. For Jan

Kott, in his influential *Shakespeare Our Contemporary*, the play forecloses all hope, worldly or otherworldly: "*King Lear* makes a tragic mockery of all eschatologies: of the heaven promised on earth, and the heaven promised after death."[60] Even Joseph Wittreich's "*Image of That Horror*," while acknowledging the tragedy's "apocalyptic framework," insists that its ironies, including Cordelia's death, "impeach the promises of Christianity."[61] Reginald Foakes argues that *King Lear* has overtaken *Hamlet* in the twentieth century, "if only because it speaks more largely than the other tragedies to the anxieties and problems of the modern world"; while action in *Hamlet* occurs within a Christian dispensation, he maintains, in *Lear* it "takes place in a secular world where the gods are verbal constructs."[62]

Stephen Greenblatt has taken the play's secularity a step farther. The tragedy, he argues, by counterfeiting the practices of the church, empties them of their sacrality: "*King Lear* is haunted by a sense of rituals and beliefs that are no longer efficacious, that have been *emptied out*."[63] The play works to disenchant medieval faith, dispelling the numinosity of its forms of worship and devotion by exposing their reliance on the same illusory techniques and resources as the theater itself. The supernatural, whether diabolic or divine, is no more than a stage effect. Edgar performs demonic possession by appearing to lose self-control, as if speech and movement had been taken over by the fiends within him— "Five fiends have been in poor Tom at once" (4.1.61–62)—and by piercing himself with pins and nails as if to force them out. Edgar also performs an act of divine intervention when he convinces his father he has survived an impossibly precipitous fall: "Thy life's a miracle" (4.6.55). The audience witnesses the disparity between the action (a forward fall on a flat stage) and what passes as a miracle, at least in the mind of Edgar's blind father. As Greenblatt remarks, Cordelia's death presents another opportunity for a miracle. If Cordelia were to return to life, as Lear craves, redemption would be at hand: "If it be so, / It is a chance which does redeem all sorrows / That ever I have felt" (5.3.263–64). But, as Greenblatt concludes, the tragedy refuses that condition: "The theatrical means that might have produced a 'counterfeit miracle' out of this moment are abjured; there will be no imposture, no histrionic revelation of the supernatural."[64] The hard fact of her death remains, the ultimate disenchantment, voided of promise. *King Lear* will feign demonic possession and a divine miracle, but not redemptive life after death.

The tragedy deploys another tactic of disenchantment. In addition to emptying out sacred forms and figures, it deforms and disfigures them. Resemblances to Christ are invited only to be baffled. When he conceals himself as Poor Tom, Edgar bears a disarming resemblance to Christ. Hailing from Bedlam, an asylum whose name is a contraction of Christ's birthplace, naked but for his blanketed loins, piercing his body with "pins, wooden pricks, nails, sprigs of rosemary" (2.2.187), Poor Tom might have been modeled after a familiar icon. The Man of Sorrows depicts Christ in a loincloth, displaying the wounds of his crucifixion, surrounded by the *arma Christi*, or instruments of his suffering or Passion (nails, hammer, pincers, spear, etc.).[65] But, as Edgar explains to the audience, Turlygod Tom intends to compel fear, not pity, as he becomes the "horrible object" he describes. Begrimed and roaring, he scares villagers into giving alms: "And with this horrible object . . . Enforce their charity" (188, 191). He thereby constrains the charity that doctrinally and proverbially is to be given freely. Lear also slips into the role of Christ when in the aftermath of the apocalyptic storm he passes judgment over the quick and the dead. But his final reckoning, rather than separating the blessed from the damned, grants amnesty to all: "None does offend, none" (4.6.164). Cordelia's Christlike pity is also off-kilter, and just at the point when it might have been effective in granting Lear the forgiveness he needs but has been too guilty to seek: "a sovereign shame so elbows him" (4.3.43). When Lear, now safely accommodated, awakens to music, rested and freshly arrayed, the scene looks set for reconciliation, but instead it hits an impasse. As Cordelia kneels to ask for blessing, Lear kneels to ask for forgiveness. With two supplicants and no absolvent, there can be no atonement. He cannot bless her until she forgives him, and she cannot forgive him until he blesses her. After their arrest, imagining their life together in prison, Lear makes a ritual of this fruitless exercise: "When thou dost ask me blessing I'll kneel down, / And ask of thee forgiveness" (5.3.10–11). At his death, he is still looking to Cordelia for the redemption she cannot deliver any more than she could express her love at the tragedy's start.

The grotesque icon, the blanket absolution, and the dead-locked sacrament: all these effects seem designed to deface and degrade what they invoke, even at the risk of sacrilege. Like Greenblatt's evacuated practices, they lend themselves to the secularizing movement that has been thought indispensable to modernity. Desecrating as well as evacuating, the tragedy redoubles its disenchantment.

But is the ungodly emptiness of *Lear* that of a disenchanted world or of a world before it has been enchanted? From the vantage of centuries after its writing, the tragedy presents us with a genuine ambiguity: a world as imagined before Revelation looks like the world that has lost faith in it. The withholding of Revelation leaves the same absences as its rejection. Yet it is the tragedy's inauspicious and vacuous setting that motivates both the extremity of its sorrow and the sorry forms by which it attempts to relieve it. It provides the farfetched pretext for what Shakespearean theater can do so brilliantly: take leave of the world, and nowhere more daringly than when Lear bids all eyes to "Look there!" for signs of the redemption that the tragedy has so artfully occluded.

King Lear is situated long before *Anno Domini* time—the era that began with the coming of Christ, or the Incarnation, and that was expected to end with his Second Coming, or Revelation. In the interest of securing its self-defined secularity, modernity has overridden both termini. To make way for its own installation, it has neutralized Christianity's incarnational incipit and dissolved its projected finis, replacing the former with a radically new start and the latter with an indefinitely open future.

In the process, faith is reduced to a mere period with faith, an age of belief, characterized by a Christian worldview. It is thus cordoned off as if it were a discrete historical unit, the medieval era. Thus defined and delimited, it could be superseded by an era whose self-proclaimed novelty depended on the disavowal of its bespoke antecedent. With faith and dogma enclosed within period parameters, modernity's own self-appointed innovations were free to emerge, among them a tragedy no longer dependent on the salvational program.

And yet *The Tragedy of King Lear* is hardly independent of that dispensation. It has been removed from the play, but only temporarily, and only from the stage. Offstage, for its early audiences, it remains as intact as it ever was. Indeed, the tragedy must assume its presence in order for its grotesque and pathetic disfigurations to register as such. For the audience, auspiciously oriented in AD time, the possibility of redemption, in the future at least, is a given. The tragedy assumes familiarity with the faith it has put in abeyance. The world that the spectators watch is not the same as the one they occupy. Unlike the Fool, they know of the Hebrew prophecies foretelling the Messiah; unlike Albany, they have seen images of the "promised end"; and unlike Lear and Cordelia's survivors, they have been led to hope for a world to come. These prospects need not be obliterated by their suspension. Indeed their value might be enhanced by the witnessing of what there is without them.

If *King Lear* assumes an audience oriented in AD time, has criticism gone astray in claiming it for modernity and secularity? Has it attributed to an earlier period its own latter-day disavowal of Christianity? If so, it would be a prime example of what the twentieth-century intellectual historian Lucien Febvre has denounced as "the worst of all sins, the sin that cannot be forgiven—anachronism."[66] The offense is the attribution of atheism to "an age of belief," the subject of Febvre's long and influential polemic, *The Problem of Unbelief in the Sixteenth Century*. For him, the predication of atheism to an earlier period dominated by faith is as bad as atheism itself, as much an abomination to historical study as deadly sin is to church doctrine.

Febvre's indictment is not of atheism but of its premature detection in the sixteenth century. The denial of God's existence must await the Enlightenment, when skepticism puts an end to faith and empirical science to superstition. To ascribe it to an earlier time is to compromise the sanctity of the historical period as a self-contained and coherent unit or, in the term coined by Febvre, as a *mentalité*. In an age that regarded the world as God's creation, he maintains, the very idea of denying the existence of God would have been "unthinkable." It exists only in the modern minds of the scholars who project it into much earlier times. This is the anachronism Febvre deems irremissible: the imposing of a later "mindset" on an earlier era.

Yet, as we have seen, the very notion of an age possessing a "mindset" or worldview is exclusive to modern epistemology. For Heidegger, only the modern age, "the age of the world picture," grasps the past as integral units set apart from its own present. To speak in terms of a medieval mentalité, whether religious or irreligious, is to cast the past into modern conceptual frames: "The world picture does not change from an earlier medieval one into a modern one, but rather the fact that the world becomes picture at all is what distinguishes the essence of the modern age."[67] By his logic, the coherent ideational and material units we call periods are themselves modern anachronistic back-formations. The same might be said of anachronisms whose detection and excoriation keep the period divisions in place.

Like Febvre's sixteenth century, *King Lear* has been caught in the periodizing schism that severs the modern from the medieval by its ostensible discrediting of faith. On which side of the epochal divide should the tragedy fall? But should a play even be asked to bear historical witness to either unbelief or belief, in either Shakespeare, his audience, or his century? After all, when *King Lear* looks secular, it is only pretending. It is making a show of irreligion. Its secular effects are theatrical. Its vacuous setting

is a fiction in keeping not with the human condition but with
what it has taken as its own impossible condition: that nothing is
yet known of Revelation. The tragedy withholds Revelation not
in deference to a secular world but in compliance with a hypo-
thetical one that would not be believed if it were not happening
on stage, for a theater that—like Revelation itself—achieves its
greatest success when it makes credible what would otherwise be
incredible, if not forever and ever, world-without-end, at least
for the time being of a few hours.

Acknowledgments

For better or worse, this book has a bold thesis. If it is at all persuasive, I owe thanks to a good number of others: To John Parker for his engagement with the book at the deepest level in matters both secular and profane. To Jessica Rosenberg for her rare ability to read for both detail and import. To Michael Dobson, James Harriman-Smith, Ivan Lupic, and Paul Werstine for bringing their expertise to bear on individual chapters. To Claire Bourne, Ian Gadd, Jonathan Keates, and Joe de Grazia for help with particular cruxes. To Crystal Bartolovich, Victoria de Grazia, Lynn Festa, Juliet Fleming, Rayna Kalas, Louisa Lane Fox, and Laurie Shannon for long walks and conversations. To Colin Burrow, David Hillman, Jay Grossman, Jeff Masten, and Carla Mazzio for being on my mind as I wrote.

To Peter Stallybrass for provoking and enriching my work throughout my career and for the trust it engendered between us. To Stephen Greenblatt for his sustained and sustaining interest in the direction of my work. To Gabriel Josipovici, whose distaste for realism in art outdoes my own. To Howard Zeiderman, who early on steered me to problems of representation. To Roger Chartier for the vitality and genius he has brought to the study of The Book. And to David Kastan for decades of support and friendship.

I also wish to acknowledge the forbearance of those who after asking "And what are you working on?" kept listening when I had no short or cogent answer: Brian Cummings, Rita Copeland, Linda Gregerson, Joanna Kavenna, Julia Lupton, Kenneth Reinhart, and David Wallace. Among them, too, belongs Alan Thomas, who even took notes. Special thanks to Randy Petilos, who cheered me on to the finish with a quality of attention I will not forget.

Thanks, too, to Bronwyn Wallace for being such a tough and kind taskmaster, to Alison Howard for her expeditious help with preparing the typescript, and to Steve LaRue for his excellent copyediting. My readers for Chicago could not have been more intelligent or helpful in their grasp of the book's import. Thanks also to Rebecca Aldi at the Beinecke Rare Book and Manuscript Library, Melanie Leung at the Folger Shakespeare Library, James E.H. Ford at Longleat House, Will Motley at Cohen and Cohen, and Denna Garrett at Chatsworth House for their prompt help in obtaining images.

To Sheli and Burt Rosenberg, who endowed the chair I held at the University of Pennsylvania and then became my very dear friends. To Austin Zeiderman for his understanding on so many levels—and for sharing Paula Durán and Eliseo.

But above all, I give thanks to Colin Thubron, who had far other worlds on his mind, yet was always ready to set them aside to hear and read about mine.

Notes

INTRODUCTION

1. See de Grazia, "Anachronism."

2. Fabian, *Time and the Other*, esp. 25–35; Levinas, *Otherwise than Being*, esp. 109–18, and the translator's preface, xxix–xxxii.

3. On the necessity for historians to be equipped with "a whole quiverful of innovative historical periods" to counter the dominance of their own, see Shagan, "Periodization and the Secular," 72–73.

4. On "psychological anachronism," see Febvre, "History and Psychology," 9.

5. Febvre, *Problem of Unbelief in the Sixteenth Century*. On the "sin" of projecting the present onto the past, see Skinner, "An Interview," 59.

6. Febvre, *Problem of Unbelief in the Sixteenth Century*, 5.

7. Aravamudan, "The Return of Anachronism"; Luzzi, "The Rhetoric of Anachronism"; Didi-Huberman, "Before the Image"; Nagel and Wood, "Towards a New Model of Renaissance Anachronism"; Rancière, "Concept of Anachronism."

8. Benjamin, "Theses on the Philosophy of History," esp. theses 7, 10, 11.

9. Bhaba, "DissemiNation"; Chakrabarty, *Provincializing Europe*, esp. 73–77, 237–55.

10. For an overview, see Dinshaw et al., "Theorizing Queer Temporalities."

11. Barthes, "The Discourse of History," 10.

12. See particularly Jacques Derrida, *Specters of Marx*, esp. chap. 1.

13. The phrase is used by Althusser to describe Hegel's philosophy of history in Althusser and Balibar, *Reading Capital*, 17.

14. See Ted Underwood's account of the emergence and durability of the period unit in literary studies in Underwood, *Why Literary Periods Mattered*, esp. 1–3.

15. See, for example, Hayot, "Against Periodization"; the cluster of essays entitled "The Long and the Short: Problems in Periodization"; Virginia Jackson, "On Periodization and its Discontents"; and Underwood, *Why Literary Periods Mattered*, esp. 157–175.

16. Jameson, *The Political Unconscious*, 28; *Postmodernism*, 282; *A Singular Modernity*, 29. For a staunch defense of periodizing in the name of social justice, see Bartolovich, "Is the Post in Posthuman the Post in Postmedieval?"

17. Davis, *Periodization and Sovereignty*, 1–6; de Grazia, "The Modern Divide."

18. Hyppolite, *Genesis and Structure of Hegel's "Phenomenology of Spirit,"* 12.

19. de Vriese, "The Charm of Disenchantment," 413n21.

20. Taylor, *A Secular Age*, 3, 539.

21. Adorno, *Aesthetic Theory*, 106.

22. On *kenosis* or the Incarnation as itself a form of secularization, see Vattimo, *After Christianity*, 67–68 and passim. On Christianity's dialectical and constitutive relation to atheism, see Parker, *Drama and the Death of God*.

23. Blumenberg, *The Legitimacy of the Modern Age*, 15, 4.

24. Blumenberg, *Legitimacy of the Modern Age* 138, 178.

25. See Stark, "Secularization, R.I.P.," and de Vriese, "The Charm of Disenchantment."

26. Taylor, *A Secular Age*, 5

27. For the identification of Valla with the detection of anachronism and modern historical consciousness, see Burke, "Sense of Anachronism"; "Sense of Historical Perspective"; *Renaissance Sense of the Past*; and "Renaissance Sense of the Past Revisited."

28. For the emergence of the modern concept of history and the concomitant awareness of anachronism in British Romanticism rather than in the Renaissance, see Chandler, *England in 1819*, 100–105.

29. Boruchoff, "Three Greatest Inventions of Modern Times."

30. Sawyer, "New Shakspere Society."

31. Taylor and Egan, *New Oxford Shakespeare: Authorship Companion*, v.

32. See, for example, Cooper, *Shakespeare and the Medieval World*; Morse, Cooper, and Holland, *Medieval Shakespeare*; and Schreyer, *Shakespeare's Medieval Craft*.

33. On the "revisionist backlash" to the secularization thesis among historians, see Walsham, "The Reformation and the 'Disenchantment of the World' Reassessed." For the "religious turn" in Shakespeare studies, see Lupton, "The Pauline Renaissance."

34. Chambers, *The Mediaeval Stage*, 1:v–vi.

35. Chambers, *The Mediaeval Stage*, 2:68–105. For a more nuanced account of secularization in Chambers, see Parker, "Who's Afraid of Darwin?," esp. 15–16.

36. Stephen Greenblatt, *Renaissance Self-Fashioning*, 7–8. For a more recent redaction, see his *Shakespeare's Freedom*, 1–5.

37. Greenblatt, *Shakespearean Negotiations*, 126.

38. Greenblatt, "Remnants of the Sacred," 344.

39. Greenblatt, *Hamlet in Purgatory*, 253.

40. Cavell, *Disowning Knowledge*, 3.

41. On the use of "ordinary language" as a defense against the "skeptical threat," see Cavell, 39.

42. Beckwith, *Shakespeare and the Grammar of Forgiveness.*

43. Lupton, *Thinking with Shakespeare*, 70. For the "imperfect translations" from theological to civic, see also Lupton, *Citizen-Saints*, 12.

44. See Lupton's review essay, "The Pauline Renaissance."

45. See DiPietro and Grady, "Presentism, Anachronism and the Case of *Titus Andronicus*."

46. On intentional anachronism as an indication of modern historical consciousness in the Renaissance, see Greene, *The Light in Troy*, 242–46. For anachronism's ideological work in Shakespeare's history plays, see Rackin, *Stages of History*, 86–145.

47. Garber, *Profiling Shakespeare*, 195–213.

48. Ruthven, "Preposterous Chatterton"; de Grazia, "Anachronism," 15–16; Munro, *Archaic Style*, 12–13.

49. See Hamlin, *The Bible in Shakespeare*, 179–230.

50. Harris, *Untimely Matter*, 171–75; Tribble and Sutton, "Minds in and out of Time."

51. Palfrey, *Shakespeare's Possible Worlds*, 147–59.

52. Derrida, "Aphorism Countertime," 430.

53. de Grazia, "Anachronism," 15–16.

54. See chapter 1.

55. Skinner, "Meaning and Understanding," esp. 32–35.

56. On the changes in the semantics of history and temporality, see Williams, *Key Words*; and Koselleck, *Futures Past*.

57. Among the many who identify Valla's *On the Donation* with the detection of anachronism are Ritter, *Dictionary of Concepts in History*, 11–13; Burke, "Sense of Anachronism," 160; Greene, *The Light in Troy*, 10, and "History and Anachronism"; Levy, *Tudor Historical Thought*, 77; Rackin, *Stages of History*, 10; Ginzburg, *History, Rhetoric, and Proof*, 64; Levine, *Humanism and History*, 71; Lynch, *Deception and Detection*, 109–14.

58. Valla, *On the Donation of Constantine*, xii, 190–91n47. Further citations to this text will appear by paragraph numbers in text.

59. Valla, 189–90n38.

60. Valla, 190–91n47.

61. On the basis of Valla's excoriation of Palea's grammar and rhetoric in Quintillian, see Hiatt, *Making of Medieval Forgeries*, 162.

62. Quintilian, *The Institutio Oratoria*, 9:2, 30–38, at 30; see also Cicero, *Rhetorica ad Herennium*, 4.53.66.

63. According to Hiatt, Palea "knew more about fourth-century imperial Latin than Valla did." Hiatt, *Making of Medieval Forgeries*, 164.

64. Valla, *On the Donation of Constantine*, 192n79. On Valla's mockery of Palea's poor performance as Constantine, see Hiatt, *Making of Medieval Forgeries*, 166.

65. Valla contests Palea's dating of the *Donation*—"*Datum Rome tertio Kalendas Aprilis*"—not for its inaccuracy but because *datum* was generally used to sign off on personal correspondence rather than to authenticate official documents (para. 70).

66. Hiatt, *Making of Medieval Forgeries*, 169–73.

67. On the completion of the fresco after Raphael's death by his workshop, see Jan L. de Jong, *Power and the Glorification*, 84–86.

68. Greene, *The Light in Troy*, 30.

69. On the term's earliest uses in Kant and Hegel, see Naugle, *Worldview*, 58n14. On "world pictures" and the nineteenth-century framing of the Renaissance as a period, see Kalas, *Frame, Glass, Verse*, 9–16.

70. *King Lear*, ed. R. A. Foakes, 3.2.95–96.

CHAPTER ONE

1. *The Tragedie of Troylus and Cressida*, Folio 1623, 3v.

2. Rowe 1709, 4:1841.

3. Pope 1725, 1:xiv.

4. According to Peter Seary, Theobald's critique impelled Pope to introduce over a hundred corrections into his 1728 edition; see Seary, *Lewis Theobald and the Editing of Shakespeare*, 97 and n26. He retained the "graver sages" emendation, however; see Pope 1728, 7:300.

5. Theobald, *Shakespeare restored*, 134–35. The appendix is reprinted in Theobald's edition of *Troilus and Cressida*, Theobad 1733, 7:42–44.

6. Theobald 1733, 7:43.

7. de Grazia, "Shakespeare's Anecdotal Character," 1–5.

8. Theobald, *Shakespeare restored*, 135. For more of Shakespeare's "grossest Offences against Chronology," see Theobald 1733, 1:xxx–xxxi.

9. Theobald, *Shakespeare restored*, 135.

10. Theobald 1733, 1:xlix

11. Theobald, *Shakespeare restored*, 135.

12. Theobald 1733, 7:44. On Theobald's translations of Greek drama, see J. Michael Walton, "Theobald and Lintott."

13. Theobald, *Shakespeare restored*, 135.

14. Theobald 1733, 4:112.

15. Johnson 1765, 1:xx–xxi.

16. George Steevens's comment is quoted in Malone-Boswell 1821, 8:297–98n8.

17. Capell, *Notes and Various Readings*, 2:123.

18. Malone-Boswell 1821, 8:313n6.

19. Malone-Boswell 1821, 16:234n9; 301n5.

20. Malone-Boswell 1821, 2:351. For Malone's three chronologies, see chapter 2, n4.

21. The *New Oxford Shakespeare* 2016 breaks with this editorial tradition, perhaps persuaded by de Grazia, "Minding Anachronism," quoted in Oxford's prefatory excerpts to *Troilus and Cressida*, 1903.

22. For the controversy over when and where *Troilus and Cressida* was first performed, see *Troilus and Cressida*, ed. Anthony B. Dawson, 6–10.

23. On the use of tents and a wall by the Lord Admiral's Men for the production of their Trojan plays, see Roger Apfelbaum, *Shakespeare's "Troilus and Cressida,"* 23, 66–69.

24. Robert I. Lublin, *Costuming the Shakespearean Stage*, 83–86.

25. The listing of "pryams hoes" in the inventory of apparel for the Admiral's Men suggests that the Trojan king was to appear in modern doublet and hose. See Henslowe, *Henslowe's Diary*, 292.

26. According to the early modern dictionaries, *senator* commonly refers to a magistrate, like an alderman or councilor, as in Robert Cawdrey, *A Table Alphabetical* (1604), *Lexicons of Early Modern English*, https://leme.library.utoronto.ca. For the inventoried senators' caps and gowns, see Hal Smith, who takes them instead as evidence that Roman apparel was worn on stage; Smith, "Some Principles of Elizabethan Stage Costume," 253.

27. For the now classic account of how acting companies acquired their wardrobes, see Jones and Stallybrass, "The Circulation of Clothes and the Making of the English Theater," *Renaissance Clothing*, esp. 176–95.

28. On the use of title page woodcuts by publishers in the first decades of the seventeenth century as a tactic for converting the experience of watching a play to one of reading a playbook, see Bourne, *Typographies of Performance*, 204–28.

29. Heywood, *The Iron Age: contayning the Rape of Hellen: The siege of Troy*, etc., F2v.

30. Heywood, *Second Part of the Iron Age*, B3v.

31. A stage direction in Heywood's *Second Part of the Iron Age* would require that Greek and Trojan attire be differentiated when a group of Trojans disguise themselves as Greeks (G4v). Perhaps the attire of the invading Greeks would have been more rudimentary than that of the Trojans, as Ajax's armor clearly is in comparison to Hector's in figure 1.2.

32. Panosky, *Renaissance and Renascences in Western Art*, 85–86.

33. For the dissemination of Panofsky's definition of the historically cognizant Renaissance against an anachronistic Middle Ages, see de Grazia, "Anachronism," 28–29.

34. As Stephen Orgel points out, the engraving cannot have been of a performance of Shakespeare's *Troilus and Cressida*, for it was not staged after the Restoration. Nor can it be of John Dryden's adaptation

of the play, *Troilus and Cressida, or Truth found too late*, in which the sleeve is replaced with the more familiar love token of a ring. See Orgel, "Shakespeare Illustrated," 70–72.

35. For the Elizabethan sleeve, and Troilus's, see Jones and Stallybrass, *Renaissance Clothing*, 4, 201–2.

36. *Lexicons of Early Modern English*, https://leme.library.utoronto.ca.

37. Douce, *Illustrations of Shakspeare*, 2:282–83.

38. Douce, "On the Anachronisms and Some Other Incongruities of Shakspeare," in *Illustrations of Shakspeare*, 2:281–96.

39. See *Troilus and Cressida*, ed. Frances A. Shirley, xiv.

40. On the possible influence of these excavations on turn-of-the-century German productions, see *Troilus and Cressida*, ed. Frances A. Shirley, 7.

41. See Harrington, "Behind the Mask of Agamemnon," 52.

42. On Poel's replication of Elizabethan stage conventions of continuous action, the thrust configuration, and the absence of scenery, see Falocco, *Reimagining Shakespeare's Playhouse*, 8–10.

43. See Apfelbaum, *Shakespeare's "Troilus and Cressida,"* 41–42.

44. See the gloss to 2.2.166–67 in "Longer Notes," *Troilus and Cressida*, ed. David Bevington, 362; and Burrow, *Shakespeare and Classical Antiquity*, 24–25.

45. William R. Elton, largely on the basis of the play's ethical and moral issues, concludes that the play's first venue was the Inns of Court, London's "third university"; see Elton, *Shakespeare's "Troilus and Cressida" and the Inns of Court Revels*, 168. For a list of parallels between the play and Aristotle's *Nicomachean Ethics*, see Elton, 183–89.

46. Schmitt, *John Case and Aristotelianism in Renaissance England*, 75, and chap. 1.

47. On this possible allusion in the folio text, see *Troilus and Cressida*, ed. David Bevington, 6–11.

48. *Troilus and Cressida*, ed. David Bevington, 5.11.54, 2.3.17–18. Unless otherwise indicated, all further references to this play will follow Bevington's edition and be cited parenthetically in the text.

49. Minton and Harvey, "'A Poor Chipochia.'"

50. On the tradition of noting this anomaly, see de Grazia, "Anachronism," 17–19, and Kalter, *Modern Antiques*, 61–65.

51. John Dryden, *The Works of Virgil*, 5:299.

52. Dryden, 5:299.

53. Dryden, 5:300.

54. Dryden, 5:301.

55. On this distinction, see Buchwald and Feingold, *Newton and the Origin of Civilization*, 8.

56. For the importance of Scaligerian chronology into the eighteenth century and beyond, see Grafton, "Scaliger's Chronology," 104–44, and *Joseph Scaliger*, 2:1–18.

57. Hearne, *Ductor historicus*, title page.

58. Coote, *The English School-Master*, 51–52.

59. Finegan, *Handbook of Biblical Chronology*, 191. On earlier precedents for Ussher's date of Creation or *Anno Mundi* at 4004 BC, see Fuller, "A Date to Remember." On Newton's controversial revisions of Ussher, see Morrison, *Isaac Newton's Temple of Solomon*, 17–21.

60. For Samuel Johnson and Edward Gibbon, see de Grazia, "Anachronism," 16–17; for Locke, see *Some Thoughts Concerning Education*, 149–50. On the study of chronology before Newton's contribution, see Buchwald and Feingold, *Newton and the Origin of Civilization*, 107–25.

61. Scaliger, *Opus de emendatione temporum*, γ3v, γ4v, and ε1r. For the Greek etymology of the word, see Rood, Atack, and Phillips, *Anachronism and Antiquity*, 11–15. For Scaliger's importance in England, see Feingold, "Scaliger in England."

62. Raleigh, *History of the World*, "To the Reader." On Raleigh's use of Scaliger, see Popper, *Walter Ralegh's "History of the World" and the Historical Culture of the Late Renaissance*, 71.

63. Drayton, *Chorographicall Description*, A2r. On Scaliger's influence on Selden, see Toomer, *John Selden*, 1:166–67; on Selden's devising of synchronisms, 112; on his "antichronismes" or conjoining of noncontemporaneous events and persons, see Kalter, *Modern Antiques*, 212n45.

64. Gregory, *Gregorii Posthuma*, 174.

65. Segrais, *Traduction de l'Eneïde de Virgile*, 27–35. For Bochart's letter on anachronism, see 89–91.

66. Scaliger, *Opus de emendatione temporum*, 1r.

67. For Helvicus's use of Scaliger's "chronological systeme," see Helvicus, *Historical and Chronological*, (a)r. On the wide publication and adoption of Helvicus, see Kalter, *Modern Antiques*, 37–42.

68. Hearne, *Ductor historicus*, 8.

69. Chambers, *Cyclopaedia*, 1:Y2.

70. For Scaliger's dating of the fall of Troy, see Grafton and Swerdlow, "Greek Chronography in Roman Epic." For Scaliger's list of eras in *Opus de emendatione*, see Grafton, *Joseph Scaliger*, 2:277–98.

71. For Eratosthenes's calculation, see Kokkinos, "Ancient Chronography."

72. *The Holy Bible* (1701). That Jepthah's and Agamemnon's reigns were thought to be concurrent gives a chronological basis to the analogy noted by Debra Kuller Shuger between Agamemnon's sacrifice of Iphigenia and Jepthah's of his unnamed daughter in George Buchanan's neo-Latin drama *Jepthah* (1554), a transposition of Euripides's *Iphigenia in Aulis*. See Shuger, *The Renaissance Bible*, 135–36.

73. Buchwald and Feingold, *Newton and the Origin of Civilization*, 203, 408–9. See also Feingold, "Newton, Historian."

74. Buchwald and Feingold, *Newton and the Origin of Civilization*, 441–56.

75. For Gibbons's and Diderot's endorsements of Newton's redating as well those of several other scholars in Spain, France, and Scotland, see Buchwald and Feingold, *Newton and the Origin of Civilization*, 418–19nn123–26.

76. Priestley, *A Description of a Chart of Biography*, 14.

77. Martyn, *Dissertations and Critical Remarks*, 22, 24.

78. Theobald, *Shakespeare restored*, 135.

79. *Poetics* XXIV, in Aristotle, *Aristotle on Poetry and Style*, 54.

80. On the role of the scholiast, see Wilson, "Scholiasts and Commentators." According to P. E. Easterling, Aristotle as well as the scholiasts thought of the Pythian Games in *Electra* as an anachronism; see Easterling, "Anachronism in Greek Tragedy," 7. But as Ebeling demonstrates, it was not until Scaliger that the word denoted "a single chronological sense." See Ebeling, "The Word Anachronism," 120.

81. Theobald, *Electra: A Tragedy*, 80–81.

82. Theobald, 80. On Theobald's translation of the Pythian games passage, see Walton, "'An Agreeable Innovation,'" 270–71.

83. Knox, *Oedipus at Thebes*, 61. See also Rood, *Anachronism and Antiquity*, 59–85, esp. 61–62.

84. Frederick Schiller, "On the Tragic Art," 363.

85. On archaism as a form of anachronism, see Munro, *Archaic Style*, 18–19.

86. Feeney, *Caesar's Calendar*, 83.

87. Horace, *Odes of Horace*, 4.9.

88. Feeney, *Caesar's Calendar*, 84.

89. Raleigh, *History of the World*, 382.

90. Ben Jonson, "Epistle to Elizabeth, Countess of Rutland," *The Forest*, in *Cambridge Edition of the Works of Ben Jonson*, 5:237, 54–58.

91. Helvicus, *Historical and Chronological Theatre*, 37.

92. Hearne, *Ductor historicus*, 6.

93. Holinshed, *Chronicles of England, Scotlande, and Irelande* (1587), vol. 1, bk. 1 ch. 3, p. 10.

94. For an example of the primacy of the date in almanacs, see Pond, *Enchiridion, or Pond his Eutheca*, A3.

95. On Geoffrey of Monmouth's placing of Lear's rule between the Hebrew prophets Elijah and Isaiah, see chapter 4, 146.

96. Feeney, *Caesar's Calendar*, 118.

97. This irony is lost when the characters are assumed to have the same epigonic, nostalgic, and overdetermined knowledge of the Troy legacy as the audience. See, for example, Freund, "'Ariachne's Broken Woof,'"; and Charnes, "'So Unsecret to Ourselves.'"

98. On the role of Hesione in classical and medieval texts about the Trojan War, including in those assumed to be Shakespeare's sources, see Hirota, "The Memory of Hesione."

99. Baldwin, *William Shakspere's Small Latine*, 1:89 and 2:239–40.

100. Among them, Edmund Spenser, Thomas Elyot, John Davies, Richard Hooker, George Chapman, and two Elizabethan homilies. See *Troilus and Cressida*, ed. H. N. Hillebrand, 404–10.

101. Tillyard, *The Elizabethan World Picture*, 12; and Lovejoy, *Great Chain of Being*, 59.

102. *Troilus and Cressida*, ed. H. N. Hillebrand, 411–15.

103. Hillman, "Worst Case of Knowing the Other?," 74.

104. Hillman, 75.

105. *The Famous Historie of Troylus and Cresseid*, B3r.

106. On the singularly heavy marking of this maxim, see Lesser and Stallybrass, "First Literary *Hamlet*," 414–15.

107. Aristotle, *Metaphysica* (*Metaphysics*), 1006a, 737.

108. *Troilus and Cressida*, ed. Frances A. Shirley, 49.

109. Ryan, "*Troilus and Cressida*: The Perils of Presentism," 170.

110. Oates, *The Edge of Impossibility*, 11.

111. Hillman, "Worst Case of Knowing the Other?," 26.

112. Miller, "Ariachne's Broken Woof."

113. de Man, *Blindness and Insight*, 148.

114. "These [present] times are the ancient times when the world is ancient, and not those which we account antient, *Ordine retrogrado*, by a computation backward from our selves." Bacon, *The Advancement of Learning*, 29.

115. As Micha Lazarus maintains in his study of Aristotle's reception in England, "every thinking Renaissance human was Aristotelian . . . . Statements were true or false by Aristotelian logic." Lazarus, "Aristotelian Criticism in Sixteenth-Century."

CHAPTER TWO

1. de Grazia, *Shakespeare Verbatim*, 143–52.

2. Edmond Malone, "Proposal for a new edition of Shakspeare" (1795), quoted by Prior, *Life of Edmond Malone*, 208n.

3. Malone-Boswell 1821, 2:467.

4. Malone's first chronology, "An Attempt to Ascertain the Order in which the Plays Attributed to Shakspeare were Written," was published in Johnson and Steevens 1778, 1:269–346. He revised and retitled the essay *An Attempt to Ascertain the Order in which the Plays of Shakespeare were written* for his own edition (1790), 1:261–386. He revised it again before his death in 1812 as it appears in Malone-Boswell 1821, 2:288–468.

5. Malone-Boswell 1821, 2:288.

6. Malone-Boswell 1821, "Advertisement," 1:xvii.

7. Chambers, *William Shakespeare*, 1:332–33, 338–39.

8. Chambers, 2:337.

9. Henslowe, *Henslowe's Diary*, 16, fol. 7.

10. On the ambiguity of "ne," see Henslowe, *Henslowe's Diary*, xxxiv–v. On "ne" as an abbreviation for Newington Butts, see Frazer, "Henslowe's 'ne.'"

11. Chambers, *William Shakespeare*, 2:331–32.

12. On the unreliability of even the dates of these accounts of payment, see Henslowe, *Henslowe's Diary*, xxx–xxxi.

13. *Henry IV, Part 1*, ed. David Kastan, 1.1.26.

14. *King Lear*, ed. R.A. Foakes, 1.2.103.

15. *Henry V*, ed. T. W. Craik, 1–2.

16. For a comprehensive overview of Shakespeare's chronology as well as recent scholarship on attribution and chronology, see Taylor

and Egan, *New Oxford Shakespeare: Authorship Companion*, particularly chapter 25, by Taylor and Rory Loughnane, "The Canon and Chronology of Shakespeare's Works," 417–602. Taylor and Loughnane take issue with the previous authority on chronology, E. K. Chambers, who was considerably more skeptical about the use of internal evidence in dating the plays. See "The Problem of Chronology," in Chambers, *William Shakespeare*, 1:243–74, and Chambers, "The Disintegration of Shakespeare."

17. For the proliferation of digitalized tests, compare the chapters on "The Canon and Chronology" in the 1986 Wells and Taylor *William Shakespeare: A Textual Companion*, 69–109, with that in the 2017 Taylor and Egan, *New Oxford Shakespeare: Authorship Companion*, 417–592: the former contains twelve tables and graphs, the latter nineteen.

18. Taylor and Egan, *New Oxford Shakespeare: Authorship Companion*, 449.

19. Kevin Gilvary also reaches this conclusion in *Dating Shakespeare's Plays*, 469.

20. E. A. J. Honigmann pushes the beginning of Shakespeare's career back to the mid-1580s in *Shakespeare's Impact on His Contemporaries*, esp. 53–66. Oxfordians, in claiming that Edward de Vere wrote the plays attributed to Shakespeare, maintain that no play can be proven to have been written after 1604, the year of de Vere's death, and thereby justify antedating the composition of the entire canon by as many as two or three decades. For comparisons of the Oxfordians with the traditional chronologies, see Gilvary, *Dating Shakespeare's Plays*.

21. On the absence of external evidence for placing *The Tempest* after *The Winter's Tale* and *Cymbeline*, see Dawson's iconoclastic "Tempest in a Teapot"; and McMullan, *Shakespeare and the Idea of Late Writing*, 78–81.

22. Taylor and Egan, *New Oxford Shakespeare: Authorship Companion*, v.

23. See Werstine, *Early Modern Playhouse Manuscripts*, 245–357. One of the eight dated playhouse manuscripts, *John a Kent*, is an exception. According to Werstine, the hand in which the date was written is not that of the Master of the Revels, Edmund Tilney, nor is it that of the author, Anthony Munday (245–47).

24. For the page layout of Harleian 7368, see *Sir Thomas More*, ed. John Jowett, 344–51.

25. *Sir Thomas More*, ed. Alexander Dyce, preface.

26. For Alfred W. Pollard's round up of scholarly support for Shakespeare's contribution in his 1923 edition of essays, *Shakespeare's Hand in the Play of "Sir Thomas More,"* see Werstine, "Shakespeare More or Less."

27. Paul Werstine, the scholar who has most closely studied early modern playhouse manuscripts from the period, remains skeptical. Werstine, *Early Modern Playhouse Manuscripts*, 252. See also James Purkis's reappraisal of Shakespeare's complexly interactive contribution to the manuscript in *Shakespeare and Manuscript Drama*, esp. 247–91.

28. The first complete works edition to include *Sir Thomas More* is Alexander 1951, as appendix; subsequent editions follow suit. See *Sir Thomas More*, ed. John Jowett, 467.

29. *Sir Thomas More*, ed. John Jowett, 5–29.

30. Taylor and Egan, *The New Oxford Shakespeare: Authorship Companion*, 548. Werstine gives 1586–1605 as the date range in *Early Modern Playhouse Manuscripts*, 250. Jowett has narrowed the gap by dating the "Original Text" 1600 and the additions 1603–1604; *Sir Thomas More*, ed. John Jowett, 425.

31. Greg, *The Shakespeare First Folio*, 102–3nH.

32. The theory of "continuous copy" maintained that playhouse promptbooks underwent repeated rehandling and by multiple hands. For its promulgation by Alfred Pollard, see Egan, *The Struggle for Shakespeare's Text*, 17–24. For a recent revival of the theory to explain the relation of the three *Hamlet* texts, see Menzer, *The Hamlets*.

33. Malone-Boswell 1821, 1:xvii.

34. Wells et al., eds., *Shakespeare: A Textual Companion*, 109.

35. Bloom, *Shakespeare*, xii–xv.

36. Garber, *Shakespeare after All*, xi–xii.

37. Traversi, *William Shakespeare: The Early Comedies; Shakespeare: The Last Phase*. See also Traversi's *An Approach to Shakespeare* that breaks into two volumes at what he accepts as the chronological midpoint of the canon, with *Twelfth Night* and *Troilus and Cressida*.

38. Bradley, *Shakespearean Tragedy*.

39. Tillyard, *Shakespeare's History Plays*.

40. Beckwith, *Shakespeare and the Grammar of Forgiveness*. For the uncertainty regarding the chronological order of the romances, see note 21 above.

41. Clemen, *The Development of Shakespeare's Imagery*; McDonald, *Shakespeare's Late Style*; Adelman, *Suffocating Mothers*; Greenblatt, *Shakespeare's Freedom*; Palfrey and Stern, *Shakespeare in Parts*; Parker, *Shakespearean Intersections*.

42. "The Avoidance of Love: A Reading of *King Lear*," in Cavell, *Disowning Knowledge*, 39–123.

43. Peter Erickson, "Introduction," in Berger, *Making Trifles of Terrors*, viii–ix.

44. Editions of Jonson's works followed Jonson's intention that they be arranged by genre from the time of the 1616 folio until the 2012 Cambridge edition, in print and online, which "breaks with this tradition by sequencing the texts chronologically," thereby overriding Jonson's generic groups that, the editors maintain, "made it difficult always to see the overall shape and progression of Jonson's career." *The Cambridge Edition of the Works of Ben Jonson Online*, https://universitypublishing online.org/cambridge/benjonson/about/general_intro/chronology/.

45. Meres, *Palladis tamia*, 282r.

46. On 1066 as a generic determinant in the first folio, see de Grazia, *"Hamlet" without Hamlet*, 52–60.

47. Holinshed, *Third Volume of Chronicles*, title page.

48. On the sixty-year duration of the "43-play canon," see Kirwan, *Shakespeare and the Idea of Apocrypha*, 18–28.

49. Nicholas Rowe's *The Works of Mr. William Shakespear* (1709) is in 6 volumes. Samuel Johnson, George Steevens, and Isaac Reed's *The Plays of William Shakspeare* (1803) is in 21.

50. On the lifting of the classicizing frame, see Boase, "Illustrations of Shakespeare's Plays," 86; Sillars, *The Illustrated Shakespeare*, 35–36; and de Grazia, "Shakespeare's Anecdotal Character," 2–3.

51. On Jacob Tonson's efforts to confer classical status on Shakespeare as well as a number of other English authors through his editions, see Hamm, "Rowe's Shakespeare (1709) and the Tonson House Style."

52. Rowe 1709, 1:xviii. All subsequent citations of Rowe 1709 will be included in text.

53. On lack of education as Shakespeare's signature characteristic up through the eighteenth century, see de Grazia, "Anecdotal Character," 3–5.

54. In his 1765 edition, Samuel Johnson alters the 1623 ordering of the comedies. In volume 1, he retains Pope's coupling of the two "original"

comedies and follows with three plays set in cities: *Merchant of Venice*, *Two Gentlemen of Verona*, and *Measure for Measure*. Volume 2 contains five plays with idyllic or country settings: *As You Like It*, *Love's Labor's Lost*, *The Winter's Tale*, *Twelfth Night*, and *The Merry Wives of Windsor*.

55. Orgel, "Shakespeare and the Kinds of Drama," in *The Authentic Shakespeare*, 143–58; and *Imagining Shakespeare*, 20–24.

56. Johnson and Steevens 1778, "An Attempt to Ascertain the Order in which the Plays Attributed to Shakspeare were Written," 1:272.

57. Letter from the Earl of Charlemont, August 18, 1777, quoted in Prior, *Life of Edmond Malone*, 51–52.

58. Johnson and Steevens 1778, 1:270–71.

59. Johnson and Steevens 1778, 1:346.

60. For Malone's final list of the play's in chronological order, see Malone-Boswell 1821, 295–96.

61. Malone, *Supplement to the edition of Shakspeare's Plays*, 1:v.

62. Malone, 1:viii. On *Pericles*'s migrations in and out of the canon, see Munro, "Young Shakespeare/Late Shakespeare." For Malone's rejection of the appended plays, see Oya, "Authenticating the Inauthentic."

63. Malone, *A Dissertation on the three parts of King Henry VI*, The Contents.

64. Malone-Boswell 1821, 2:334, 327, 318. Subsequent references to this volume appear parenthetically in text.

65. On Malone's late and dismissive use of Henslowe's papers, see Schoch, *Writing the History of the British Stage: 1660–1900*, 284–87.

66. Malone-Boswell 1821, introductory note to historical plays, 5:n.p.

67. For Boswell's dilemma, see de Grazia, *Shakespeare Verbatim*, 148.

68. Malone-Boswell 1821, introductory note to the historical plays, 15:n.p.

69. There are a few minor unexplained divergences, however, between Malone's chronology (2:295–96) and the order in which the plays were printed (cf. table of contents, 1:lxxiv–lxxvi). The order of *Macbeth*, *Julius Caesar*, and *Twelfth Night* is altered and that of *Coriolanus* and *Timon of Athens* is inverted.

70. Hurdis, *Cursory remarks*, 5. Subsequent references appear parenthetically in text.

71. Coleridge, *Literary Remains of Samuel Taylor Coleridge*, 2:84–97. Coleridge's three orders are most conveniently accessed in *Coleridge's*

Shakespearean Criticism, 1:237–42. The 1802 chronology derived from Coleridge's manuscript, now in the British Library (Add MS 34225, ff. 52), may have been written in preparation for an edition. The 1810 and 1819 lectures are based on notes from his lectures; see Foakes's headnote to the 1819 lecture in Coleridge, *Lectures 1808–1819*, 2:370–72 at 371. John Payne Collier records another list, from his mother, in Coleridge, *Coleridge on Shakespeare*, app. A, 132–33n1.

72. Coleridge, *Coleridge's Shakespearean Criticisms*, 1:238, 241–42.

73. Advertisement for the 1819 lectures, quoted in, Coleridge, *Lectures 1808–1819*, 2:370.

74. He appears to have been referring to either Wordsworth's poems or his own, in Coleridge, *Table Talk*, 1:453 and n5. For "Coleridge's projected edition of Shakespeare," see Badawi, *Coleridge: Critic of Shakespeare*, app. B, 204–17.

75. From *The Notebooks of Samuel Taylor Coleridge* as quoted by Han, *Romantic Shakespeare*, 73.

76. Coleridge, *Lectures 1808–1819*, 1:240.

77. Coleridge, *Coleridge's Shakespearean Criticism*, 1:236.

78. Coleridge, *Table Talk*, 1:468.

79. Coleridge, *Coleridge's Criticism of Shakespeare*, 1:187. On Coleridge's coinage of "psychological," see p. 1.

80. Coleridge, *Lectures 1808–1819*, 1:306.

81. Coleridge, 1:153

82. Coleridge, 2:374 and n6.

83. See H. J. Jackson, "Coleridge's Biographia," 54.

84. *Biographia Literaria*, quoted by Jackson, who notes the discrepancy, "Coleridge's Biographia," 63.

85. See, for example, Sylvan Barnet, who is confident that "today we run no such danger as that which in the eighteenth century beset James Hurdis"; Signet 1963, v.

86. Several editors worked on Shakespeare's chronology—Alexander Chalmers, Nathan Drake, Alexander Dyce, and John Payne Collier—but their editions all loosely follow the folio order.

87. Collier, *Reasons for a New Edition of Shakespeare's Works*, 52.

88. See Murphy, *Shakespeare in Print*, 176–77.

89. Furnivall, "The Founder's Prospectus," 6.

90. Furnivall, 6–7

91. Furnivall, 6–7n3.

92. Gervinus, *Shakespeare Commentaries*, 22.

93. Furnivall, "*The Succession of Shakspere's Works*," xlvi.

94. *The Leopold Shakspere* (1877) was reprinted as *The Royal Shakspere* in 1881.

95. Furnivall, *The Succession of Shakspere's Works*, xix–xlix.

96. On metrical tests as an English rather than German fixation, see Marvin Spevack, "Furnivall, Gervinus, and the Germanization of the New Shakspere Society," 3–4.

97. Furnivall, "The Founder's Prospectus," 6.

98. Furnivall, 7.

99. Bathurst, *Remarks on the Differences*, 6.

100. Bathurst appears to have relied on the 1790 and 1821 chronologies of Malone (see note 4 above) as well as that of Chalmers reproduced by Boswell in Malone-Boswell 1821, 2:470–71.

101. Bathurst, *Remarks on the Differences*, 1.

102. Furnivall, "The Founder's Prospectus," 7.

103. Furnivall, 8.

104. Fleay, "On Metrical Tests," 2.

105. Fleay, "On Metrical Tests," 2, and *Shakespeare Manual*, 122.

106. Fleay, *Shakespeare Manual*, 134, 126.

107. Chambers, "The Disintegration of Shakespeare."

108. For the Furnivall-Dowden connection, see Murphy, "Shakespeare and Chronology," 131–32.

109. Dowden, *Shakspere: His Mind and Art*. For the trial table, see xvi–vii. Subsequent references to this work appear parenthetically in text.

110. For Dowden's appreciation of the metrical tests from Malone to Fleay, see *Shakspere: His Mind and Art*, 6–7n.

111. On the association of Shakespeare's genius with the Reformation, "the boundary line which divides two periods, at the point of transition from medieval to modern," see Gervinus, *Shakespeare Commentaries*, 872.

112. Dowden, *Shakspere: His Mind and Art*, 47–48.

113. Dowden, "Shakspere's Last Plays," in *Shakspere: His Mind and Art* (1875), 378–430.

114. Dowden, *Shakspere: His Mind and Art*, 56. For a probing critique of Dowden's genre and the idea of authorial lateness it promulgated, see McMullan, *Shakespeare and the Idea of Late Writing*, 50–78.

115. Several recent editions of Dowden's *Shakespeare: A Critical Study of His Mind and Art*—Routledge and Kegan Paul (1971), Atlantic (2003, 2009), Cambridge University Press (2009), and Andesite Press (2015, 2017)—return to the 1875 first edition, omitting the work's most significant and enduring contribution: the naming of the "Romances."

116. Dowden, *Shakspere: His Mind and Art*, 339.

117. Orgel, "Desire and Pursuit of the Whole," esp. 292.

118. Dowden also adds a biography and notes to Irving 1888 in which the plays are "arranged as nearly as possible to the order they were supposed to have been written by Shakespeare," 1:x.

119. See Samuel Schoenbaum, *Shakespeare's Lives*, 359.

120. Alexander 1951, xxxiv–xl.

121. Steve Sohmer, "'Double Time' Crux in *Othello* Solved," 214. For a full account of the "discovery" of the double-time theory, see *Othello*, New Variorum Edition, ed. H. H. Furness, 358–72.

122. Graham Bradshaw, "Obeying the Time in *Othello*."

123. Sohmer, "'Double Time' Crux in *Othello* Solved, 214–38.

124. Allen, "The Two Parts of *Othello*."

125. Jonathan Gil Harris, "Crumpled Handkerchiefs: William Shakespeare's and Michel Serres's Palimpsested Time," in *Untimely Matter*, 182–84; Hutson, "'Lively Evidence.'"

126. RSC 2007, 2471–75.

127. New Oxford 2017.

128. New Oxford 2016, inside flap.

129. Taylor and Egan, *New Oxford Shakespeare: Authorship Companion*, 485, 526. See also Gilvary, *Dating Shakespeare's Plays*, where each chapter on the dating of a play is preceded by the earliest and latest possible date of composition.

CHAPTER THREE

1. Figure 3.1 is an anonymous engraving of James Quin's performance at Covent Garden in 1749 of *Coriolanus, or the Roman Matron*, an adaptation of Shakespeare's play by Thomas Sheridan. See Ripley, *"Coriolanus" on Stage*, 91–94.

2. Figure 3.2 is an engraving by James Caldwell from a painting by Gavin Hamilton, exhibited in 1790 and now lost. The engraving was published in Boydell, *A Collection of Prints*, xxix. For Hamilton's painting, see Cassidy, *Life & Letters of Gavin Hamilton*, 82.

3. For an account of the gradual development from the makeshift staging of the Restoration theater to the picture-perfect realistic productions of the Kembles at the turn of the nineteenth century, see Lily Bess Campbell, *A History of Costuming on the English Stage between 1660 and 1823*.

4. On Garrick's distaste for "the Roman shape," see Pentzell, "Garrick's Costuming," 1, 26–30, 39. For an engraving of a young Garrick in a balletic *tonnelet* skirt similar to Quin's, see Orgel, *Imagining Shakespeare*, 54, fig. 2.10.

5. For an account of the drawing and a reproduction of the manuscript page on which it appears, see Foakes, *Illustrations of the English Stage*, 48–51.

6. On the emergence of world pictures in the eighteenth century, see Wilhelm Dilthey, "The Types of World-View and Their Development." For a mid-twentieth-century account of a world picture as a "fixed system" that "inspired the minds and imaginations of all men of the Renaissance," including Shakespeare, see Tillyard, *The Elizabethan World Picture*. For a recent use of the same model, though pluralized to cover early modern Europe and the Americas, see Roland Greene, who identifies five key words as "the working terms on which worldviews are established"; Greene, *Five Words*, 14.

7. For a list of historians and theorists who have located "a fundamental change in the recognition and representation of historical time *in* a time that is either called 'Romantic' or dated to a period (roughly 1770 to 1830)," see Chandler, *England in 1819*, 101.

8. Jameson, *A Singular Modernity*, 29, 28.

9. For the theatrical *habit* or *costume à la Romaine*, also known as the "Roman shape," consisting of cuirass, skirt, buskins, and heavily plumed helmet, see Odell, *Shakespeare from Betterton to Irving*, 1:207–9.

10. Plutarch, *The Lives of the Noble Grecians and Romanes, Compared*, quoted in *Coriolanus*, ed. Peter Holland, 434.

11. Motley, *Baroque & Roll*, 106.

12. Volumnia's ten lines printed beneath the engraving correspond to *Coriolanus*, ed. Peter Holland, 5.3.167–77.

13. *Coriolanus*, ed. Peter Holland, 5.3.168, 169, 175.

14. See Naiden, *Ancient Supplication*, 51–55, and app. 1b, "Acts of Supplication in Latin Authors," 338–63.

15. For Raphael's influence on Hamilton, see Boase, "Illustrations of Shakespeare's Plays," 99; and Irwin, "Gavin Hamilton," 96, 99; for the

influence of Poussin on eighteenth-century staging of *Coriolanus*, see George, "Poussin's Coriolanus," 2–10.

16. On the drawing's costumes, see Cerasano, "'Borrowed Robes,'" 45–48; Foakes, *Illustrations of the English Stage*, 49–51; and *Titus Andronicus*, ed. Jonathan Bate, 38–43.

17. On the *Figurenposition* of the Vice on both the medieval scaffold and the Shakespearean platform stage, see Weimann, *Shakespeare and the Popular Tradition*, 115–16, 224–37. On the "sword of lath," see Crosbie, "The Longleat Manuscript Reconsidered," 225–33.

18. See Smith, "Some Principles of Elizabethan Stage Costume," 242 and n10.

19. See Astington, *Stage and Picture in the English Renaissance*, 195.

20. For Jacques Petit's letter to Anthony Bacon, dated January 1596, see Ungerer, "Unrecorded Elizabethan Performance," 107–8; see also *Titus Andronicus*, ed. Bate, 43. The spelling in the quotation above has been modernized.

21. See Cerasano, "'Borrowed Robes,'" 51. On an acting company's investment in their wardrobe, see Jones and Stallybrass, *Renaissance Clothing*, 178–79.

22. See Jones and Stallybrass, *Renaissance Clothing*, 25–26, 190–91.

23. Lublin, "Shakespearean Visual Semiotics," 245. See also Lublin, *Costuming the Shakespearean Stage*, 83–86. Lublin does not discuss Shakespeare's two "toga/tongue" cruxes: Coriolanus's "wolvish toge" and the Venetian "toged consuls"; see *Coriolanus*, ed. Peter Holland, 2.3.113 and Long Note 425, and *Othello*, ed. E. A. J. Honigmann, 1.1.24, n24.

24. Henslowe, *Henslowe's Diary*, 109, 110, fol. 56.

25. Norland, "Neo-Latin Drama in Britain," 473.

26. For the St. John's costume inventories, see Billington, "Sixteenth-Century Drama in St. John's College," 6–8.

27. See Smith, "Some Principles of Elizabethan Stage Costume," 252.

28. Peacock, "Inigo Jones and the Arundel Marbles," 75–90.

29. Diana de Marly discusses and reproduces both sketches in "The Establishment of Roman Dress in Seventeenth-Century Portraiture," 445, 447.

30. Samuel Pepys records having seen Corneille's tragedy in London on March 8, 1664; Pepys, *Diary of Samuel Pepys*, 5:79.

31. See *OED Online*, s.v. "costume," n.2b, https://www.oed.com/. On the distinction between *clothes* and *costumes*, see Jones and Stallybrass, *Renaissance Clothing*, 182–83.

32. Henslowe, *Henslowe's Diary*, app. 2, 316–25.

33. Malone, "Historical Account," in Malone-Boswell 1821, 3:115, 118, 178.

34. Orgel, *Imagining Shakespeare*, 47.

35. Josiah Boydell reproduces his uncle's letter dated May 1, 1789, in the preface to *A Collection of Prints*. On the inception of the gallery, see Ashton, "The Boydell Shakespeare Gallery," 37–43.

36. Orgel, *Imagining Shakespeare*, 50, 56.

37. On Hamilton's study, excavation, restoration, and sale of antiquities, see Irwin, "Gavin Hamilton."

38. Strong, *Painting the Past*, 28.

39. Hammerschmidt-Hummel, "Boydell's Shakespeare Gallery," 34–35, 39.

40. On Kemble's familiarity with Hamilton's work, see Sachs, *Roman Antiquity*, 195.

41. Boaden, *Memoirs of the Life of John Philip Kemble*, 1:425.

42. Boaden, *Memoirs of the Life of John Philip Kemble*, 1:239.

43. Boaden, *Memoirs of Mrs. Siddons*, 2:290–91.

44. Kemble was also celebrated in the role of two other Romans: Cato in Joseph Addison's *Cato* and Brutus in Shakespeare's *Julius Caesar*.

45. In *Minerva*, New York, October 4, 1823, quoted by Ripley, *"Coriolanus" on Stage*, 137.

46. See Ripley, *"Coriolanus" on Stage*, 120.

47. Kemble, *John Philip Kemble's Promptbook*, 1, 45.

48. Hazlitt, "Mr. Kemble's Retirement," 8:375.

49. Walter Scott, "Life of Kemble," 198. For additional examples of Kemble's patrician self-Romanizing, see Sachs, *Romantic Antiquity*, 197–200.

50. Thomas Lawrence, *John Philip Kemble as Coriolanus at the Hearth of Tullus Aufidius*, in the Guildhall Art Gallery, London; Peter Francis Bourgeois, *John Philip Kemble as Coriolanus with a Statue of Mars*, in John Soane's Museum, London; an engraved portrait by Thomas Cook, frontispiece to *Coriolanus* in Inchbald, *The British Theatre*, v.

51. Now in the Guildhall Art Gallery, London. https://commons
.wikimedia.org/wiki/File:Thomas_Lawrence_-_John_Philip_Kemble
_as_Coriolanus_(1798).jpg.

52. Now in John Soane's Museum, London. http://collections.soane
.org/object-p99.

53. From Scott's review in the *Quarterly Review* (June 1826), reprinted in Wells, *Shakespeare in the Theatre*, 33. On the interest in the
"authentic" past shared by Kemble, Scott, and Malone, and their counterrevolutionary inclinations, see Watson, "Kemble, Scott, and the
Mantle of the Bard."

54. According to Ripley, the procession was introduced by Thomas
Sheridan in his adaptation performed in 1754 at Covent Garden, 105–6.

55. For a facsimile of Kemble's numbered manuscript list of forty-
seven entries for the ovation procession, see Kemble, *John Philip Kemble
Promptbook*, ed. Shattuck, vol. 2, app.

56. See Martindale, *Triumphs of Caesar*, 109–11.

57. Caesar, *Commentaries of Caesar*, 336. A copy of this lavish folio
was owned by the antiquarian and neoclassical architect John Soane;
for Soane and Kemble, see Dobson, "John Philip Kemble," 96.

58. See Halliday, "Literary Sources."

59. Boaden, *Memoirs of the Life of John Philip Kemble*, 1:280.

60. Ripley reproduces the 1811 prints in *"Coriolanus" on Stage*, 124–35.
For the origin of the prints and their fidelity to Kemble's production,
see Rosenfeld, *Georgian Scene Painters and Scene Painting*, 146.

61. Baugh, "Stage Design from Loutherbourg to Poel," 314.

62. Odell, *Shakespeare from Betterton to Irving*, 2:104.

63. John Finlay, *Miscellanies* (1835), quoted in Moody, "Romantic
Shakespeare," 45.

64. For details of Robert Smirke's rebuilding of the theater, see Dobson, "Nationalisms," 44.

65. From Bell's *Weekly Messenger*, June 29, 1817, quoted in Ripley,
"Coriolanus" on Stage, 136.

66. Thomas Gilliland, quoted in Baker, *John Philip Kemble*, 268.

67. Suetonius, *Lives of the Caesars*, 58.

68. From the *Examiner*, March 18, 1838, reprinted in Wells, *Shakespeare in the Theatre*, 77–78. On the pressure to come up with a "more
historically accurate Rome," with both scenery and costume faithful to
a republican rather than an imperial Rome, see Sachs, 206.

69. Advertisement, *Shakspeare's Coriolanus*, ed. R. W. Elliston

70. Advertisement, *Shakspeare's Coriolanus*, ed. R. W. Elliston, vi.

71. John Cole in *The Life and Theatrical Times of Charles Kean* (1860), quoted in Robinson, "John Philip Kemble," 728.

72. J. R. Planché, introductory notice to *Julius Caesar*, *The Pictorial Edition of the Works of Shakspere*, ed. Charles Knight, 2:220.

73. *Shakspeare's Coriolanus*, ed. R. W. Elliston, vi.

74. From Charles Knight's 1838 prospectus to the *Pictorial Edition of the Works of Shakspere*, quoted in Murphy, *Shakespeare in Print*, 174.

75. Knight, *The Pictorial Edition of the Works of Shakspere*, 2:149.

76. J. R. Planché, introductory notice to *Julius Caesar*, *The Pictorial Edition of the Works of Shakspere*, ed. Charles Knight, 2:219.

77. Niebuhr, *Roman History*, 1:xxix, 444–59, quote from 450.

78. *The Pictorial Edition of the Works of Shakspere*, ed. Charles Knight 2:148.

79. *Coriolanus*, ed. H. H. Furness Jr., xi.

80. Elizabeth Inchbald, preface to *Coriolanus; or The Roman Matron*, in *The British Theatre*, 5:5.

81. On Kemble's placating cuts, see Ripley, *"Coriolanus" on Stage*, 117–23; and Bate, "The Romantic Stage," 99–100.

82. *Coriolanus*, ed. Peter Holland, 1.1.13–23, 74–81.

83. Ripley, *"Coriolanus" on Stage*, 123.

84. William Hazlitt, "Coriolanus," in Hazlitt, *Collected Works*, 1:214. For Kemble's counterrevolutionary inclinations, see Dobson, "Nationalisms," 43–46.

85. Hazlitt, "An Authentic Narrative," in Hazlitt, *Collected Works*, 8:348.

86. On the Old Price Riots that disrupted sixty-seven productions of *Macbeth*, see Bate, *Shakespearean Constitutions*, 42–45.

87. Planché, *Recollections and Reflections*, 1:52–53.

88. See Schoch, *Shakespeare's Victorian Stage*, 74–79.

89. Anonymous review, *The New York Mirror*, September 29, 1832, 98.

90. Orgel, *Spectacular Performances*, 52–53.

91. Planché, *Recollections and Reflections*, 1:52.

92. For a reproduction of the playbill for Kemble's 1823 *King John*, see *King John*, ed. Jesse M. Lander and J. J. M. Tobin, fig. 9.

93. Planché, *Recollections and Reflections*, 1:56–57.

94. Planché, *Recollections and Reflections*, 1:57.

95. Douce, *Illustrations of Shakspeare*, 2:283.

96. For the coinage of "the spirit of the age" at the turn of the nineteenth century, see Chandler, *England in 1819*, 105–14. For uses of the phrase in England, see Himmelfarb, *Spirit of the Age*, 1–18.

97. John Stuart Mill, *Spirit of the Age*, 1.

98. See Story, "Hazlitt's Definition of the Spirit of the Age," 101–2.

99. Orgel, *Imagining Shakespeare*, 47.

100. Planché, *History of British Costume*, xi.

101. Douce, *Illustrations of Shakspeare*, 2:285n.

102. Planché, *History of British Costume*, xi.

103. Planché, xi, note.

104. Unless otherwise specified, all quotations from Douce are to *Illustrations of Shakspeare*, 2:281–84.

105. In the illustrations to Rowe 1709, the characters in bespoke costumes are supernatural (the witches in *Macbeth*, the ghosts in *Richard III*), Greek and Roman characters are in costume *à la Romaine*, and the king in *Henry VIII* is positioned and dressed after Holbein's portrait, with other court figures in periwigs and waistcoats. On these illustrations and their rich sourcing in the traditions of painting and engraving, see Sillars, *The Illustrated Shakespeare*, 31–72.

106. Review of Planché's *Dramatic Costume*, *Gentleman's Magazine*, January 1825), 53.

107. Douce, *Illustrations of Shakspeare*, 2:283.

108. Hegel, *Hegel's Aesthetics*, 1:264. Subsequent page numbers to this work will be given parenthetically in text.

109. For the use of a Marxist inflection of Hegel's "necessary anachronism" to resolve the clash of periods in Scott's historical novels, see Lukács, *The Historical Novel*, 61–63.

110. Martin Heidegger, "The Age of the World Picture," 115–154. Subsequent page numbers will appear parenthetically in the text.

111. Blumenberg, *Legitimacy of the Modern Age*, 457–81, esp. 457–63. Cf. Chandler, "The Age of the Spirit of the Age," in Chandler, *England in 1819*, 105–6.

112. The proscenium stage has the same visual effect as the picture frame in Rayna Kalas's *Frame, Glass, Verse*: to abstract its subject from the world, to represent it as complete and true to itself and therefore real. See Kalas, 5–9, 22–35.

113. Jameson, *A Singular Modernity*, 51. Subsequent citations to this work appear parenthetically in text.

114. Jameson, *Postmodernism*, 3.

115. Jameson, xi.

116. Jameson, *A Singular Modernity*, 28.

117. Jameson, 26.

118. Ripley, *"Coriolanus" on Stage*, 114, 114–42.

CHAPTER FOUR

1. For Hector's anachronism, see chapter 1, 23–29.

2. *King Lear*, ed. R. A. Foakes, 3.2.79–80. All further references to this play are to this edition and will be cited parenthetically in the text.

3. The prophecy, while absent from the 1608 quarto of *King Lear*, appears in the 1623 folio and in the traditional or composite editions of the play introduced in the eighteenth century.

4. Geoffrey of Monmouth, *The "Historia regum Britannie" of Geoffrey of Monmouth V*, bk. 2, chap. 10, p. 29.

5. Geoffrey of Monmouth, bk. 7, chap. 2, pp. 108–30.

6. For a catalog of the 217 surviving manuscripts of the *Historia* and a list of the 90 surviving independent manuscripts of the *Prophetie Merlini*, see Geoffrey of Monmouth, *The "Historia regum Britannie" of Geoffrey of Monmouth III*, 330–32.

7. H. Howard, *A Defensative against the Poyson of Supposed Prophecies* (1620), as quoted by Thomas, *Religion and the Decline of Magic*, 467.

8. On the dismissal of the Fool's prophecy as spurious or corrupt and its printing as two discrete prophecies in the eighteenth and twentieth century editions, see de Grazia, "The Fool's Promised Exit," 303–5, 349n4.

9. See, for example, *King Lear*, ed. R. A. Foakes, 269n95.

10. Holinshed, *Chronicles of England, Scotlande, and Irelande*, vol. 1, bk. 2, ch. 5, p. 12.

11. Holinshed, vol. 2, bk. 2, ch. 36, p. 53.

12. On the surprisingly late standardization of AD time and the even later standardization of BC time, see Blackburn and Holford-Strevens, *Oxford Companion to the Year*, 781.

13. On the use of the 6000 year schema by both chronologists and theologians, see Westman, *The Copernican Question*, 119–21. On its

importance for the English Reformation, see Firth, *Apocalyptic Tradition in Reformation Britain*, 5–22.

14. Abodah Zarah 9a, *Hebrew-English Edition of the Babylonian Talmud: Abodah Zarah*, 2:16. I am indebted to John Parker for having located this source.

15. Philip Melanchthon, quoted by Barr, "Why the World Was Created in 4004 B.C.," 575, 581. For a description of the 6000 year schema and prophecy—"two thousand Vayne, two thousand Lawe two thousand Christe"—.see Scheltco à Geveren, *Of the ende of this worlde*, 12v, and Firth, *Apocalyptic Tradition in Reformation Britain*.

16. See Leigh, *The Christians Watch*, E4r–E5v, emphasis added.

17. Lucretius, *De rerum natura*, 1.146; Epicurus, *Letter to Herodotus*, in *Epicurus: The Extant Remains*, para. 39, 21.

18. On the dictum's association with heathenism and skepticism, see Elton, *"King Lear" and the Gods*, 181–88.

19. See the title page of the 1608 quarto: "*M. William Shak-speare: His True Chronicle Historie of the life and death of King LEAR.* . . . As it was played before the Kings Maiestie at Whitehall vpon S. Stephans night in Christmas Hollidayes."

20. Lancelot Andrewes, *XCVI Sermons*, 163, F3r.

21. Augustine, *City of God against the Pagans*, 12.14.517.

22. Croce, *Theory and History of Historiography*, 112.

23. Jaspers, "The Axial Period," *Origin and Goal of History*, 1–25, 12. Jaspers replaces the Christian BC-AD axis with a "deeper cut off point": "the Axial age," spanning from 200 BC to 800 BC, to include China and India as well as the West. For a recent revival of this axis, see Taylor, *A Secular Age*, 151, 792n9.

24. *Henry IV, Part 1*, ed. David Scott Kastan, 1.1.25–27.

25. On the beginning of counting time from the Incarnation by Bede in the eighth century, see Cheney, *A Handbook of Dates*, 1–2.

26. Friedrich Nietzsche, *The Anti-Christ*, 66.

27. Nietzsche, *The Anti-Christ*, 64.

28. On the question of where to locate the threshold of modernity, see Koselleck, *The Practice of Conceptual History*, 156–60.

29. As his translator maintains in his introduction, Hans Blumenberg's defense of modernity specifically targets Karl Löwith's thesis in *Meaning in History* (1949) that the modern idea of progress is a secularization of Christian eschatology. Blumenberg, *Legitimacy of the Modern*

Age, xiv–xvii. For Blumenberg's critique of Carl Schmitt's contention in *Political Theology* (1922) that modern concepts of the state are secularizations of theological concepts, see Blumenberg, 14–15, 89–102.

30. Blumenberg, 15.

31. For Blumenberg's inventory of modern secularizations, see *Legitimacy of the Modern Age*, 14–18.

32. Blumenberg, 138, 178.

33. Blumenberg, 549.

34. Koselleck, *Futures Past*, 232.

35. *Progress* and *development* are among the temporalizing concepts Koselleck sees as emergent along with modernity or the *neue Zeit* in his analysis of "the semantics of historical time." See, for example, Koselleck, "Historical Criteria of Temporalization," in *Futures Past*, 236–48.

36. Koselleck, *Practice of Conceptual History*, 165.

37. See "The Unknown Future and the Art of Prognosis," in Koselleck, *Practice of Conceptual History*, 131–47.

38. Kermode, *Sense of an Ending*, 27. Further references will be cited parenthetically in the text.

39. Bloom, *Shakespeare*, 339.

40. For the performance of *Christus Triumphans* in 1562–1563 at Trinity College, Cambridge, and possibly also at Magdalen College, Oxford, see J. H. Smith's introduction to Foxe, *Two Latin Comedies*, 34, and 215n1. For how the play might have been staged at Magdalen College, see Blank, "Performing Exile." Recent discussions of Foxe's apocalyptic play also include Leo, *Tragedy as Philosophy*, 61–65; Höfele, "John Foxe, *Christus Triumphans*"; and Norland, "John Foxe's Apocalyptic Comedy."

41. *Christus Triumphans*, in Foxe, *Two Latin Comedies*, 209. Further references to Smith's edition will be cited parenthetically in the text.

42. See the definition of both *apocalypse* and *revelation* in *Lexicons of Early Modern English*, http://leme.library.utoronto.ca.

43. In his dedicatory epistle, Foxe refers to Paul's warning to the Thessalonians (2 Thess. 2:1–3) that Christ would not return "before that hellish Antichrist should appear," 207.

44. On the identification of the papacy with the Antichrist, see Bauckham, *Tudor Apocalypse*, 99–108. The play's dramatic peripeteia also marks the turning point of Foxe's ecclesiastical history: the Reformation.

As a messenger announces to Pseudamnus, "Everywhere [men are] being refined by letters and languages. Everywhere they're farting on your orders and shitting on your bulls," *Christus Triumphans*, 351. On the topicalities that draw the play's action to the moment of its writing and staging, see Norland, "John Foxe's Apocalyptic Comedy," 82–83.

45. On the fig tree as a sign of the apocalypse in Augustine, the Old Testament, and the Gospels, see Freccero, "The Fig Tree and the Laurel," 141–42.

46. For the lowering of Christ by pulleys from above on a rainbow of painted boards in productions of the Corpus Christi plays, see Schreyer, *Shakespeare's Medieval Craft*, 112, 218n34.

47. Translated in the Vulgate and in Foxe as "Factum est."

48. For the dramatic use of *catastrophe* derived from Donatus, see Leo, *Tragedy as Philosophy*, 17–20, 51. For its presence in Shakespeare, see de Grazia, "Four Shakespearean Catastrophes."

49. For astronomical catastrophes portending apocalypse, see Granada, "Kepler v. Roeslin." Thanks to John Parker for this reference.

50. In his edition of *King Lear*, Foakes forecloses the possibility by interpolating the stage direction "[*He lays her down*]" at 5.3.259.

51. On the survival of the icon in England after the Reformation—in wood, alabaster, stained glass, and woodcuts, some defaced and others intact—see de Grazia, "*King Lear* in BC Albion," 148–52.

52. For the category of "impossible deictics" in Marlowe's theater, see John Parker, *The Aesthetics of Antichrist*, 236.

53. See, for example, the Penguin *King Lear*, ed. George Hunter, and the note keyed to line 308: "Clearly Lear imagines he sees Cordelia coming to life again," 311.

54. *The Bodleian First Folio, Tragedies*, fol.ss3r.

55. *The Book of Common Prayer*, ed. Brian Cummings, 172.

56. *The History of King Lear*, ed. Nahum Tate, dedicatory epistle.

57. Samuel Johnson, *Johnson on Shakespeare*, 704.

58. Bradley, *Shakespearean Tragedy*, 245. Further references to this work will be cited parenthetically in the text.

59. Elton, *"King Lear" and the Gods*, 334.

60. Kott, *Shakespeare Our Contemporary*, 147

61. Wittreich, *"Image of That Horror,"* 124, 122.

62. Foakes, *Hamlet versus Lear*, 224, 203.

63. Greenblatt, *Shakespearean Negotiations*, 119.

64. Greenblatt, *Shakespearean Negotiations*, 124.

65. For woodcuts of the Man of Sorrows and his *arma*, see Dodgson, *English Devotional Woodcuts*, plates 35–36.

66. Febvre, *Problem of Unbelief in the Sixteenth Century*, 5.

67. Heidegger, "Age of the World Picture," 130.

Bibliography

Editions of Shakespeare

COMPLETE WORKS

Folio 1623: Heminges, John, and Henry Condell, eds. *Mr. William Shakespeares Comedies, Histories, & Tragedies, Published according to the True Originall Copies.* London: Isaac Jaggard and Edward Blount, 1623.

Rowe 1709: Rowe, Nicholas, ed. *The Works of Mr. William Shakespear.* 6 vols. London: Jacob Tonson, 1709.

Pope 1725: Pope, Alexander, ed. *The Works of Shakespear.* 6 vols. London: Jacob Tonson, 1725.

Pope 1728 : Pope, Alexander, ed. *The Works of Shakespear.* 10 vols. London: Jacob Tonson, 1728.

Theobald 1733: Theobald, Lewis, ed. *The Works of Shakespeare.* 7 vols. London: A. Bettesworth, and C. Hitch, J. Tonson, F. Clay, W. Feales, and R. Wellington, 1733.

Johnson 1765: Johnson, Samuel, ed. *The Plays of William Shakespeare.* 8 vols. London: J. and R. Tonson, C. Corbet, H. Woodfall, et al., 1765.

Johnson and Steevens 1778: Johnson, Samuel, and George Steevens, eds. *The Plays of William Shakspeare.* 2nd ed. 10 vols. London: C. Bathurst, 1778.

Malone 1790: Malone, Edmond, ed. *The Plays and Poems of William Shakspeare*. 10 vols. London: H. Baldwin for J. Rivington and Sons, L. Davis, B. White and Son, et al., 1790.

Malone-Boswell 1821: Malone, Edmond, and James Boswell, eds. *The Plays and Poems of William Shakspeare*. 21 vols. London: F. C. and J. Rivington, T. Egerton, J. Cuthell, et al., 1821.

Cambridge 1863–1866: Clark, W. G., and W. A. Wright, eds. *The Works of William Shakespeare*. 9 vols. Cambridge: Cambridge University Press, 1863–1866.

Irving 1888: Irving, Henry, and Frank A. Marshall, eds. *The Henry Irving Shakespeare*. 8 vols. London: Blackie & Son, 1888.

Alexander 1951: Alexander, Peter, ed. *The Complete Works of William Shakespeare: The Alexander Text*. Glasgow: Harper Collins, 2006 (1951).

Signet 1963: Barnet, Sylvan, ed. *The Complete Signet Classic Shakespeare*. New York: Harcourt Brace, 1972 (1963).

Riverside 1974: Evans, G. Blakemore, gen. ed. *The Riverside Shakespeare*. Boston: Houghton Mifflin, 1997 (1974).

Oxford 1987: Wells, Stanley, and Gary Taylor, gen. eds. *The Complete Oxford Shakespeare*. Oxford: Oxford University Press, 1987.

Pelican 2002: Orgel, Stephen, and Albert Braunmuller, eds. *The Complete Pelican Shakespeare*. New York: Penguin, 2002.

RSC 2007: Bate, Jonathan, and Eric Rasmussen, eds. *The RSC Shakespeare: The Complete Works*. Basingstoke: Palgrave Macmillan, 2007.

Bevington 2013: Bevington, David, ed. *The Complete Works of Shakespeare*. 7th ed. London: Pearson, 2013 (1980).

New Oxford 2016: Taylor, Gary, gen. ed. *The New Oxford Shakespeare. Complete Works: Modern Critical Edition*. Oxford: Oxford University Press, 2016.

New Oxford 2017: Taylor, Gary, gen. ed. *The New Oxford Shakespeare. The Complete Works: Critical Reference Edition*. 2 vols. Oxford: Oxford University Press, 2017.

Norton 2016: Greenblatt, Stephen, gen. ed. *The Norton Shakespeare*. New York: W. W. Norton, 2016 (1997).

Arden 2017: Proudfoot, Richard, Ann Thompson, and David Scott Kastan, eds. *The Arden Shakespeare Complete Works*. London: Bloomsbury Arden Shakespeare, 2017 (1998).

The Bodleian First Folio: Digital facsimile of the First Folio of
  Shakespeare's plays, Bodleian Arch. G c.7. http://firstfolio.
  bodleian.ox.ac.uk/.

SINGLE PLAYS

Coriolanus
*Shakspeare's Coriolanus: An Historical Play; From the Prompt Copy of the
  Theatre Royal, Drury Lane.* Edited by R. W. Elliston. London:
  J. Tabby, 1820.
The Tragedie of Coriolanus. Edited by H. H. Furness Jr. New Variorum
  Edition. Philadelphia: J. B. Lippincott, 1928.
Coriolanus. Edited by Peter Holland. Arden Shakespeare, 3rd ser.
  London: Bloomsbury, 2013.

Henry IV, Part I
King Henry IV, Part 1. Edited by David Scott Kastan. Arden Shakespeare, 3rd ser. London: Bloomsbury, 2002.

Henry V
King Henry V. Edited by T. W. Craik. Arden Shakespeare, 3rd ser.
  London: Bloomsbury, 1995.

King John
King John. Edited by Jesse M. Lander and J. J. M. Tobin. Arden
  Shakespeare, 3rd ser. London: Bloomsbury, 2018.

King Lear
The History of King Lear. Revised by Nahum Tate. London: E. Flesher,
  1681.
King Lear. Edited by R. A. Foakes. Arden Shakespeare, 3rd ser.
  London: Thomas Nelson and Sons, 1997.
King Lear. Edited by George Hunter. London: Penguin, 2005.
The Tragedy of King Lear. Edited by Jay L. Halio. Cambridge:
  Cambridge University Press, 2005.

Othello
Othello. Edited by H. H. Furness. New Variorum Edition.
  Philadelphia: J. B. Lippincott, 1886.

Othello. Edited by E. A. J. Honigmann. Arden Shakespeare, 3rd ser. London: Bloomsbury, 1996.

Sir Thomas More

Sir Thomas More: A Play. Edited by Alexander Dyce. London: The Shakespeare Society, 1844.

Sir Thomas More, original text by Anthony Munday and Henry Chettle, censored by Edmund Tilney, revisions co-ordinated by Hand C, revised by Henry Chettle, Thomas Dekker, Thomas Heywood and William Shakespeare. Edited by John Jowett. Arden Shakespeare, 3rd ser. London: Bloomsbury, 2011.

Titus Andronicus

Titus Andronicus. Edited by Jonathan Bate. Arden Shakespeare, 3rd ser. London: Bloomsbury, 2018 (1995).

Troilus and Cressida

The Famous Historie of Troylus and Cresseid. London: George Eld for R. Bonian and H. Walley, 1609.

Troilus and Cressida: First quarto, 1609 / with an introductory note by W. W. Greg. London: Shakespeare Association, 1952.

Troilus and Cressida. Edited by H. N. Hillebrand. Philadelphia: J. B. Lippincott, 1953.

Troilus and Cressida. Edited by Kenneth Muir. Oxford: Clarendon Press, 1982.

Troilus and Cressida. Edited by Anthony Dawson. Cambridge: Cambridge University Press, 2003.

Troilus and Cressida. Edited by Frances A. Shirley. Shakespeare in Production. Cambridge: Cambridge University Press, 2005.

Troilus and Cressida. Edited by David Bevington. Rev. ed. Arden Shakespeare, 3rd ser. London: Bloomsbury, 2014.

Primary and Secondary Sources

Adelman, Janet. *Suffocating Mothers: Fantasies of Maternal Origin in Shakespeare's Plays, "Hamlet" to "The Tempest."* London: Routledge, 1992.

Adorno, Theodor. *Aesthetic Theory.* Edited by Gretel Adorno and Rolf Tiedemann. Translated by Robert Hullot-Kentor. Minneapolis: University of Minnesota Press, 1997.

Alexander, Peter. *A Shakespeare Primer*. London: Nisbet, 1951.

Allen, Ned B. "The Two Parts of *Othello*." *Shakespeare Survey* 21 (1969): 13–30.

Althusser, Louis, and Étienne Balibar. *Reading Capital*. Translated by Ben Brewster. London: Verso, 1979.

Andrewes, Lancelot. *XCVI Sermons*. 2nd ed. London: Richard Badger, 1631.

Apfelbaum, Roger. *Shakespeare's "Troilus and Cressida": Textual Problems and Performance Solutions*. Newark: University of Delaware Press, 2004.

Aravamudan, Srinivas. "The Return of Anachronism." *Modern Language Quarterly* 62, no. 4 (2001): 331–53.

Aristotle. *Aristotle on Poetry and Style*. Translated by G. M. A. Grube. Indianapolis, IN: Bobbs-Merrill, 1958.

Aristotle. *Metaphysica* (*Metaphysics*). In *The Basic Works of Aristotle*, edited by Richard McKeon with an introduction by C. D. C. Reeve and translated by Oxford translators, 685–934. New York: Modern Library, 2009 (1941).

Ashton , Geoffrey. "The Boydell Shakespeare Gallery: Before and After." In *The Painted Word: British History Painting, 1750–1830*, edited by Peter Cannon-Brookes, 37–43. Woodbridge, UK: Boydell, 1991.

Astington, John H. *Stage and Picture in the English Renaissance: The Mirror up to Nature*. Cambridge: Cambridge University Press, 2017.

Augustine. *The City of God against the Pagans*. Edited and translated by R. W. Dyson. Cambridge: Cambridge University Press, 1998.

Bacon, Francis. *The Advancement of Learning*. Edited by Michael Kiernan. Oxford: Clarendon Press, 2000.

Badawi, Muhammad Mustafa. *Coleridge: Critic of Shakespeare*. London: Cambridge University Press, 1973.

Baker, Herschel C. *John Philip Kemble: The Actor in His Theatre*. Cambridge, MA: Harvard University Press, 1942.

Baldwin, T. W. *William Shakspere's Small Latine & Lesse Greeke*. 2 vols. Urbana: University of Illinois Press, 1944.

Barr, James. "Why the World Was Created in 4004 B.C.: Archbishop Ussher and Biblical Chronology." *Bulletin of the John Rylands University Library of Manchester* 67, no. 2 (1985): 575.

Barthes, Roland. "The Discourse of History." Translated by Stephen Bann. *Comparative Criticism* 3 (1981): 7–20.

Bartolovich, Crystal. "Is the Post in Posthuman the Post in Post-medieval?" *Postmedieval: A Journal of Medieval Cultural Studies* 1, no. 1 (April 2010): 18–31.

Bate, Jonathan. "The Romantic Stage." In *Shakespeare: An Illustrated Stage History*, edited by Jonathan Bate and Russell Jackson, 92–111. Oxford: Oxford University Press, 1996.

Bate, Jonathan. *Shakespearean Constitutions: Politics, Theatre, Criticism, 1730–1830*. Oxford: Clarendon Press, 1989.

Bathurst, Charles. *Remarks on the Differences in Shakespeare's Versification in Different Periods of His Life*. London: J. W. Parker & Son, 1857.

Bauckham, Richard. *Tudor Apocalypse: Sixteenth Century Apocalypticism, Millennarianism and the English Reformation from John Bale to John Foxe and Thomas Brightman*. Oxford: Sutton Courtenay Press, 1978.

Baugh, Christopher. "Stage Design from Loutherbourg to Poel." In *The Cambridge History of British Theatre*, edited by Joseph Donohue, 2:309–30. Cambridge: Cambridge University Press, 2004.

Beckwith, Sarah. *Shakespeare and the Grammar of Forgiveness*. Ithaca, NY: Cornell University Press, 2011.

Benjamin, Walter. "Theses on the Philosophy of History." In *Illuminations: Essays and Reflections*, edited by Hannah Arendt and translated by Harry Zohn, 253–64. New York: Schocken Books, 1969.

Berger, Harry, Jr. *Making Trifles of Terrors: Redistributing Complicities in Shakespeare*. Edited by Peter Erickson. Stanford, CA: Stanford University Press, 1997.

Bhabha, Homi K. "DissemiNation." In *Nation and Narration*, edited by Homi K. Bhaba, 291–332. New York: Routledge, 1990.

Billington, Sandra. "Sixteenth-Century Drama in St. John's College, Cambridge." *Review of English Studies* 29, no. 113 (February 1978): 1–10.

Blackburn, Bonnie, and Leofranc Holford-Strevens. *Oxford Companion to the Year*. New York: Oxford University Press, 1999.

Blank, Daniel. "Performing Exile: John Foxe's *Christus Triumphans* at Magdalen College, Oxford." *Renaissance Studies* 30, no. 4 (2016): 581–601.

Bloom, Harold. *Shakespeare: The Invention of the Human.* London: Fourth Estate, 1998.

Blumenberg, Hans. *The Legitimacy of the Modern Age.* Translated by Robert M. Wallace. Cambridge, MA: MIT Press, 1983.

Boaden, James. *Memoirs of Mrs. Siddons Interspersed with Anecdotes of Authors and Actors.* 2 vols. London: Henry Colburn, 1827.

Boaden, James. *Memoirs of the Life of John Philip Kemble, Esq. Including a History of the Stage, from the Time of Garrick to the Present Period.* London: Longman, 1825.

Boase, T. S. R. "Illustrations of Shakespeare's Plays in the Seventeenth and Eighteenth Centuries." *Journal of the Warburg and Courtauld Institutes* 10 (1947): 83–108.

Boruchoff, David. "The Three Greatest Inventions of Modern Times: Scientific Culture and the Cult of Modernity." In *Entangled Knowledge: Scientific Discourses and Cultural Difference,* edited by Klaus Hock and Gesa Mackenthun, 133–63. Münster: Waxmann, 2012.

Bourne, Claire M. L. *Typographies of Performance in Early Modern England.* Oxford: Oxford University Press, forthcoming 2020.

Boydell, Josiah. *A Collection of Prints, from Pictures Painted for the Purpose of Illustrating the Dramatic Works of Shakspeare, by the Artists of Great-Britain.* 2 vols. London: J. & J. Boydell, 1803.

Bradley, A. C. *Shakespearean Tragedy: Lectures on "Hamlet," "Othello," "King Lear," "Macbeth."* London: Penguin, 2005 (1904).

Bradshaw, Graham. "Obeying the Time in *Othello*: A Myth and the Mess It Made." *English Studies* 73, no. 3 (1998): 211–28.

Buchwald, Jed Z., and Mordechai Feingold. *Newton and the Origin of Civilization.* Princeton, NJ: Princeton University Press, 2013.

Burke, Peter. *The Renaissance Sense of the Past.* London: Edward Arnold, 1969.

Burke, Peter. "The Renaissance Sense of the Past Revisited." *Culture and History* 12 (1994): 42–56.

Burke, Peter. "The Sense of Anachronism from Petrarch to Poussin." In *Time in the Medieval World,* edited by C. Humphrey and W. M. Ormrod, 157–73. Rochester, NY: York Medieval Press, 2001.

Burke, Peter. "The Sense of Historical Perspective in Renaissance Italy." *Journal of World History* 11 (1968): 615–32.

Burrow, Colin. *Shakespeare and Classical Antiquity.* Oxford: Oxford University Press, 2013.

Caesar, Julius. *The Commentaries of Caesar*. Translated by William Duncan. London: J. & R. Tonson, 1753.

Campbell, Lily B. *A History of Costuming on the English Stage between 1660 and 1823*. Madison: University of Wisconsin Press, 1918.

Capell, Edward. *Notes and Various Readings to Shakespeare*. 3 vols. London: Edward and Charles Dilly, 1783.

Cassidy, Brendan. *The Life & Letters of Gavin Hamilton (1723–179): Artist & Art Dealer in Eighteenth-Century Rome*. Edited by Brendan Cassidy. London: Harvey Miller, 2011.

Cavell, Stanley. *Disowning Knowledge in Seven Plays of Shakespeare*. Cambridge: Cambridge University Press, 2003 (1987).

Cerasano, Susan P. "'Borrowed Robes,' Costume Prices, and the Drawing of *Titus Andronicus*." *Shakespeare Studies* 22 (1994): 45–57.

Chakrabarty, Dipesh. *Provincializing Europe: Postcolonial Thought and Historical Difference*. Princeton, NJ: Princeton University Press, 2000 (1987).

Chambers, E. K. "The Disintegration of Shakespeare." British Academy Annual Shakespeare Lecture (1924). In *Shakespearean Gleanings*, 1–21. London: Oxford University Press, 1944.

Chambers, E. K. *The Mediaeval Stage*. 2 vols. London: Oxford University Press, 1903.

Chambers, E. K. *William Shakespeare: A Study of Facts and Problems*. 2 vols. Oxford: Clarendon Press, 1930.

Chambers, Ephraïm. *Cyclopædia; or, An Universal Dictionary of Arts and Sciences*. 2 vols. London: D. Midwinter, W. Innys, C. Rivington, et al., 1741.

Chandler, James. *England in 1819: The Politics of Literary Culture and the Case of Romantic Historicism*. Chicago: University of Chicago Press, 1998.

Charnes, Linda. "'So Unsecret to Ourselves': Notorious Identity and the Material Subject in *Troilus and Cressida*." In *Notorious Identity: Materializing the Subject in Shakespeare*, 70–102. Cambridge, MA: Harvard University Press, 1995.

Cheney, C. R., ed. *A Handbook of Dates: For Students of British History*. Cambridge: Cambridge University Press, 2000.

Cicero. *Rhetorica ad Herennium*. Translated by Harry Caplan. Loeb Classical Library. Cambridge, MA: Harvard University Press, 1954.

Clemen, Wolfgang H. *The Development of Shakespeare's Imagery*. London: Methuen, 1963 (1951).

Coleridge, Samuel Taylor. *Coleridge on Shakespeare: The Text of the Lectures of 1811–12*. Edited by R. A. Foakes. London: Routledge, 1971.

Coleridge, Samuel Taylor. *Coleridge's Criticism of Shakespeare: A Selection*. Edited by R. A. Foakes. London: Athlone Press, 1989.

Coleridge, Samuel Taylor. *Coleridge's Shakespearean Criticism*. Edited by Thomas Middleton Raysor. 2 vols. London: Constable, 1930.

Coleridge, Samuel Taylor. *Lectures & Notes on Shakespeare and Other English poets*. London: G. Bell & Sons, 1907.

Coleridge, Samuel Taylor. *Lectures 1808–1819: On Literature*. Edited by R. A. Foakes. Vol. 5, bk. 1–2 of *The Collected Works of Samuel Taylor Coleridge*, gen. ed. Kathleen Coburn, associate ed. Bart Winer. London: Routledge & Kegan Paul; Princeton, NJ: Princeton University Press, 1987.

Coleridge, Samuel Taylor. *The Literary Remains of Samuel Taylor Coleridge*. Collected and edited by Henry Nelson Coleridge. 4 vols. London: William Pickering, 1836–1839.

Coleridge, Samuel Taylor. *Shakespeare, Ben Jonson, Beaumont and Fletcher: Notes and Lectures*. Liverpool: Edward Howell, 1881.

Coleridge, Samuel Taylor. *Specimens of the Table Talk of the Late Samuel Taylor Coleridge*. 2 vols. London: John Murray, 1835.

Coleridge, Samuel Taylor. *Table Talk*. Edited by Carl Woodring. Vol. 14, bk. 1–2, of *The Collected Works of Samuel Taylor Coleridge*, gen. ed. Kathleen Coburn, associate ed. Bart Winer. London: Routledge & Kegan Paul; Princeton, NJ: Princeton University Press, 1990.

Collier, John Payne. *Reasons for a New Edition of Shakespeare's Works*. London: Whittaker, 1841.

Cooper, Helen. *Shakespeare and the Medieval World*. London: Arden Shakespeare, 2014.

Coote, Edmund. *The English School-Master*. London: R. & W. Leybourn for the Company of Stationers, 1656.

Croce, Benedetto. *Theory and History of Historiography*. Translated by Douglas Ainslie. London: George G. Harrap, 1921.

Crosbie, Christopher. "The Longleat Manuscript Reconsidered: Shakespeare and the Sword of Lath." *English Literary Renaissance* 44, no. 2 (2014): 221–40.

Cummings, Brian, ed. *The Book of Common Prayer: The Texts of 1549, 1559, and 1662*. Oxford: Oxford University Press, 2011.

Danby, John F. *Shakespeare's Doctrine of Nature: A Study of "King Lear."* London: Faber and Faber, 1949.

Davidson, Clifford. *Corpus Christi Plays at York: A Context for Religious Drama.* With a contribution in collaboration with Sheila White. AMS Studies in the Middle Ages, no. 30. New York: AMS Press, 2013.

Davies, Thomas. *Memoirs of the Life of David Garrick, Esq. interspersed with characters and anecdotes of his theatrical contemporaries.* 3rd ed. 2 vols. London: Printed for the author, 1781.

Davis, Kathleen. *Periodization and Sovereignty: How Ideas of Feudalism and Secularization Govern the Politics of Time.* Philadelphia: University of Pennsylvania Press, 2008.

Dawson, Anthony B. "Tempest in a Teapot: Critics, Evaluation, Ideology." In *Bad Shakespeare: Revaluations of the Shakespeare Canon,* edited by Maurice Charney, 61–73. Rutherford, NJ: Fairleigh Dickinson University Press, 1988.

de Grazia, Margreta. "Anachronism." In *Cultural Reformations: Medieval and Renaissance in Literary History,* edited by Brian Cummings and James Simpson, 13–32. Oxford: Oxford University Press, 2012.

de Grazia, Margreta. "The Fool's Promised Exit." In *Shakespeare Up Close: Reading Early Modern Texts,* edited by Russ McDonald, Nicholas D. Nace, and Travis D. Williams, 303–8. London: Bloomsbury, 2012.

de Grazia, Margreta. "Four Shakespearean Catastrophes." In *Histories of the Future, c. 1600: On Shakespeare and Thinking Ahead,* edited by Carla Mazzio. Philadelphia: University of Pennsylvania Press, forthcoming.

de Grazia, Margreta. *"Hamlet" without Hamlet.* Cambridge: Cambridge University Press, 2007.

de Grazia, Margreta. "King Lear in BC Albion." In *Medieval Shakespeare: Pasts and Present*s, edited by Ruth Morse, Helen Cooper, and Peter Holland, 138–56. Cambridge: Cambridge University Press, 2013.

de Grazia, Margreta. "The Modern Divide: From Either Side." *Journal of Medieval and Early Modern Studies* 37, no. 3 (2007): 453–67.

de Grazia, Margreta. "Shakespeare's Anecdotal Character." *Shakespeare Survey* 68 (2015): 1–14.

de Grazia, Margreta. *Shakespeare Verbatim: The Reproduction of Authenticity and the 1790 Apparatus.* Oxford: Oxford University Press, 1991.

de Jong, Jan L. *The Power and the Glorification: Papal Pretensions and the Art of Propaganda in the Fifteenth and Sixteenth Centuries.* University Park: Pennsylvania State University Press, 2013.

de Man, Paul. *Blindness and Insight: Essays in the Rhetoric of Contemporary Criticism,* 2nd ed. Minneapolis: University of Minnesota Press, 1995.

de Marly, Diana. "The Establishment of Roman Dress in Seventeenth-Century Portraiture." *Burlington Magazine* 117, no. 868 (July 1975): 442–51.

Derrida, Jacques. "Aphorism Countertime." Translated by Nicholas Royle. In *Acts of Literature,* edited by Derek Attridge, 414–34. London: Routledge, 1992.

Derrida, Jacques. *Specters of Marx: The State of Debt, the Work of Mourning, and the New International.* Translated by Peggy Kamuf. New York: Routledge, 1993.

de Vriese, Herbert. "The Charm of Disenchantment: A Quest for the Intellectual Attraction of Secularization Theory." *Sophia* 49 (2010): 407–28.

Didi-Huberman, Georges. "Before the Image, Before Time: The Sovereignty of Anachronism." In *Compelling Visuality: The Work in and out of History,* edited by Claire Farago and Robert Zwijnenberg, 31–44. Minneapolis: University of Minnesota Press, 2003.

Dilthey, William. "The Types of World-View and Their Development in the Metaphysical Systems." In *Selected Writings,* edited by H. P. Rickman, 133–54. Cambridge: Cambridge University Press, 1976.

Dinshaw, Carolyn, Lee Edelman, Roderick A. Ferguson, Carla Freccero, Elizabeth Freeman, Judith Halberstam, Annamarie Jagose, Christopher Nealon, and Nguyen Tan Hoang. "Theorizing Queer Temporalities: A Roundtable Discussion." *GLQ: A Journal of Gay and Lesbian Studies* 13, no. 2/3 (2007): 177–95.

DiPietro, Cary, and Hugh Grady. "Presentism, Anachronism, and the Case of *Titus Andronicus.*" *Shakespeare* 8, no. 1 (2012): 44–73.

Dobson, Michael. "John Philip Kemble." In *Garrick, Kemble, Siddons, Kean: Great Shakespeareans,* edited by Peter Holland, 2:55–104. London: Continuum, 2010.

Dobson, Michael. "Nationalisms, National Theatres, and the Return of *Julius Caesar.*" In *Roman Shakespeare: Intersecting Times, Spaces, Languages*, edited by Daniela Guardamagna, 33–56. Oxford: Peter Lang, 2018.

Dodgson, Campbell. *English Devotional Woodcuts of the Late Fifteenth Century, With Special Reference to Those in the Bodleian Library.* London: Walpole Society, 1929.

Douce, Francis. *Illustrations of Shakspeare and of Ancient Manners.* 2 vols. London: Longman, 1807.

Dowden, Edward. *Shakspere: A Critical Study of His Mind and Art.* London: H. S. King, 1875.

Dowden, Edward. *Shakspere: A Critical Study of His Mind and Art.* 3rd ed. New York: Harper & Brothers, 1881.

Dowden, Edward. *Shakspere.* Literature Primers. New York: D. Appleton, 1878.

Drayton, Michael. *Poly-olbion. Or A Chorographicall Description of all the Tracts, Rivers, Mountains, Forests, and Other Parts of this Renowned Isle of Great Britain.* London: John Mariott, John Grismand, and Thomas Dewe, 1622.

Dryden, John. *The Works of John Dryden.* Vol. 5, *Poems: The Works of Virgil in English*, edited by William Frost and Vinton A. Dearing. Berkeley: University of California Press, 1987 (1697).

Easterling, P. E. "Anachronism in Greek Tragedy." *Journal of Hellenic Studies* 105 (1985): 1–10.

Ebeling, Herman L. "The Word Anachronism." *Modern Language Notes* 52, no. 2 (1937): 120–21.

Egan, Gabriel. *The Struggle for Shakespeare's Text: Twentieth-Century Editorial Theory and Practice.* Cambridge: Cambridge University Press, 2010.

Elton, William R. *"King Lear" and the Gods.* Lexington: University Press of Kentucky, 1988 (1966).

Elton, William R. *Shakespeare's "Troilus and Cressida" and the Inns of Court Revels.* Brookfield, VT: Ashgate, 1999.

Epicurus. *Letter to Herodotus.* In *Epicurus: The Extant Remains*, edited and translated by Cyril Bailey, 18–55. Oxford: Clarendon Press, 1926.

Fabian, Johannes. *Time and the Other: How Anthropology Makes Its Object.* New York: Columbia University Press, 2002.

Fabricius, Johannes. *Syphilis in Shakespeare's England.* London: Jessica Kingsley, 1994.

Falocco, Joe. *Reimagining Shakespeare's Playhouse: Early Modern Staging Conventions in the 20th Century*. Cambridge: D. S. Brewer, 2010.

Febvre, Lucien. "History and Psychology." In *A New Kind of History from the Writings of Febvre*, edited by Peter Burke and translated by K. Folca, 1–11. New York: Harper & Row, 1973 (1938).

Febvre, Lucien. *The Problem of Unbelief in the Sixteenth Century: The Religion of Rabelais*. Translated by Beatrice Gottlieb. Cambridge, MA: Harvard University Press, 1982.

Feeney, Denis. *Caesar's Calendar: Ancient Time and the Beginnings of History*. Berkeley: University of California Press, 2007.

Feingold, Mordechai. "Newton, Historian." In *The Cambridge Companion to Newton*, edited by Rob Iliffe and George E. Smith, 524–55. Cambridge: Cambridge University Press, 2016.

Feingold, Mordechai. "Scaliger in England." In *For the Sake of Learning: Essays in Honor of Anthony Grafton*, edited by Ann Blair and Anja-Silvia Goeing, 1:55–72. Zurich: Brill, 2016.

Finegan, Jack. *Handbook of Biblical Chronology: Principles of Time Reckoning in the Ancient World and Problems of Chronology in the Bible*. Princeton, NJ: Princeton University Press, 1964.

Firth, Katharine R. *The Apocalyptic Tradition in Reformation Britain, 1530–1645*. Oxford: Oxford University Press, 1979.

Fleay, F. G. "On Metrical Tests as Applied to Dramatic Poetry." In *Transactions of the New Shakspere Society*, 1:1, 1–72. London: N. Trübner & Co., 1874.

Fleay, F. G. *Shakespeare Manual*. London: Macmillan, 1876.

Foakes, R. A. *Hamlet versus Lear: Cultural Politics and Shakespeare's Art*. Cambridge: Cambridge University Press, 1993.

Foakes, R. A. *Illustrations of the English Stage 1580–1642*. London: Scolar, 1985.

Foxe, John. *Two Latin Comedies by John Foxe the Martyrologist: Titus et Gesippus, Christus Triumphans*. Edited, translated, and with an introduction and notes by John Hazel Smith. Ithaca, NY: Cornell University Press in association with the Renaissance Society of America, 1973.

Frazer, Winifred. "Henslowe's 'ne.'" *Notes and Queries* 38 (1991): 34–35.

Freccero, John. "The Fig Tree and the Laurel." In *Dante's Wake: Navigating from Medieval to Modern in the Augustinian Tradition*, edited by Danielle Callegari and Melissa Swain, 137–50. New York: Fordham University Press, 2015.

Freund, Elizabeth. "'Ariachne's Broken Woof': The Rhetoric of Citation in *Troilus and Cressida*." In *Shakespeare and the Question of Theory*, edited by Patricia Parker and Geoffrey Harman, 19–36. New York: Methuen, 1985.

Fuller, J. G. C. M. "A Date to Remember: 4004 BC." *Earth Sciences History* 24, no. 1 (2005): 5–14.

Furnivall, F. J. "The Founder's Prospectus." *Publications of the New Shakspere Society* 1 (1874): app. 6–10.

Furnivall, F. J. *The Succession of Shakspere's Works and the Use of Metrical Tests in Settling It*. London: Smith, Elder, 1874. Reprint, New York: AMS Press, 1972.

Garber, Marjorie. *Profiling Shakespeare*. London: Routledge, 2008.

Garber, Marjorie. *Shakespeare after All*. New York: Pantheon Books, 2004.

The Geneva Bible: A Facsimile of the 1560 Edition. Introduction by Lloyd E. Berry. Madison: University of Wisconsin Press, 1969.

Geoffrey of Monmouth. *The "Historia regum Britannie" of Geoffrey of Monmouth III: A Summary Catalogue of the Manuscripts*. Edited by Julia C. Crick. Cambridge: D. S. Brewer, 1989.

Geoffrey of Monmouth. *The "Historia regum Britannie" of Geoffrey of Monmouth V: "Gesta regum Britannie."* Edited and translated by Neil Wright. Cambridge: D. S. Brewer, 1991.

George, David. "Poussin's Coriolanus and Kemble's Roman Matron." *Theatre Notebook* 48, no. 1 (1994): 2–10.

Gervinus, Georg Gottfried. *Shakespeare Commentaries*. Translated by F. E. Bunnett. London: Smith, Elder, 1875.

Geveren, Sheltco à. *Of the ende of this worlde, and the seconde commyng of Christ a comfortable and necessary discourse, for these miserable and daungerous days*. London: T. Gardyner and T. Dawson for Andrew Maunsel, 1577.

Gilvary, Kevin, ed. *Dating Shakespeare's Plays: A Critical Review of the Evidence*. Kent: Parapress, 2010.

Ginzburg, Carlo. *History, Rhetoric, and Proof*. Hanover, NH: University Press of New England, 1999.

Grafton, Anthony. *Joseph Scaliger: A Study in the History of Classical Scholarship*. Vol. 2, *Historical Chronology*. Oxford: Clarendon Press, 1993.

Grafton, Anthony. "Scaliger's Chronology: Philology, Astronomy, World History." In *Defenders of the Text: The Traditions of Scholarship in an Age of Science, 1450–1800*, 104–44. Cambridge, MA: Harvard University Press, 1991.

Grafton, Anthony, and N. M. Swerdlow. "Greek Chronography in Roman Epic: The Calendrical Date of the Fall of Troy in the *Aeneid*." *Classical Quarterly*, n.s., 36, no. 1 (1986): 212–18.

Granada, Miguel A. "Kepler v. Roeslin on the Interpretation of Kepler's nova: (1) 1604–1606." *Journal for the History of Astronomy* 36, no. 3 (2005): 299–319.

Greenblatt, Stephen. *Hamlet in Purgatory*. Princeton, NJ: Princeton University Press, 2014.

Greenblatt, Stephen. "Remnants of the Sacred in Early Modern England." In *Subject and Object in Renaissance Culture*, edited by Margreta de Grazia, Maureen Quilligan, and Peter Stallybrass, 337–45. Cambridge: Cambridge University Press, 1996.

Greenblatt, Stephen. *Renaissance Self-Fashioning: From More to Shakespeare*. Chicago: University of Chicago Press, 1980.

Greenblatt, Stephen. *Shakespearean Negotiations: The Circulation of Social Energy in Renaissance England*. Berkeley: University of California Press, 1988.

Greenblatt, Stephen. *Shakespeare's Freedom*. Chicago: University of Chicago Press, 2010.

Greene, Roland. *Five Words: Critical Semantics in the Age of Shakespeare and Cervantes*. Chicago: University of Chicago Press, 2013.

Greene, Thomas. "History and Anachronism." In *The Vulnerable Text: Essays on Renaissance Literature*, 218–35. New York: Columbia University Press, 1986.

Greene, Thomas. *The Light in Troy: Imitation and Discovery in Renaissance Poetry*. New Haven, CT: Yale University Press, 1982.

Greg, W. W. *The Shakespeare First Folio: Its Bibliographical and Textual History*. Oxford: Clarendon Press, 1955.

Gregory, John. *Gregorii Posthuma: or certain learned tracts written by John Gregorie*. London: J. G[urgany], 1649.

Halliday, Anthony. "The Literary Sources of Mantegna's 'Triumphs of Caesar.'" *Annali Della Scuola Normale Superiore Di Pisa, Classe Di Lettere E Filosofia*, 3rd ser., 24, no. 1 (1994): 337–96.

Hamlin, Hannibal. *The Bible in Shakespeare*. Oxford: Oxford University Press, 2013.

Hamm, Robert B., Jr. "Rowe's Shakespeare (1709) and the Tonson House Style." *College Literature* 31 (2004): 179–205.

Hammerschmidt-Hummel, Hildegard. "Boydell's Shakespeare Gallery and Its Role in Promoting English History Painting." In *The Boydell Shakespeare Gallery*, edited by Walter Pape and Frederick Burwick. Bottrop: Pomp, 1996.

Han, Younglim. *Romantic Shakespeare: From Stage to Page*. Cranbury, NJ: Fairleigh Dickinson University Press, 2001.

Harrington, Spencer P. M., William M. Calder, David A. Traill, Katie Demarkopoulou, and Kenneth D. S. Lapatin. "Behind the Mask of Agamemnon." *Archaeology* 52, no. 4 (1999): 51–59.

Harris, Jonathan Gil. *Untimely Matter in the Time of Shakespeare*. Philadelphia: University of Pennsylvania Press, 2009.

Hayot, Eric. "Against Periodization." In *On Literary Worlds*, 147–60. Oxford: Oxford University Press, 2012.

Hazlitt, William. *The Collected Works of William Hazlitt*. Edited by A. R. Waller and A. Glover. 12 vols. London: J. M. Dent, 1902.

Hazlitt, William. "Mr. Kemble's Retirement." In *The Collected Works of William Hazlitt in Twelve Volumes: A View of the English Stage*, edited by A. R. Waller and Arnold Glover, 8:374–79. London: J. M. Dent, 1903.

Hearne, Thomas. *Ductor historicus, or, A short system of universal history and an introduction to the study of that science containing a chronology of the most celebrated persons and actions from the creation to this time*. London: Timothy Childe, 1698.

Hegel, G. W. F. *Hegel's Aesthetics: Lectures on Fine Art*. 2 vols. Translated by T. M. Knox. Oxford: Clarendon Press, 1975.

Heidegger, Martin. "The Age of the World Picture." In *The Question Concerning Technology and Other Essays*, translated by William Lovitt, 115–54. New York: Harper & Row, 1977.

Helvicus, Christopher. *The Historical and Chronological Theatre of Christopher Helvicus*. Oxford: George West & John Crosley, 1687.

Henslowe, Philip. *Henslowe's Diary*. Edited by R. A. Foakes. 2nd ed. Cambridge: Cambridge University Press, 2002 (1961).

Heywood, Thomas. *The Iron Age: Contayning the Rape of Hellen: The siege of Troy: The combate betwixt Hector and Aiax [. . .] &c.* London: Nicholas Okes, 1632.

Heywood, Thomas. *The Second Part of the Iron Age: Which contayneth the death of Penthesilea, Paris, Priam, and Hecuba; The burning of*

Troy; The deaths of Agamemnon, Menelaus [. . .] *&c.* London: Nicholas Okes, 1632.

Hiatt, Alfred. *The Making of Medieval Forgeries: False Documents in Fifteenth-Century England.* London: British Library and University of Toronto Press, 2004.

Hillman, David. "The Worst Case of Knowing the Other? Stanley Cavell and *Troilus and Cressida.*" *Philosophy and Literature* 32, no. 1 (2008): 74–86.

Himmelfarb, Gertrude, ed. *The Spirit of the Age: Victorian Essays.* New Haven, CT: Yale University Press, 2007.

Hirota, Atsuhiko. "The Memory of Hesione: Intertextuality and Social Amnesia in *Troilus and Cressida.*" *Actes des congrès de la Société française Shakespeare* 30 (2013). http://shakespeare.revues .org/1920.

Höfele, Andreas. "John Foxe, *Christus Triumphans.*" In *The Oxford Handbook of Tudor Drama,* edited by Thomas Betteridge and Greg Walker, 123–43. Oxford: Oxford University Press, 2012.

Holinshed, Raphael. *The Firste Volume of the Chronicles of England, Scotlande, and Irelande.* London: John Harrison, 1577.

Holinshed, Raphael. *The Third volume of Chronicles, beginning at duke William the Norman, commonlie called the Conqueror.* London: John Harrison, 1587.

The Holy Bible. 2 vols. London: C. Bill and the executrix of T. Newcomb, 1701.

Honigmann, E. A. J. *Shakespeare's Impact on His Contemporaries.* London: Macmillan, 1982.

Horace. *Odes of Horace.* Translated by Jeffrey H. Kaimowitz. Baltimore: Johns Hopkins University Press, 2008.

Hunter, G. K. "The Social Function of Annotation." In *Arden: On Editing; Essays in Honour of Richard Proudfoot,* edited by Ann Thompson and Gordon McMullan, 177–90. London: Arden Shakespeare, 2003.

Hurdis, James. *Cursory remarks upon the arrangement of the plays of Shakespear occasioned by reading Mr. Malone's essay on the chronological order of those celebrated pieces.* London: J. Johnson, 1792.

Hutson, Lorna. "'Lively Evidence': Legal Inquiry into the *Evidentia* of Shakespearean Drama." In *Shakespeare and the Law: A Conversation among Disciplines and Professions,* edited by Bradin

Cormack, Martha C. Nussbaum, and Richard Strier, 72–97. Chicago: University of Chicago Press, 2013.

Hyppolite, Jean. *Genesis and Structure of Hegel's "Phenomenology of Spirit."* Translated by Samuel Cherniak and John Heckman. Evanston, IL: Northwestern University Press, 1974.

Inchbald, Elizabeth. *The British Theatre; or, A Collection of Plays, Which Are Acted at the Theatres Royal, Drury Lane, Covent Garden, and Haymarket.* With biographical and critical remarks by Mrs. Inchbald. 25 vols. London: Longman, Hurst, Rees, and Orme, 1808.

Irwin, David. "Gavin Hamilton: Archaeologist, Painter, and Dealer." *Art Bulletin* 44, no. 2 (1962): 87–102.

Jackson, H. J. "Coleridge's Biographia: When Is an Autobiography Not an Autobiography?" *Biography* 20, no. 1 (1997): 54–71.

Jackson, Virginia. "On Periodization and Its Discontents." In *On Periodization: Selected Essays from the English Institute,* edited by Virginia Jackson, 2–17. Cambridge, MA: English Institute in Collaboration with the American Council of Learned Societies, 2010. http://hdl.handle.net/2027/heb.90047.0001.001.

Jameson, Fredric. *The Political Unconscious: Narrative as a Socially Symbolic Act.* Ithaca, NY: Cornell University Press, 1981.

Jameson, Fredric. *Postmodernism; or, The Cultural Logic of Late Capitalism.* Durham, NC: Duke University Press, 1991.

Jameson, Fredric. *A Singular Modernity: Essay on the Ontology of the Present.* London: Verso, 2002.

Jaspers, Karl. *The Origin and Goal of History.* Translated by Michael Bullock. London: Routledge & Kegan Paul, 1953.

Johnson, Samuel. *Johnson on Shakespeare.* Edited by Arthur Sherbo. Vol. 8 of *The Yale Edition of the Works of Samuel Johnson.* New Haven, CT: Yale University Press, 1968.

Jones, Ann Rosalind, and Peter Stallybrass. *Renaissance Clothing and the Materials of Memory.* Cambridge: Cambridge University Press, 2000.

Jonson, Ben. *The Cambridge Edition of the Works of Ben Jonson.* Edited by D. M. Bevington, M. Butler and I. Donaldson. 7 vols. Cambridge: Cambridge University Press, 2012.

Jonson, Ben. *The Cambridge Edition of the Works of Ben Jonson Online.* Edited by Martin Butler, David Bevington, Karen

Britland, Ian Donaldson, David L. Gants, and Eugene Giddens. Cambridge: Cambridge University Press, 2014. https://univer sitypublishingonline.org/cambridge/benjonson/.

Kalas, Rayna. *Frame, Glass, Verse: The Technology of Poetic Invention in the English Renaissance*. Ithaca, NY: Cornell University Press, 2007.

Kalter, Barrett D. *Modern Antiques: The Material Past in England, 1660–1780*. Lewisburg, PA: Bucknell University Press, 2012.

Kemble, John Philip. *An Authentic Narrative of Mr. Kemble's Retirement from the Stage* [. . .] *Selected from Various Periodical Publications* [. . .] *To Which Is Prefixed, an Essay, Biographical and Critical, etc*. London: John Miller, 1817.

Kemble, John Philip. *John Philip Kemble's Promptbook of William Shakespeare's "Coriolanus; or, the Roman Matron."* Vol. 2 of *John Philip Kemble Promptbooks*, edited by Charles H. Shattuck. Charlottesville: University Press of Virginia for the Folger Shakespeare Library, 1974.

Kermode, Frank. *The Sense of an Ending: Studies in the Theory of Fiction (with a New Epilogue)*. Oxford: Oxford University Press, 2000 (1967).

Kirwan, Peter. *Shakespeare and the Idea of Apocrypha: Negotiating the Boundaries of the Dramatic Canon*. Cambridge: Cambridge University Press, 2015.

Knapp, Jeffrey. *Shakespeare's Tribe: Church, Nation, and Theater in Renaissance England*. Chicago: University of Chicago Press, 2002.

Knight, Charles, ed. *The Pictorial Edition of the Works of Shakspere*. 8 vols. London: Charles Knight, 1838–1842.

Knox, Bernard. *Oedipus at Thebes: Sophocles' Tragic Hero and His Time*. New Haven, CT: Yale University Press, 1998.

Kokkinos, Nikos. "Ancient Chronography, Eratosthenes and the Dating of the Fall of Troy." *Ancient West and East* 8 (2009): 37–56.

Koselleck, Reinhart. *Futures Past: On the Semantics of Historical Time*. Translated by Keith Tribe. Cambridge, MA: MIT Press, 1985.

Koselleck, Reinhart. *The Practice of Conceptual History: Timing History, Spacing Concepts*. Translated by Todd Presner, Kerstin Behnke, and Jobst Welge. Stanford, CA: Stanford University Press, 2002.

Kott, Jan. *Shakespeare Our Contemporary*. Translated by Boleslaw Taborski. London: Doubleday, 1966.

Lazarus, Micha. "Aristotelian Criticism in Sixteenth-Century England." Oxford Handbooks Online. https://www.oxfordhandbooks.com /view/10.1093/oxfordhb/9780199935338.001.0001/oxfordhb-978 0199935338-e-148.

Leigh, William. *The Christians Watch: or, An Heavenly Instruction to all Christians, to expect with patience that happy day of their change by death or doome.* London: E. White, 1605.

Leo, Russ. *Tragedy as Philosophy in the Reformation World.* Oxford: Oxford University Press, 2019.

Lesser, Zachary, and Peter Stallybrass. "The First Literary *Hamlet* and the Commonplacing of Professional Plays." *Shakespeare Quarterly* 59, no. 4 (2008): 371–420.

Levinas, Emmanuel. *Otherwise than Being; or, Beyond Essence.* Translated by Alphonso Lingis. The Hague: Nijhoff, 1981.

Levine, Joseph M. *Humanism and History: Origins of Modern English Historiography* Ithaca, NY: Cornell University Press, 1987.

Levy, Fred Jacob. *Tudor Historical Thought.* San Marino, CA: Huntington Library, 1967.

Lexicons of Early Modern English. Edited by Ian Lancashire. University of Toronto. http://leme.library.utoronto.ca/.

Locke, John. *Some Thoughts Concerning Education.* Edited by John William Adamson. Mineola, NY: Dover, 2007 (1693).

"The Long and the Short: Problems in Periodization." *PMLA* 127, no. 2 (2012): 301–56.

Lovejoy, A. O. *The Great Chain of Being: A Study in the History of an Idea.* Cambridge, MA: Harvard University Press, 1936.

Löwith, Karl. *Meaning in History: The Theological Implications of the Philosophy of History.* Chicago: University of Chicago Press, 1949.

Lublin, Robert I. *Costuming the Shakespearean Stage: Visual Codes of Representation in Early Modern England.* London: Routledge, 2016.

Lublin, Robert I. "Shakespearean Visual Semiotics and the Silver Screen." In *Reinventing the Renaissance: Shakespeare and His Contemporaries in Adaptation and Performance*, edited by Sarah Brown, Robert I. Lublin, and Lynsey McCulloch, 242-54. New York: Palgrave Macmillan, 2013.

Lucretius. *De rerum natura.* Translated by W. H. D. Rouse. Cambridge, MA: Harvard University Press, 1924.

Lukács, Georg. *The Historical Novel.* Translated by Hannah and Stanley Mitchell. Harmondsworth: Penguin, 1981 (1962).

Lupton, Julia Reinhard. *Citizen-Saints: Shakespeare and Political Theology*. Chicago: University of Chicago Press, 2005.

Lupton, Julia Reinhard. "The Pauline Renaissance: A Shakespearean Reassessment." *European Legacy* 15, no. 2 (2010): 215–20.

Lupton, Julia Reinhard. *Thinking with Shakespeare: Essays on Politics and Life*. Chicago: University of Chicago Press, 2011.

Luzzi, Joseph. "The Rhetoric of Anachronism." *Comparative Literature* 61, no. 1 (2006): 69–84.

Lynch, Jack. *Deception and Detection in Eighteenth-Century Britain*. Aldershot: Ashgate, 2008.

Malone, Edmond. "An Attempt to Ascertain the Order in which the Plays Attributed to Shakspeare were Written." In *The Plays of William Shakespeare*, edited by Samuel Johnson and George Steevens, 2nd ed., 1:269–346. London: C. Bathurst, 1778.

Malone, Edmond. "An Attempt to Ascertain the Order in which the Plays Attributed to Shakspeare were Written." In *The Plays and Poems of William Shakspeare*, edited by Edmond Malone, 1:261–386. London: J. Rivington and Sons et al., 1790.

Malone, Edmond. *A Dissertation on the three parts of King Henry VI., tending to shew that those plays were not written originally by Shakspeare*. London: Henry Baldwin, 1787.

Malone, Edmond, ed. *Supplement to the edition of Shakspeare's plays published in 1778 by Samuel Johnson and George Steevens*. 2 vols. London: C. Bathurst, W. Strahan, J.F. and C. Rivington, et al., 1780.

Martindale, Andrew. *The Triumphs of Caesar by Andrea Mantegna in the Collection of Her Majesty the Queen at Hampton Court*. London: Harvey Miller, 1979.

Martyn, James. *Dissertations and Critical Remarks upon the Æneids of Virgil, containing [. . .] a full vindication of the poet from the charge of an anachronism with regard to the foundation of Carthage*. London: Lockyer Davis, 1770.

McDonald, Russ. *Shakespeare's Late Style*. Cambridge: Cambridge University Press, 2006.

McMullan, Gordon. *Shakespeare and the Idea of Late Writing: Authorship in the Proximity of Death*. Cambridge: Cambridge University Press, 2007.

Menzer, Paul. *The Hamlets: Cues, Qs, and Remembered Texts*. Newark: University of Delaware Press, 2008.

Meres, Francis. *Palladis tamia Wits treasury being the second part of Wits common wealth.* London: Cuthbert Burbie, 1598.

Mill, John Stuart. *The Spirit of the Age.* With an introductory essay by Frederick A. von Hayek. Chicago: University of Chicago Press, 1942.

Miller, J. Hillis. "Ariachne's Broken Woof." *Georgia Review* 31, no. 1 (1977): 44–60.

Minton, Gretchen E., and Paul B. Harvey, Jr. "'A Poor Chipochia': A New Look at an Italian Word in *Troilus and Cressida* 4.2." *Neophilologus* 88 (2004): 307–14.

Moody, Jane. "Romantic Shakespeare." In *The Cambridge Companion to Shakespeare on Stage,* edited by Stanley Wells and Sarah Stanton, 37–57. Cambridge Companions to Literature. Cambridge: Cambridge University Press, 2002.

Moorehead, Caroline. *Priam's Gold: Schliemann and the Lost Treasures of Troy.* London: Tauris Parke Paperback, 2016.

Morrison, Tessa. *Isaac Newton's Temple of Solomon and His Reconstruction of Sacred Architecture.* Basel: Birkhäuser, 2011.

Morse, Ruth, Helen Cooper, and Peter Holland, eds. *Medieval Shakespeare: Pasts and Presents.* Cambridge: Cambridge University Press, 2013.

Motley, William. *Baroque & Roll.* Reigate: Cohen & Cohen, 2015.

Munro, Lucy. *Archaic Style in English Literature, 1590–1674.* Cambridge: Cambridge University Press, 2013.

Munro, Lucy. "Young Shakespeare/Late Shakespeare: The Case of *Pericles.*" *Actes des congrès de la Société française Shakespeare* 34 (2016): 1–18.

Murphy, Andrew. "Shakespeare and Chronology: Edward Dowden's Biographical Readings." *Forum for Modern Language Studies* 46, no. 2 (2010): 130–37.

Murphy, Andrew. *Shakespeare in Print: A History and Chronology of Shakespeare Publishing.* Cambridge: Cambridge University Press, 2003.

Nagel, Alexander, and Christopher Wood. "Towards a New Model of Renaissance Anachronism." *Art Bulletin* 87, no. 3 (2005): 403–15.

Naiden, F. S. *Ancient Supplication.* New York: Oxford University Press, 2006.

Naugle, David. *Worldview: The History of a Concept.* Grand Rapids, MI: William B. Eerdmans, 2002.

Niebuhr, Barthold Georg. *Roman History*. Translated by F. A. Walter. 2 vols. London: C. and J. Rivington, 1827.

Nietzsche, Friedrich. *The Anti-Christ*. In *The Anti-Christ, Ecce Homo, Twilight of the Idols, and Other Writings*, edited by Aaron Ridley and Judith Norman and translated by Judith Norman, 3–67. Cambridge: Cambridge University Press, 2005.

Norland, Howard B. "John Foxe's Apocalyptic Comedy." In *The Early Modern Cultures of Neo-Latin Drama*, edited by Philip Ford and Andrew Taylor, 75–84. Leuven: Leuven University Press, 2013.

Norland, Howard B. "Neo-Latin Drama in Britain." In *Neo-Latin Drama and Theatre in Early Modern Europe*, edited by Jan Bloemendal and Howard B. Norland, 471–544. Leiden: Brill, 2013.

Oates, Joyce Carol. *The Edge of Impossibility: Tragic Forms in Literature*. New York: Vanguard Press, 1972.

Odell, George Clinton Densmore. *Shakespeare from Betterton to Irving*. 2 vols. London: Constable, 1921.

Orgel, Stephen. *The Authentic Shakespeare, and Other Problems of the Early Modern Stage*. New York and London: Routledge, 2002.

Orgel, Stephen. "The Desire and Pursuit of the Whole." *Shakespeare Quarterly* 58, no. 3 (Fall 2007): 290–310.

Orgel, Stephen. *Imagining Shakespeare: A History of Texts and Visions*. Houndmills: Palgrave, 2003.

Orgel, Stephen. "Shakespeare Illustrated." In *The Cambridge Companion to Shakespeare and Popular Culture*, edited by Robert Shaughnessy, 67–92. Cambridge: Cambridge University Press, 2007.

Orgel, Stephen. *Spectacular Performances: Essays on Theatre, Imagery, Books and Selves in Early Modern England*. Manchester: Manchester University Press, 2011.

Oya, Reiko. "Authenticating the Inauthentic: Edmond Malone as Editor of the Apocryphal Shakespeare." *Shakespeare Survey* 69 (2016): 324–33.

Palfrey, Simon. *Shakespeare's Possible Worlds*. Cambridge: Cambridge University Press, 2014.

Palfrey, Simon, and Tiffany Stern. *Shakespeare in Parts*. Oxford: Oxford University Press, 2010.

Panofsky, Erwin. *Renaissance and Renascences in Western Art*. New York: Harper & Row, 1972.

Parker, John. *The Aesthetics of Antichrist: From Christian Drama to Christopher Marlowe*. Ithaca, NY: Cornell University Press, 2007.

Parker, John. *Drama and the Death of God: Secularization before Shakespeare*. Forthcoming.

Parker, John. "Who's Afraid of Darwin? Revisiting Chambers and Hardison . . . and Nietzsche." *Journal of Medieval and Early Modern Studies* 40, no. 1 (2010): 7–35.

Parker, Patricia. *Shakespearean Intersections: Language, Contexts, Critical Key Words*. Philadelphia: University of Pennsylvania Press, 2018.

Peacock, John. "Inigo Jones and the Arundel Marbles." *Journal of Medieval and Renaissance Studies* 16 (1986): 75–90.

Pentzell, Raymond J. "Garrick's Costuming." *Theatre Survey* 10, no. 1 (May 1, 1969): 18–42.

Pepys, Samuel. *The Diary of Samuel Pepys*. 11 vols. Edited by Robert Latham and William Matthews. London: Bell & Hyman, 1985.

Planché, J. R. *History of British Costume, from the Earliest Period to the Close of the Eighteenth Century*. London: C. Cox, 1847.

Planché, J. R. *Recollections and Reflections*. 2 vols. London: Tinsley Brothers, 1872.

Pollard, Alfred W., ed. *Shakespeare's Hand in the Play of "Sir Thomas More."* Cambridge: Cambridge University Press, 1923.

Pond, Edward. *Enchiridion, or, Pond his Eutheca 1604 a new almanacke for this prese[n]t yeare of our Lord MDCIIII*. London: Edward Allde, 1604.

Popper, Nicholas. *Walter Raleigh's "History of the World" and the Historical Culture of the Late Renaissance*. Chicago: University of Chicago Press, 2012.

Priestley, Joseph. *A Description of a Chart of Biography*. London: J. Johnson, 1764.

Prior, James. *Life of Edmond Malone, Editor of Shakespeare*. London: Smith, Elder, 1680.

Purkis, James. *Shakespeare and Manuscript Drama: Canon, Collaboration and Text*. Cambridge: Cambridge University Press, 2016.

Quintilian. *The Institutio Oratoria*. Edited and translated by Donald A. Russell. 2 vols. Loeb Classical Library 124–27 and 494. Cambridge, MA: Harvard University Press, 2001.

Rackin, Phyllis. *Stages of History: Shakespeare's English Chronicles*. Ithaca, NY: Cornell University Press, 1990.

Raleigh, Walter. *The History of the World*. London: Walter Burre, 1614.

Rancière, Jacques. "The Concept of Anachronism and the Historian's Truth." Translated by Tim Stott. *InPrint* 3, no. 1 (2015): 21–52.

Ripley, John. *"Coriolanus" on Stage in England and America, 1609–1994.* Madison, NJ: Fairleigh Dickinson University Press; London: Associated University Presses, 1998.

Ritter, Harry. *Dictionary of Concepts in History.* New York: Greenwood Press, 1986.

Robinson, Terry F. "John Philip Kemble." In *The Encyclopedia of Romantic Literature*, edited by Frederick Burwick, Nancy Moore Goslee, and Diane Long Hoeveler, 2:723–30. Malden, MA: Wiley-Blackwell, 2012.

Rood, Tim, Carol Atack, and Tom Phillips. *Anachronism and Antiquity.* London: Bloomsbury, 2019.

Rosenfeld, Sybil, *Georgian Scene Painters and Scene Painting.* Cambridge: Cambridge University Press, 1981.

Ruthven, K. K. "Preposterous Chatterton." *English Literary History* 71 (2004): 345–75.

Ryan, Kiernan. *"Troilus and Cressida*: The Perils of Presentism." In *Presentist Shakespeares*, edited by Hugh Grady and Terence Hawkes, 164–83. New York: Routledge, 2006.

Sachs, Jonathan. *Romantic Antiquity: Rome in the British Imagination, 1789–1832.* Oxford: Oxford University Press, 2010.

Sawyer, Robert. "The New Shakspere Society, 1873–1894." *Borrowers and Lenders* 2, no. 2 (2006). http://www.borrowers.uga.edu/781463/pdf.

Scaliger, Joseph. *Opus de emendatione temporum.* Leiden: Franciscus Raphelengius, 1598.

Schiller, Frederick. "On the Tragic Art." In *Aesthetical and Philosophical Essays*, translated by J. C. F. Schiller, 346–66. New York: Harvard, 1895.

Schmitt, Carl. *Political Theology: Four Chapters on the Concept of Sovereignty.* Translated by George Schwab. Chicago: University of Chicago Press, 2005 (1922).

Schmitt, Charles. *John Case and Aristotelianism in Renaissance England.* Montreal: McGill-Queen's University Press, 1983.

Schoch, Richard. "Performing History on the Victorian Stage." In *Conjuring the Real: The Role of Architecture in Eighteenth- and Nineteenth-Century Fiction*, edited by Rumiko Handa and James Porter. Lincoln: University of Nebraska Press, 2011.

Schoch, Richard. "Pictorial Shakespeare." In *The Cambridge Companion to Shakespeare on Stage*, edited by Stanley Wells and

Sarah Stanton, 58–75. Cambridge Companions to Literature. Cambridge: Cambridge University Press, 2002.

Schoch, Richard. *Shakespeare's Victorian Stage: Performing History in the Theatre of Charles Kean.* Cambridge: Cambridge University Press, 1998.

Schoch, Richard. *Writing the History of the British Stage: 1660–1900.* Cambridge: Cambridge University Press, 2016.

Schoenbaum, Samuel. *Shakespeare's Lives.* Oxford: Oxford University Press, 1991 (1970).

Schreyer, Kurt. *Shakespeare's Medieval Craft: Remnants of the Mysteries on the London Stage.* Ithaca, NY: Cornell University Press, 2014.

Scott, Walter. "Life of Kemble." In *Periodical Criticism.* Vol. 4 of *The Miscellaneous Prose Works,* edited by Robert Cadell, 152–232. Edinburgh: Robert Cadell, 1835.

Seary, Peter. *Lewis Theobald and the Editing of Shakespeare.* Oxford: Clarendon Press, 1990.

Segrais, Jean Regnault de. *Traduction de l'Eneïde de Virgile, par Mr. De Segrais.* Paris: Claude Barbin, 1668.

Shagan, Ethan H. "Periodization and the Secular." In *Early Modern Histories of Time: The Periodizations of Sixteenth- and Seventeenth-Century England,* edited by Kristen Poole and Owen Williams, 72–87. Philadelphia: University of Pennsylvania Press, 2019.

Sheridan, Thomas. *Coriolanus; or, the Roman Matron. A tragedy. Taken from Shakespear and Thomson. As it is acted at the Theatre-Royal in Covent-Garden. To which is added, the order of the Ovation.* London: A. Millar, 1755.

Shuger, Debora Kuller. *The Renaissance Bible: Scholarship, Sacrifice, and Subjectivity.* Berkeley: University of California Press, 1994.

Sillars, Stuart. *The Illustrated Shakespeare, 1709–1875.* Cambridge: Cambridge University Press, 2008.

Skinner, Quentin. "An Interview." *Finnish Year Book of Political Thought* 6 (2002): 32–63.

Skinner, Quentin. "Meaning and Understanding." In *Meaning and Context: Quentin Skinner and his Critics,* edited by James Tully, 29–67. Princeton, NJ: Princeton University Press, 1988.

Smith, Hal. "Some Principles of Elizabethan Stage Costume." *Journal of the Warburg and Courtauld Institutes* 25, no. 3/4 (1962): 240–57.

Sohmer, Steve. "The 'Double Time' Crux in *Othello* Solved." *English Literary Renaissance* 32, no. 2 (2002): 214–38.

Spevack, Martin. "Furnivall, Gervinus, and the Germanization of the New Shakspere Society." *Shakespeare Newsletter* 52, no. 1 (Spring 2002): 3–4.

Stark, Rodney. "Secularization, R.I.P." *Sociology of Religion* 60, no. 3 (Autumn 1999): 249–73.

Story, Patrick. "Hazlitt's Definition of the Spirit of the Age." *Wordsworth Circle* 6, no. 2 (Spring 1975): 97–108.

Strong, Roy C. *Painting the Past: The Victorian Painter and British History*. London: Pimlico, 2004.

Suetonius. *Lives of the Caesars*. Translated by Catharine Edwards. Oxford: Oxford University Press, 2008.

Taylor, Charles. *A Secular Age*. Cambridge, MA: Belknap Press, 2007.

Taylor, Gary, and Gabriel Egan, eds. *The New Oxford Shakespeare: Authorship Companion*. Oxford: Oxford University Press, 2017.

Theobald, Lewis, ed. and trans. *Electra: A Tragedy. Translated from Sophocles, with Notes by Mr. Theobald*. London: Bernard Lintott, 1714.

Theobald, Lewis. *Shakespeare restored: or, a specimen of the many errors, as well committed, as unamended, by Mr Pope in his late edition of this poet*. London: R. Francklin, J. Woodman and D. Lyon, and C. Davis, 1726.

Thomas, Keith. *Religion and the Decline of Magic: Studies in Popular Beliefs in Sixteenth- and Seventeenth-Century England*. London: Penguin Books, 1991 (1971).

Tillyard, E. M. W. *The Elizabethan World Picture: A Study of the Idea of Order in the Age of Shakespeare, Donne & Milton*. London: Macmillan, 1942.

Tillyard, E. M. W. *Shakespeare's History Plays*. New York: Chatto & Windus, 1980 (1944).

Toomer, G. J. *John Selden: A Life in Scholarship*. 2 vols. Oxford: Oxford University Press, 2009.

Traversi, Derek. *An Approach to Shakespeare*. 2nd ed. Glasgow: Sands, 1957 (1938).

Traversi, Derek. *Shakespeare: The Last Phase*. London: Hollis, and Carter, 1969 (1954).

Traversi, Derek. *William Shakespeare: The Early Comedies*. London: Longmans Green & Co. for the British Council, 1969.

Tribble, Evelyn B., and John Sutton. "Minds in and out of Time: Memory, Embodied Skill, Anachronism, and Performance." *Textual Practice* 26, no. 4 (2012): 587–607.

Underwood, Ted. *Why Literary Periods Mattered: Historical Contrast and the Prestige of English Studies.* Stanford, CA: Stanford University Press, 2013.

Ungerer, Gustav. "An Unrecorded Elizabethan Performance of *Titus Andronicus.*" *Shakespeare Survey* 14 (1961): 102–9.

Valla, Lorenzo. *On the Donation of Constantine.* Translated by G. W. Bowersock. I Tatti Renaissance Library. Cambridge, MA: Harvard University Press, 2007.

Vattimo, Gianni. *After Christianity.* Translated by Luca D'Isanto. New York: Columbia University Press, 2002.

Walsham, Alexandra. "The Reformation and the 'Disenchantment of the World' Reassessed." *Historical Journal* 51, no. 2 (2008): 497–528.

Walton, Michael. "'An Agreeable Innovation': Play and Translation." In *Translation and the Classic: Identity as Change in the History of Culture,* edited by Alexandra Lianeri and Vanda Zajko, 261–78. Oxford: Oxford University Press, 2008.

Walton, Michael. "Theobald and Lintott: A Footnote on Early Translations of Greek Tragedy." *Arion: A Journal of Humanities and the Classics,* 3rd ser., 16, no. 3 (2009): 103–10.

Watson, Nicola. "Kemble, Scott, and the Mantle of the Bard." In *The Appropriation of Shakespeare: Post-Renaissance Reconstructions of the Works and the Myth,* edited by Jean Marsden, 73–92. New York: Harvester Wheatsheaf, 1991.

Weimann, Robert. *Shakespeare and the Popular Tradition in the Theater: Studies in the Social Dimension of Dramatic Form and Function.* Translated and edited by Robert Schwartz. Baltimore: Johns Hopkins University Press, 1978.

Wells, Stanley, ed. *Shakespeare in the Theatre: An Anthology of Criticism.* Oxford: Clarendon Press, 1997.

Wells, Stanley, and Gary Taylor with John Jowett and William Montgomery, eds. *William Shakespeare: A Textual Companion.* London: W. W. Norton, 1997 (1987).

Werstine, Paul. *Early Modern Playhouse Manuscripts and the Editing of Shakespeare.* Cambridge: Cambridge University Press, 2013.

Werstine, Paul. "Shakespeare More or Less: A.W. Pollard and Twentieth-Century Shakespeare Editing." *Florilegium* 16 (1999): 125–45.

Westman, Robert S. *The Copernican Question: Prognostication, Skepticism, and Celestial Order*. Berkeley: University of California Press, 2011.

Williams, Raymond. *Key Words: A Vocabulary of Culture and Society*. Rev. ed. Oxford: Oxford University Press, 1983.

Wilson, Nigel. "Scholiasts and Commentators." *Greek, Roman, and Byzantine Studies* 47 (2007): 39–70.

Wittreich, Joseph. *"Image of That Horror": History, Prophecy, and Apocalypse in "King Lear."* San Marino, CA: Huntington Library, 1984.

Index

Page numbers in italics refer to images.

dating of plays (*cont.*)
  More, 67; in Stationers' Reg-
    ister entries, 64; stylometrics,
    66; termini, 64, 65, 66; topical
    references, 65–66. *See also* "Booke
    of Sir Thomas More"; editions of
    complete works of Shakespeare;
    Malone, Edmond
deictics: "impossible deictics,"
    206n52; "look there," 164; "mod-
    ern" as, 16; "now" as, 44
Delius, Nicolaus, 94
de Man, Paul, 57
Derrida, Jacques, 1, 5, 57
Descartes, René, 6, 7, 13, 140–41,
    142
development, 11, 105; and bildungs-
    roman, 6; of Hegelian history,
    139; and modernity, 155; of plot,
    102; semantics of, 155, 205n35; of
    Shakespeare, 11, 20, 60, 68, 69, 99,
    81–83, 91, 93, 96–99, 105; toward
    realism on stage, 107–10, 197n3
Diderot, Denis, 42
Donation of Constantine, 8–9, 17–18.
    See also dates; Valla, Lorenzo
doomsday. *See* end-time
double time, 101–2
Douce, Francis, 36, 134, 135–37
Dowden, Edward: breaking of "his-
    torical chain," 100; influence of,
    100–101; naming of "Romances,"
    99; *Shakspere* (primer), 98–100;
    *Shakspere: A Critical Study of His
    Mind and Art*, 96–98, 99, 100,
    109, 196n115. *See also* chronology;
    development; genre; Hegel,
    G. W. F.; New Shakspere Society
dramatic irony, 19, 47–52, 59, 188n96
Dryden, John, 38–39, 41, 184–85n34
duration of dramatic action, 101–2.
    See also *Othello*

early modern. *See* Renaissance
editions of complete works of Shake-
    speare, 10, 11–12, 20, 28–29, 60–64,
    67, 100; Alexander, 101; Arden,
    12, 28, 102; Leopold, 94; New
    Cambridge, 29; New Oxford, 12,
    63, 66–67, 68, 103–4, 183n21; New
    Variorum, 101–2, 130; Norton, 29,
    63, 67, 69, 103; Oxford, 28, 63, 67,
    69; Pelican, 63; Riverside, 28, 63,
    69; Royal Shakespeare Company
    (RSC), 12, 29, 102–3; Signet, 61,
    63
eighteenth century, 19, 22, 38, 40, 43,
    58; editions, 20, 24–28, 74–81. *See
    also* dates: 1800
Elliston, Robert, 128
Elton, William R., 170
end-time: always prorogued, 154,
    160–61; and fictional endings,
    155–57, 158; imminence of, 154–56,
    161; and Last Things, 155, 156, 158;
    and marriage of Christ and the
    Church, 159; millenarian expecta-
    tion, 154–55. *See also* apocalypse;
    Christus Triumphans; *King Lear*:
    Koselleck, Reinhart; "promised
    end"; prophecy; revelation
Enlightenment, 39, 175
episteme. *See* worldview
epochal divides, 1, 5, 6–7, 9; and *The
    Anti-Christ*, 152; axial age, 204n23;
    between medieval and modern,
    5–6, 9; between medieval and
    Renaissance, 184n33; Descartes's
    cogito, 6, 7, 13, 140, 142; 1800,
    197n7 (*see also* eighteenth cen-
    tury); Incarnation, 150–54; *King
    Lear* as, 156–57; Norman con-
    quest, 73; Reformation, 6, 12, 14,
    98, 195n111. *See also* dates: of Fall
    of Troy (Trojan War)